Agamben and Theology

Other titles in the Philosophy and Theology series include:

Agamben and
Theology

Colby Dickinson

t&t clark

Published by T&T Clark International
A Continuum Imprint
The Tower Building, 11 York Road, London SE1 7NX
80 Maiden Lane, Suite 704, New York, NY 10038

www.continuumbooks.com

British Library Cataloguing-in-Publication Data
A catalogue record for this book is available from the British Library

ISBN 13: 978-0-567-22138-4 (hardback)
ISBN 13: 978-0-567-62224-2 (paperback)

Typeset by Newgen Imaging Systems Pvt Ltd, Chennai, India
Printed and bound in India

For Elisabeth & Rowan

Contents

Contents

Acknowledgments

I am extremely grateful for the multiple counts of assistance given to my work by Lieven Boeve, Frederiek Depoortere, Joeri Schrijvers, and the various members of the research group "Theology in a Postmodern Context" within the Faculty of Theology, K.U. Leuven, as they have provided valuable feedback and insight on the research undertaken for this book at multiple stages in its formation. I am also deeply indebted to the K.U. Leuven Research Fund for their generous support which has made my research possible. The many conferences where I have presented various stages of this book were excellent springboards from which to ponder the directions I should take. In particular, I would like to thank the organizers of the following venues for allowing me to participate and to share the research I was then conducting: "Towards a Philosophy of Life" held at Liverpool Hope University, England (2009), "Real Objects or Material Subjects?" held at the University of Dundee, Scotland (2010), the Catholic Theological Society of America's annual conference (2010), and the Colloquium on Violence and Religion held at Notre Dame University (2010). In addition, I would also like to acknowledge those who have given their time by looking over earlier versions of this book and offering their comments and suggestions, including Ken Surin, Peter Langford, and Elisabeth Bayley, as well as Adam Kotsko, for his assistance with translational queries.

Abbreviations

B	*Bartleby, la formula della creazione (con Gilles Deleuze)*
CC	*The Coming Community*
EP	*The End of the Poem: Studies in Poetics*
HS	*Homo Sacer: Sovereign Power and Bare Life*
IH	*Infancy and History: On the Destruction of Experience*
IP	*The Idea of Prose*
LD	*Language and Death: The Place of Negativity*
MC	*The Man without Content*
ME	*Means without Ends: Notes on Politics*
N	*Nudités*
O	*The Open: Man and Animal*
P	*Potentialities: Collected Essays in Philosophy*
PR	*Profanations*
RA	*Remnants of Auschwitz: The Witness and the Archive, Homo sacer III*
RG	*Le Règne et la gloire. Pour une généalogie théologique de l'économie et du gouvernement. Homo Sacer II, 2*
S	*Stanzas: Word and Phantasm in Western Culture*
SA	*The Signature of All Things: On Method*
SE	*State of Exception, Homo sacer II, 1*
SL	*Le sacrement du langage. Archéologie du serment. Homo sacer II, 3*
TR	*The Time That Remains: A Commentary on the Letter to the Romans*
WA	*What is an Apparatus? and Other Essays*

Introduction

In a staged dialogue with Juliane Schiffers for the journal *Law Critique*, Alice Lagaay speaks about the experience of reading Giorgio Agamben through a childhood image which seems, for her, to evoke a similar existential "dissolution" of the will as she encounters it in reading his work.[1] As she describes it, and as it bears repeating,

> [i]t's a sudden, physical encounter with a sense of the profound foreignness of the world (or the foreignness of my own being-in-the-world). In this state, which even as a child would sometimes overcome me, the activities of every day life are suddenly put on hold, making space for the perception of a state of bare existence, whatever that may be, yes something like neutral, meaningless, material existence. This state corresponds to a very intimate, indeed quite unique (and at the same time uncannily "general") and perhaps even (despite this attempt here) quite *incommunicable* feeling. It is on the one hand an individual, personal experience, in the sense that it has to do with a sensing of my own being. Yet on the other hand, there is something about it that is clearly more impersonal, more general than perhaps any other experience I've ever had, for, when under the grips of this mystery, it feels as if all that is personal and individual in me were suddenly to dissolve, as if my very being were about to merge with the concrete walls of the room that my fingers may just be brushing.[2]

At which point an unnamed interlocutor (simply designated as "voice off") asks "[w]hat sense can it possibly make to talk about such a personal and indescribable event in an academic context such as this? Where will it lead?" Her dialogue partner seemingly responds for her by pointing out that the recounting of such an experience, no matter how indescribable, points to the limits of language, as well as of academic discourse. That is, the experience which has just been recounted is one which seems to indicate a place where the typical divisions between the individual and the universal are dissolved. This, she indicates, is what Agamben's work is all about.

What this event signals, no less, is the dissolution of the boundaries typical of thought, not to mention academia in general. Schiffers can therefore state that what an event such as this directs our attention to is not the "pros and cons of an argument"; rather, thought is turned toward itself. It "becomes self-referential and thus, to a certain extent, without distance to itself."[3] It is a radical passivity which has often been labeled by Agamben as a state of "infancy" if you will, a returning to a realm within us that is prior to the divisions of thought we so often overlay upon our experiences.[4] And as Lagaay summarizes, Agamben's philosophy seems to evoke not only this state of existence, but also a "strange suspension" of the "familiar categories and strategies of argumentation" that we otherwise rely on: "Everything suddenly appears to be possible and impossible at the same time!"[5] A strange state indeed.

Considering that his work in general attempts to defy those reductionistic representations or labels we so often apply to people in the academic world, and that the experience of reading Agamben apparently lends itself to dissolving those traditional boundaries anyway, it perhaps would be in bad taste to begin this study of Giorgio Agamben and his relation to theology with a few quick gestures toward whichever fields of inquiry would seem to be most receptive to his writings. Political theory, philosophy, law, theology, poetry, literary studies, linguistics, philology, history, cultural studies, film and visual arts, as well as a host of others to be sure, could all lay claim to his work, which, for its part, seems content to crisscross through

Introduction

each and every one of these disciplinary boundaries. But, just as assuredly, none of these disciplines could be said to typify his writing which seems to address the heart of each theoretical realm and yet transcend the very boundaries of every one. And, as we will soon see, crossing over borders and boundaries is precisely what he has foremost in mind.

Throughout his life, he has certainly crossed over numerous cultural landscapes, teaching and/or researching in Germany at Heinrich Heine University, Düsseldorf, in the United States at the University of California, Berkeley, and Northwestern University, Evanston, in London at the Warburg Institute, and in his home country of Italy at the universities located in Macerata, Verona, and Venice, where he currently holds a post. He also holds positions at present in Paris at the Collège International de Philosophie and in Switzerland at the European Graduate School.

His early work, through various periods of his life, seems to have centered around figures such as Simone Weil, Hannah Arendt, and especially Martin Heidegger, with whom he studied for a short period in Freiburg during the late 1960s. His Italian influences and collaborations run deep, as one might expect, placing him in league with its rich literary scene ranging from Italo Calvino to Giorgio Caproni and from the poetic work of Giovanni Pascolini to the novelist Elsa Morante. He is also the Italian editor and translator of the works of Walter Benjamin, a monumental influence upon his thought, and a figure whose name will ceaselessly creep up in nearly all of Agamben's writing. His later work has borne an increasing influence from the work of Michel Foucault, though this is not to suggest that Foucault is the only French theorist juxtaposed with his various projects. Indeed, traces of Guy Debord, Jacques Derrida, Maurice Blanchot, Jean-Luc Nancy, Jean-François Lyotard, Georges Bataille, and Gilles Deleuze, with whom he coauthored a short book on Melville's character of "Bartleby," likewise play a role in his work. It is certainly safe to say that his work is centered upon what is considered in the Anglo-American world to be "continental thought."

3

On the whole, his is a remarkably cohesive body of work, one which links his early writings in near seamless fashion with his later projects, one of the themes I will be pursuing subtly under the text of this book. This consistency of thought, if it can be labeled as such, means that it is often possible to find the same or similar themes present in varying contexts from publication to publication. In recent years, his writing has become immensely popular in a remarkably short span of time, and has seemingly gone beyond the traditional disciplinary boundaries that so often characterize academic discourse and into a vaster, fuller interdisciplinary dimension which perhaps better characterizes the world that he addresses.[6]

To attempt to isolate something like the "theological" in his work, at the expense of so much else essential to comprehending his work, would be a somewhat reductionistic endeavor. At most, what this book will attempt to be is little more than a specifically focused introduction to his work, a theologically inflected and all-too-brief study of what could be said to constitute the major "theological" lines of thought within his corpus that have surfaced thus far. What will not be offered here is an in-depth critical analysis of his work, something which I will perform only minimally and at times often simply in the footnotes. Nor will this book be an offering of a theological evaluation of his most basic premises, no matter how tempted I might be at times to do so. In essence, it seemed somewhat impossible to form an original synthesis of his "theological" thoughts while also providing a rigorous critical evaluation of those same ideas in such a brief work. I am here rather attempting to present Agamben's work as it is, or as much as this can be shown, to trace the themes as they appear within his writings and as faithfully as I can in order to allow his work to resonate within the reader of its own accord. That is, I hope to let the profundity and radicality of his thought produce scores of its own music without some of the critical dissonance being present that often hampers creative thought.

Chapter 1

The State of Original Sin, or On Language

The Quest for Language

In a rather fragmentary appendix to his work *The End of the Poem*, Agamben briefly pauses to reflect upon the *Inferno* of the medieval Italian poet Dante Alighieri, specifically its portrait of a helpless soul named Nemrod who is languishing for eternity in hell. Nemrod, we soon discover, is the biblical figure legendarily cast as both a masterful hunter and as the instigator of the building of the tower at Babel.[1] In Dante's version, Nemrod is forever being punished for the latter act with "the loss of meaningful language," a fitting punishment, we are left to presume, for someone associated with the arrogance of trying to construct a tower to the heavens. Nemrod is consequently portrayed as capable of understanding no one and is thus eternally isolated from everyone. Hence, as Dante tells it, "every language is to him as his is to others, which is known to none" (*EP* 124). In his commentary on Nemrod's tale, Agamben lingers upon this nightmarish scene in particular, in effect wondering aloud what the prey which Nemrod sought actually was and why his hunt was traditionally said to be "against God." He concludes that "[i]f the punishment of Babel was the confusion of languages, it is likely that Nemrod's hunt had to do with an artificial improvement of the one human language that was to grant reason unlimited power" (*EP* 124). If the building of the tower of Babel was the visible evidence of this crime, was Nemrod's actual sin, in fact, and as Agamben speculates, the act of trying to surpass the one language given to humanity, the language of God, and that which, in fact, gave rise to the (overly) rational propensities of humankind?

This reading of Nemrod's character stands to reason, Agamben suggests, especially if considered within the context of Dante's admission of his own personal "hunt for language," a hunt which crisscrossed throughout many of his works, and which, we might add, seems to bear a fitting witness to the necessary, but often perilous, task of writing. According to Agamben's retelling, Dante might perhaps have been seeking an answer to the potentially insurmountable question of why we, as a unique species of animal, often find ourselves more than just somewhat compelled to write. From the letters and emails we send to the books and magazines we read, and from the blogs that proliferate on the web to the latest status updates on Facebook, we write and write and write. Yet how often do we actually stop to reflect upon what it is exactly that we seek to convey through our use of language. How indeed are we to capture the essence of things in language at all? Or, we might add, what is it that we are really trying to express through our use of words?

These questions, of course, become central to Agamben's reading of Dante, though they essentially remain implied in this immediate context. There is a subtle impulse under Agamben's text that quickly expands beyond this medieval poetic framework and blossoms into new inquiries for the present day, such as: What does our desire to use language ultimately say about us in the end? Or, more to the point, how do we seek to construct ourselves *through* language? These are questions which Agamben will bring up time and again elsewhere in his writings (cf. *LD*; *P* 37ff.; *RA*; *SL*) and which seem to frame this singular inquiry into Nemrod's potential sin.

The figure of Nemrod fascinated Dante because his sin is that of which Dante himself appears to be guilty. Nemrod had sought, and perhaps got too close, to the limits of language, a task that every serious author must confront either sooner or later. And it appears thus as the ultimate confrontation with which Agamben himself seems eager to engage. Hence, Agamben concludes here that the quest for a poetic language is best symbolized by the "disturbing sign of Nemrod and his titanic hunt," because it is this hunt which signifies the "mortal risk implicit in every search for language that seeks in some way to restore its originary splendor" (*EP* 125). It is the fire behind a passion then that, one could say, might burn down the entire house. Perhaps it is also, however, as if Dante himself were saying, through his use of Nemrod's legendary character: *search, if you will, for the origins of language, but be careful, for this desire for language may in the end consume you.*

Indeed, if we adhere to Agamben's reading, how must we imagine Dante to have felt to construct such a scene in an imaginary hell, one wherein his own desire to form an "illustrious poetic language" is torn between its disastrous consequence (the Babelic loss of meaning) and its exalted form of poetic endurance (what Dante hoped his work might become)? Perhaps akin to the dual reactions many authors experience upon viewing their own work, that it is either a magnificent expression of the human condition or a pile of rubbish meaningful to no one (two reactions often felt in close proximity to one another I might add), Dante's quest for language is torn from within from the very beginning. In many ways, his struggle is nothing new to our times which are perhaps best characterized by a host of self-reflexive authors who are willing to write themselves into their work as figures in search of the limits to which language can be pushed.[2] This fact of our epoch, accompanied by the proliferation of poetic works which seem to pass beyond all comprehensible meaning, seems only to confirm Dante's initial suspicions about Nemrod's "hunt."[3] In many ways, what Dante seems to discover in Nemrod's tale is a fundamental and highly problematic truth concerning all of humanity. He invokes what might be called a perplexing difficulty, or aporia, of our being animals who use language and who try in some sense to constitute ourselves *through* language. This is a feat which often leaves us contemplating which came first, the selves which we are or the words which we use to describe those selves. Or, as Agamben may in the end have it, perhaps these are merely two sides to the same action which we struggle to articulate. It is an inexpressible aporia *of* language, then, which has been uncovered by this literary hunt *for* language. It is, we are told, "an antidivine arrogance that exalts the calculating power of the word and an amorous search that wants to remedy Babelic presumption" (*EP* 125). It is an inescapable risk that everyone who enters language must undertake.

I can think of no better way to introduce a work devoted to the study of Agamben's relation to theology than this. As my analysis of his work gradually unfolds within these pages, I hope it will become clear that Agamben almost ceaselessly "runs up to" and "bumps into" the history and inner workings of language whenever he comes closest to taking up the major themes running through the history of theology. And, if we consider his work seriously, then this interaction is no coincidence, but rather occurs with good reason, as we shall see. The inexpressibility of the existence of language, which he will elsewhere call the very essence of "revelation" (cf. *P* 39ff.), allows us to see theology from another perspective, to question its most basic and cherished terms in an effort to re-envision its history and purpose. Indeed, Agamben's work, on the whole, seems to be given over more and more in recent years to the contemplation of traditional theological concepts and themes, a project which appears to make him as eager to examine theology as to completely redefine it. Hence, another risk is constantly being run: that Agamben's philosophy suggestively "undoes" theology, at least as we historically have known it, or that it perhaps threatens to remove its content while preserving its empty shell alone.

This "profanation," as he will come to call it, of our most significant, Western theological concepts has not diverted Agamben's interest from the history of theology proper. In fact, his work has only drawn closer to theology over the years, with his most recent works focusing on some of the richest tapestries woven within the theological tradition, and with all of its various central arguments yet put on display in his writings (cf. *RG, SL, N*). Agamben's confrontation with theology, for it is no less a confrontation than a near total reformulation, becomes immediately discernable in his attempt to reveal the tensions present within every search for language, in our every effort to cement ourselves *in* and *through* language, which is for him the religious task par excellence. This perspective opens up an entire hermeneutical field through which Agamben reads other literary historical figures, though this time in direct relation to what constitutes the grounds of the theological.

This is, to extend his analysis of Nemrod and language further, how he, for example, brings the work of the late Italian poet Giorgio Caproni within the scope of Nemrod's (and Dante's) hunt for language.[4] In the same subsection of *The End of the Poem* where he address Dante's *Inferno*, Agamben subsequently relates how it is in Caproni's late poetry that "an obsessive and ferocious hunt" likewise develops, one "whose object is language itself." Moreover, it is "a hunt that unites the biblical giant's challenge to the limits of language with Dante's pious veneration." It therefore involves "two aspects of human language (Nemrod's naming and the poet's amorous search)" which, for all intents and purposes, "have now become indistinguishable" (*EP* 125). The inclusion of Caproni within this list of figures and suggestions, however, marks a significant shift away from Dante's understanding of the poetic endeavor, something which, for him, appears to stand much closer to granting at least some allowance for divine activity. There is something else in Caproni's work, however, that Agamben wishes to dwell upon for a while, something which in fact brings the theological implications of this fracture in our desire for language to the forefront.

The quest for language, Agamben explains, becomes in Caproni's eyes a "mortal experience" whose prey is speech itself, a searching for the thing which cannot ever properly be said in language, and, for this reason, any "saying of speech" itself is fleeting, completely ephemeral: "Speech now turns to its own logical power; it says *itself* and, in this extreme poetic gesture, grasps only its own foolishness and appears only in its own dispersion" (*EP* 125). This is to say, whenever we try to capture the bare existence of language *through* language, we run up against the limits of language as well as the uttermost limits of our humanity as we have defined it. We can try to express nearly anything in and through language *except the very fact that language itself exists*, which is a fact we can only assume with our being. It is this truth as it were that also potentially serves to undo our linguistically constructed selves. To confront language is to confront ourselves, to reveal the essence of what makes us human. In so many words, it is also, as he will elsewhere state through the use of an analogy, an attempt to pronounce the unpronounceable name of God that is at stake historically within this search for language, a task we find ourselves challenged with again and again (cf. *CC* 76–77). In a very direct sense, then, our efforts to pronounce the existence of language are bound up with our (in)ability to express our own being, the realm of the divine and our relationship to it.

It is Caproni's poetry which signals for Agamben a modern transition to another way of expressing the inexpressible situation in which humanity finds itself, defined *in* and *through* language.[5] But this time, opposed to Dante's attempt to bring the quest within the sphere of some divine order, a state of being now exists that coincides with what Caproni once referred to as a "solitude without God," including, as Agamben summarizes it, the experience of the freedom to believe in God while knowing that there is no God (*EP* 91–92). This is the state that humanity fundamentally rests within as an aporia of our existence, something it constructs itself *out from* in the form of a project which Agamben sees as often having been confused with various religious or theological endeavors enacted throughout history.

The State of Original Sin, or On Language

Rather than promote some form of a "negative theology," or a theology which attempts to circumscribe the boundaries of what cannot be said about God, however, in the poetry of Caproni there is what Agamben calls a poetic "atheology" that takes place, one that is "in flight beyond every familiar figure of the human and the divine" (*EP* 90). This initial starting point will, as Agamben's work progresses, become the central principle that serves to dismantle the boundaries which have been constructed along the borders of so many classifications and divisions that seemingly hold the representations of our world together, such as between the human and the animal, the subject and the object, or even the human and the divine. For these are the boundaries which we make *in* language in order to construct our self-image *through* language, to fabricate humanity as it were. In this respect, his contextualized retelling of Dante's tale is emblematic of his entire theoretical undertaking, from its beginning to the present day. As we see time and again, he mines the theological heritage, as with the biblical one here or as with the literary scene of his Italian heritage (cf. *S*), in a "hunt for language" which appears at once as the necessary and yet blasphemous task of all human beings: to push language (and consequently theology) to its limits. It is the risk continuously placed before humanity that Agamben does not wish to set aside: the challenge of illuminating a poetic language in the face of a "fallen" and increasingly desperate humanity, one prone to Nemrod's sin of attempting to complete the one given language that Adam used to name the animals in Eden (cf. *SA* 33). The sin, as Nemrod testifies and as we will continue to see unfold before us, was an understanding of language as being a useful tool for establishing ourselves as sovereign over the insecurities that otherwise rage through the "human animal." Nemrod's sin, then, was of trying to "complete" what could not, and will never, be completed: of classifying, reordering, indeed, resignifying the human animal itself.

In no uncertain terms, this sin, embodied as a "hunt for language," and as that which haunts many religious traditions still, is the "original sin" that Agamben seeks to illuminate ever more brightly as the cornerstone for his critique of all society, one which is not just "Western" and not just "civilized." Just as with even the grandest historical narratives that attempt to present religious truths, there is certainly a universal appeal to his claims. Our "original sin," as he tells us elsewhere, is the state wherein we dwell as human beings caught within this quest for a language to complement the language we have already been given but cannot ever fully express, a frustrating and yet interminable state that comes to define our existence as creatures immersed in a medium (language) that we rely upon to posit what we have come to call "humanity."

Falling into a State of "Original Sin"

The twentieth century saw the rise of a number of profound evolving theories on the nature of language and its effects upon how we understand our world. One of the most enduring has been semiotics, or the study of cultural signs systems, and how these systems convey meaning in our (symbolic) world. These studies arise, for the most part, from looking at the processes of assigning meaning and value to things within our world, the historical acts of "naming" things as it were. This process, also called "signification," is what gives words their values, what, in essence, allows us to use anything like language in the first place.[6]

What we call or name things takes on a concrete reality in the world before us. That is, a symbolic world, with its various and often political tensions, is itself constructed according to how things have been initially ascribed their value. Exemplified, for example, through the acts of reducing a diverse ethnic population to a singular label or of drawing arbitrary national boundaries through multiple, varied terrains, signification is a force that grants us a certain sense of "cultural intelligibility" though at a reductionistic, and often violent, cost.[7] The power to "know" and "say" what things are, in effect to *name* them as such, is thereby revealed by semiotics as more than an act of "taking part" in a neutral language handed on from generation to generation. Language, in any form, is essentially a fluid, hybrid conglomeration of stakes and tensions which contains as many unjust (racist, sexist, imperialist, etc.) acts of naming as ones that give life to our most basic hopes and desires.[8]

For the most part, linguists and philosophers alike have chosen to accept that this is the situation which we are dealt, and in which we find ourselves, and, in truth, that there is very little we can do about it other than strive, in whatever way possible, to make our acts of naming things more just than they previously were. In Agamben's eyes, philosophical projects such as Jacques Derrida's deconstructionist one, for example, fall into line with this fundamentally misleading assumption about how we are supposed to relate to language. On more than one occasion, Agamben accordingly devotes a good deal of space to distancing himself from what he sees as a wrongful condoning of language's ability to signify reality, no matter how "just" it strives to become.[9] Indeed, from his point of view, what is in fact sinful, *originally* sinful, is that signification exists at all, that we need rely on any form of communicativity which automatically does a demonstrable harm to people in any respect through its reduction of their uniqueness to a given cultural stereotype or representation.

Our "original sin," for him, is therefore to reside within a "state of the spectacle," as he will call it, that "is language, the very communicativity or linguistic being of humans" (*CC* 80; cf. *RG* 15).[10] In his work on the arbitrary partition between the human and the animal titled *The Open*, moreover, Agamben in fact goes to great lengths in order to illustrate how the construction of the human subject in its very essence is built upon this foundation of division and separation, one which has no substance in and of itself other than its ability to signify a (yet heavily contestable) reality. Indeed, the space that is said to offer such a signification is decidedly empty, having no content per se, only bearing its position as a pure functionality of separating and dividing. And this is where our linguistic nature appears perhaps most profoundly, as well as most forcefully: in the construction of the human subject over and against the (or even *its*) world of animality. That is, the human subject, in order to appear as a "human being," must continuously distinguish itself from the other animals, even if such distinctions become more and more difficult, or even impossible to make. The human being must remove him/herself from the animal world, an original act of *transcendence* that Agamben will read as intimately intertwined with the deep theological resonance this word traditionally bears, as well as with its linguistic power to name things and thereby ascribe them with meaning.

The aporia within us that divides us from ourselves and that seems forever unresolved despite our many attempts to resolve it through language is what pushes us to separate ourselves from the animal world. As he describes it, "[t]he division of life into vegetal and relational, organic and animal, animal and human, therefore passes first of all as a mobile border within living man, and without this intimate caesura the very decision of what is human and what is not would probably not be possible" (*O* 15). Here there is a "division of life" itself, one made by human subjects, which is without justification or even the potential for being clearly delineated as identifiable. Thus, for Agamben, life is "*what cannot be defined, yet, precisely for this reason, must be ceaselessly articulated and divided*" (*O* 13, emphasis in the original). Language must survive, indeed it must *thrive*, through its "ceaseless" acts of articulation and division if the human being is to be established as such.

The need to rearticulate the boundaries between human and animal, a boundary which cannot really be said to exist as such, is hereby exposed by what Agamben will call the "anthropological machine," the various mechanisms (or apparatuses) that produce what we have come to know as "humanity" (cf. *O* 33–38). Perhaps somewhat analogous to what Louis Althusser once referred to as "Ideological State Apparatuses," the "anthropological machinery" of our world appears to work most effectively within those social formations which we have traditionally relied upon to give us a strong sense of self: family, nation-states, schools, and churches, among others, for example.[11] Spinning the aporia at the heart of our existence into a space where the "anthropological machine" can construct human subjects is what language then is all about. As a sort of trapdoor exit from the "indiscernability" and "unpronounceability" of our fundamental condition as animals, language is what allows us *as humans* to declare ourselves as sovereign masters capable of naming, or signifying, the rest of the world around us. It is precisely a "zone of indifference" within us, what he will elsewhere call a "zone of indistinguishability" or a place of "pure potentiality," that allows the anthropological machinery of language to engage in a ceaseless production of our being in the space between human and animal, or humanity and its "others" (O 37–38). Humankind thus becomes sovereign within (or *over*) the animal kingdom because it alone can draw a distinction of some sort between what is considered as "human" and what is left to be "animal," despite the fact that no substantial or quantifiable distinction can really be established as such simply through our being, that is *ontologically*.[12]

What becomes evident for Agamben on this point then is that a deeper ontological rift is opened up through this investigation into the boundary between animal and human, a rift which likewise threatens to engulf the entirety of the Western rational and theological project inasmuch as it calls into question our very reliance upon language or the *logos* behind our significations. As he aptly defines the nature of the situation:

> It is as if determining the border between human and
> animal were not just one question among many
> discussed by philosophers and theologians, scientists and
> politicians, but rather a fundamental metaphysico-
> political operation in which alone something like "man"
> can be decided upon and produced. If animal life and
> human life could be superimposed perfectly, then

15

neither man nor animal—and, perhaps, not even the divine—would any longer be thinkable. (*O* 21)

What is clear to Agamben is that, much like Michel Foucault's famous conclusion to *The Order of Things* in which he declares that "man" is a recent invention, the invention of *homo sapiens* is itself "neither a clearly defined species nor a substance; it is, rather, a machine or device for producing the recognition of the human" (*O* 26).[13] And if this "anthropological machinery" could be exposed for what it is, for the damage it has done in determining our "sinful" situation, then perhaps metaphysics as a whole can be "undone" as it were, bringing theology and even religion to a halt along with it. Such would seem to be the conclusion that Agamben is stretching toward in this context.

There is more than simply an uncanny parallel here between the articulation (or "division") of life and the decision of the sovereign (as king, God, or humanity in general) that will come to play so central a role in his later work (cf. *HS*, *SE*). Though Agamben does not explicitly express the connection here as such in these terms, the decision regarding life and death which sovereign power holds over the general populace, and which is grounded in a state of "undecidability" (as a "state of exception" to any governing norm), is the same structural feature which governs the boundary between the human and the animal. In this sense, the significations themselves may be arbitrary or empty, but they do indeed reflect the coordinates of established power relations. As the German political theorist Carl Schmitt emphasized repeatedly, and which Agamben has not failed to notice (cf. *SE* 1ff.), the person who casts the decision for the state of exception is the sovereign power.[14] And, we might only here add in this context, that the animal who can decide that it is not an animal like all the others is sovereign over the other animals, simply, as it were, by declaring it to be so. In truth, however, the space that affords us to make such a decision is actually empty, devoid of the "special" content we often assume it has. The only content it seemingly contains consists in our decision to be different, to be in fact sovereign (*O* 38). As Agamben will phrase this situation elsewhere, and with a more distinctly political undertone of how this principle has become exposed within our age in a new way: "The historic-social experience of our time is that of an original partition, an *Ur-teilung*, that has no appropriation to accomplish, a sending that has no message, a destiny that does not originate in any foundation" (*P* 112). It is now only the establishment of a defining boundary without any significant meaning or reason for its existence being attached to it that has come to define our age.

This same theme is picked up by Agamben in a series of essays gathered under the title of *Profanations,* a title which certainly indicates the overall projected horizon of where these thoughts have taken him with regard to what has thus far been considered sacred. There, again, we hear a similar refrain regarding the classifications and equivalences of the work of identification, here referenced under the label of "species." The "species," accordingly, is what humanity attempts to fix as a substance, to attain an identity as such (*PR* 59). Our very intelligibility in cultural terms depends upon it, and in some sense at least this would seem to be relatively all that matters, that something *is* signified and that someone gains (sovereign) power through the very act of signification, even if that sovereign figure is known to be unreliable, incompetent, or simply ineffective. Perhaps akin to watching a so-called reality show on television where people become famous simply because they are declared to be famous by the media, this same signifying act, though on a different scale, is indeed, for Agamben, what coordinates the construction of the differing political realities in which we live.

The reality of signification in which we dwell, moreover, is therefore not merely a demonstrable political act, for Agamben is quick to remind his reader that they should bear in mind that the implications of this act of identification are "theological, psychological, and social." It is in fact a unique intermixture of the three, formed in such a way that the difficulty subsequently

17

becomes one of trying to untangle the effects of one domain upon another. Indeed, there is little to distinguish one from the other, and this will constitute the profundity of his point: "The transformation of the *species* into a principle of identity and classification is the original sin of our culture, its most implacable apparatus. Something is personalized—is referred to as an identity—at the cost of sacrificing its specialness" (*PR* 59). Or, as Agamben elsewhere defines it, original sin is the post-Kantian "reunification of the transcendental subject and empirical consciousness in a single absolute subject" (*IH* 37). In this manner, the limits of our "inexperience" are surpassed through what can only be seen as immanently "experienceable" and therefore classifiable as being under a species. The actuality of a signified world wins out over an unsignified potentiality, we might add, using the same Aristotelian categories (potentiality/ actuality) which Agamben finds so useful in other contexts (cf. *P* 177–184). In this sense, actuality holds the creative naming power over the "other," whether the "other" in question be animals or other human animals often denigrated as "less than human" to those wielding such power (cf. the conceptualization of "bare life" in *HS*). It is not a coincidence, then, that the power of naming things is often perceived as a godlike power, the power of a Creator who is transcendent to (as it has often been put) "His" world.

In a world of actuality, one where theo-political forms of sovereignty continue to reign, each thing must be signified, must be named in language, *by* language, even if this act is a violent reduction of the thing itself. In so many ways, Agamben tells us, all we are left with is the reign of "the spectacle," the lot given over to those immersed in a world lost to original sin. This is an experience of the spectacle which is "the separation of generic being" (what he elsewhere calls "whatever being" (cf. *CC* 2ff.)) and which is said by him to signal "the impossibility of love and the triumph of jealousy" (*PR* 60). It is the denial of the amorous search by the violence which would, in drastic measure, reduce the beloved's particularity that would otherwise present itself beyond what any language could do justice to.

Following the lead of the Situationist Guy Debord, Agamben refers to this fallen state of humanity as a "pure form of separation" (CC 79). And this is the actuality with which Agamben is here concerned: an actuality that is in fact an image come to life, a virtual (phantasmic, mythical) decision that reality be so because someone declares that it should be. It is a reality, in other words, that is, and could only be a fictional bid for sovereign power. Hence, this power is isolated, closed to the "other power" (presumably) of love, its amorousness, that single characteristic perhaps beyond jealousy and its desire to establish itself in language.

Beyond the Spectacle of Paradise

As Moses proclaimed to the Israelites in the wilderness, what we have before us (i.e., signification, language, even law) is both a "blessing" and a "curse," perhaps in the end nothing more than a demonstration of the risk that lies buried in the precarity of our existence as human beings.[15] As Agamben himself will elsewhere reiterate, every act of naming, of labeling, or representing through language, is both "a blessing and a curse" (SL 108). This is the situation we find ourselves in as creatures who have "fallen" into the state of this "original sin." This linguistic being that we bear witness to at the core of our represented selves is thereby also, for Agamben, a mark of our total immanence and yet evidence of our desire to transcend it. Everything remains within language and nothing could therefore be said to transcend our linguistic habitat; and so the desire grows larger, again and again, *ceaselessly*, to transcend what cannot ultimately be transcended. We wish to make language do what language cannot do, to speak itself into existence and thereby to posit us along with it. But we are trapped within language, within these representations we have given birth to, and therefore, as Derrida famously put it, "there is nothing outside the text." As he elaborates in his often enigmatic work *The Coming Community*, it is in this "society of the spectacle," our state of being immersed in language and therefore "sin," that the existence of language is concealed from us and is separated from our being, thrusting us into a shared (political) existence that attempts to legitimate our being-separate from "others" whether they be animal or human (cf. *CC* 82). Politics, it would seem, is a doomed enterprise from the start, a result of the failure of humanity to cling to its divinely granted and shared language, something which perhaps other animals have not yet shed from themselves, thus allowing them to avoid politics tout court. It is humanity's sole shared "destiny," as it were, under this sign of the spectacle, to be alienated even further from its linguistic habitat, driven together and residing together politically as a result of our shared alienation.

The only thing which could be said to "transcend" our linguistic boundaries, and thereby to preempt any serious threat of nihilism, is the possibility that the existence of language itself could be said. This is, of course, an otherwise impossible proposition toward which religious desire has tried to point throughout history, but which has thus far been unable to state. This exception, however, is the very principle which allows Agamben to maintain such a close proximity to theological discourse and to mirror at times its most intricate inner workings. It is what also appears to shut the door on the entrance of the transcendent altogether, if only, Agamben hopes, we could realize the true nature of what we have come to identify as transcendent in the first place.

With this view in mind, the hinge upon which everything turns reappears: the logic of a "double bind," being caught between a blessing and a curse in our hunt for language, a dilemma that would present both life and death through the risk of pronouncing our linguistic being. And, thus, it is here that the problem is found, but also here that a solution can perhaps be recognized as well, for, if Agamben is to be understood at all on this point, this is the first time in history that we stand capable of declaring the existence of language itself as the real (religious) content that we have been searching after (cf. *CC* 83). The fact of the existence of language—this is the treasure that Agamben will attempt to extract from historical religion, which is specifically, for him, the monotheistic heritage. Indeed, he will attempt to extract it from the *logos* itself which animates this recovery of the amorous search but which also, and seemingly paradoxically, leads us to the profaned truth of our being which cannot be voiced.

This veiling of language's existence is aptly expressed through the many theological attempts made throughout the centuries to come to terms with the source of all mystery, the being of God who can be said to reside entirely within the mystery that God is. And yet, for Agamben, no religious tradition seems to capture this seminal truth as well as Christianity, a religious movement that holds a special place within his writings. For example, and with reference to Saint Paul's association of "mystery" (*to mysterion*) and "the word of God" (*to logon tou theou*) in Colossians 1.26, Agamben makes a fundamental connection which brings about his formulation of the "idea of language" as being nothing more than an inexpressible fact of our existence: "The mystery that was hidden and that is now made manifest concerns not this or that worldly or otherworldly event but, simply, the word of God" (*P* 40), the word of God that is yet without content, a *logos* without transcendent being.

Though perhaps this will appear to some, especially those firmly rooted within the Western theological tradition, as painting too broad a stroke or at times maybe as being itself overly reductionistic, Agamben presses onward to discern the implications of this profound truth:

> If the theological tradition has therefore always understood revelation as something that human reason cannot know on its own, this can only mean the following: the content of revelation is not a truth that can be expressed

in the form of linguistic propositions about a being
(even about a supreme being) but is, instead, a truth that
concerns language itself, the very fact that language (and
therefore knowledge) exists. (*P* 40)

The sole meaning which Agamben thus accords to revelation is
that it exposes a phenomenon which was concealed and, in a
sense, points toward the otherwise incommunicable (immanent) existence of language itself, rather than a (transcendent)
being said through language. Language itself, then, is revealed at
the same time as the foundation of religious thought, here
ascribed to the place held by (the name of) God, otherwise
concealed in "mystery" (cf. *P* 40). Hence, there is a direct continuity established by Agamben between the profane world that
is the immanent world of language, and the "sacred" world
beyond, that is, the "transcendent" realm of God's dwelling and
theology's stated focus. *This* continuity, and nothing else, is what
revelation points to and *it* is the truth that matters, the hinge
upon which all truth ultimately turns. It is manifestly discernable in his numerous propositions that render all religious
content superfluous insofar as any such articulation is intimately
bound up with this fundamental disclosure (cf. *TR* 136–137).
That is, religion does express a profound truth about our reality,
but it also serves to mask this truth at the same time.

Accordingly, Agamben reads the existence of religious doctrine through this singularizing lens and it is on these grounds,
in the hopes of making economic sense of its formulations, that
he posits the rise of Trinitarian theology as "the most rigorous
and coherent way to consider the paradox of the word's primordial status" (*P* 40). As he so remarkably and yet clearly
considers it, the Trinity is the summit of the expression of the
existence of language (cf. *RG* 75ff.):

The Trinitarian movement of God that has become
familiar to us through the Nicene Creed . . . says nothing
about worldly reality; it has no ontic content. Instead it

registers the new experience of the word that Christianity brought to the world. To use Wittgenstein's terms, it says nothing about *how* the world is, but rather reveals *that* the world is, that language exists. The word that is absolutely in the beginning, that is therefore the absolute presupposition, presupposes nothing if not itself; it has nothing before itself that can explain it or reveal it in turn (there is no word for the word); its Trinitarian structure is nothing other than the movement of its own self-revelation. And this revelation of the word, this presupposition of nothing, which is the sole presupposition, is God: "and the Word was God." (*P* 41)

Likewise, any justification given for the existence of God must rely upon these same formulations between language and the divine. This is the "fact" of existence that can only be expressed indirectly and thus what constitutes the basic difficulty in positing arguments concerning the existence of God. Thus, subsequently, in the context of commenting on Anselm's ontological proof for the existence of God, with its focus upon the "greatest thoughts" that can be thought, Agamben is quick to point out

[w]hat the ontological argument proves is therefore that the speech of human beings and existence of rational animals necessarily imply the divine word, in the sense that they presuppose the signifying function and openness to revelation (only in this sense does the ontological argument prove the existence of God—only, that is, if God is the name of the preexistence of language, or his dwelling in the *arkhē*). (*P* 41)

This is the pure place of a Voice which speaks without uttering any meaningful speech per se, a Voice that "signifies signification" itself (*P* 42). The role of Voice here is crucial, because it alone is that which attempts to remove us from the (symbolic) significations of language. For this reason, this focus on Voice is also indicative of certain contemporary trends in thought which would see a shift from language (*langue*) to voice (*parole*), an indicator perhaps of the regression to speech that Agamben seems at times keen to promote (cf. *IH* 60ff.; *LD* 53; *CC* 99–100; *EP* 66 and 75).[16] It is, in this sense, a "gift of the voice by language" which is the establishment of God as divine word (*logos*), recalling the stress often placed upon God's name, or even the more recent psychoanalytic traditions of referring to the "name-of-the-father."[17] "The name of God, that is, the name that names language, is therefore a word without meaning," the place of pure signification without anything yet being signified (*P* 42). It is a Voice which does not yet speak any (signified) language.

What Agamben has here been heading toward, and what in fact is the crux of the matter for him, is something found in the structures of religious thought as a whole, the "logic of faith" that these propositions signal. This is to say that *the* truth of religion par excellence, for him, is to establish the human being *in* and *through* language ("through, with and in" the *logos*, as some Christian liturgies would have it) and thereby set a boundary between humanity and God. It is the Voice that religion hears calling to it without that Voice yet expressing anything in particular, perhaps somewhat akin to God's calling of a person's name without any command or directive yet being given. Religion then builds a system of doctrine upon such a Voice itself devoid of linguistic signification. That is, there is a solitary Voice apparently calling out to us which is itself sufficient to express the place which God holds in relation to humanity, as removed from the symbolic realm of language. It is a Voice, however, which is then reduced into a linguistic form, a Voice incarnated into its fleshly living. This is the real annunciation that Agamben discerns in the Christian message, one often seemingly at odds with other (Pauline) readings of the "Christ event," as we will soon see.

The Real Birth of Tragedy

This universal state of our linguistic being, as well as his adaptation of the phrase "original sin" has much in common with the lineage of thought bequeathed to the world by Christianity. Christianity in fact laid the groundwork for a modern conception of the tragic through its doctrine of "original sin," a point which Agamben himself is quick to incorporate into this analysis of language's role in our lives. Turning to the Church Fathers and Thomas Aquinas as his primary examples, in fact, Agamben begins his exploration of the tragic in his work *The End of the Poem* by stating that: "in its attempt to explain the paradox of guilt that is transmitted independently of individual responsibility through the distinction of natural sin and personal sin, Christian theology lay [*sic*] the foundations for the categories through which modern culture was to interpret tragic conflict" (*EP* 11). This is not, however, an effort to develop something akin to classical, Greek tragedy where the focus was placed upon a character's individual fate, and thus highlighting their inability to escape its pull. Rather, by pointing toward our shame in nakedness after the Fall as illustrative of the situation of human finitude, the Church Fathers were wont to develop, as he emphasizes, a "dark, 'tragic' background that Christ's passion radically alters" (*EP* 12). The Christian narrative, hence, could be seen to rely upon the tragic background of "original sin" in order to surpass it with and *through* Christ's salvific grace, a consistent thematic that has often been portrayed as a contrast between our naked sin and our being clothed in grace (cf. *N* 95ff.). Or, as he renders the thought, "[t]ransforming the conflict between natural guilt and personal innocence into the division between *natural* innocence and *personal* guilt, Christ's death thus liberates man from tragedy and makes comedy possible" (*EP* 13, emphasis in the original). This is the comic element, of course, that Dante had seized upon in his *Divine Comedy*, a movement which seemed to take the then popular literature from its more "serious" tragic focus to an equally serious "comic" one.

For the most part, however, the history of Christianity did not necessarily succeed in effacing the sinful state of language through its comic alternative to the tragic state of original sin. Rather, if anything, subsequent receptions of the Christian message may have in fact distorted its original intent to "go beyond" language and thus sought to maintain a middle ground between the tragic and the comic which yet insists on the quest for language, now simultaneously identified as the *logos* of Christ, or as the ultimate goal of all human desiring to establish itself in language. It is subsequently in this historical shift from tragedy to comedy that Agamben again discerns the importance of Dante's fundamental poetic gesture. Dante, who is to be understood here as the medieval source of the "categorical revolution" that took place in the movement from tragedy to comedy, is framed by him as the instigator of a contrast between the "public" material of tragedy and the "private" world of comedy, wherein Christianity remains as the worldly institution somehow in-between original sin and Christ's salvific act (cf. *EP* 5). Of course, this contrast between public and private seemingly mirrors Dante's private undisclosed love for Beatrice, a woman he ardently admired, but never, as far as we know, approached with his true feelings. This undisclosed desire, it would seem, also defined the generation of the poets who worked under the banner of Dante's love poetry which came to be known as "Dolce Stil Novo," and the influence of this thirteenth-century Italian poetic focus upon love would thus reverberate throughout all of Europe, entering deep within the popular imagination and creating a lasting impression of what should constitute a more proper (Christian) subjectivity (cf. *S* 23–26).

In so many words, Dante's poetry initiated a shift in the journey of the subject, a movement from tragedy, which was a progression from innocence to guilt before the divine, to comedy, which became a progression from guilt to innocence: "Dante thus joined the categories of the tragic and the comic to the theme of the innocence and guilt of the human creature, such that *tragedy appears as the guilt of the just and comedy as the justification of the guilty"* (*EP* 8, emphasis in the original). This is the revelation that Christ's death affords humanity in Dante's eyes. It is in fact the "comic possibility opened to man by Christ's passion" (*EP* 10). A dramatic rereading of sin therefore lays at the center of all these formulations concerning the Christian narrative and the transition from tragedy to comedy. Referring to Aristotle's *Poetics* and the distinctions it makes between tragedy and comedy, Agamben senses the profundity of what he is attempting to formulate and thus states:

> Here the center of both the tragic and the comic
> experience is expressed with a word that is none other
> than the tone by which the New Testament indicates
> sin: *hamartia*. It is curious that this terminological
> coincidence, by virtue of which tragedy and comedy
> could appear as the two poetic genres of antiquity at
> whose center lay *peccatum* (sin), has not been taken into
> account by scholars. (*EP* 9)

His emphasis, as we will continue to see throughout this study of his relationship to theology, is decidedly upon the manner in which the historical lessons of these basic poetic gestures are entirely caught up within the most elemental progressions of religious faith, specifically the Christian tradition, though, as in Dante's case, their import has subsequently been somewhat distorted. And, as before, everything that lay between them becomes consolidated upon the horizon of language, for "after the Fall, human language cannot be tragic; before the Fall, it cannot be comic" (*EP* 10, deemphasized from the original).

As human beings who are always yet on the verge of sin, indeed on the verge of recreating the conditions under which the Fall took place, we are, according to Dante, caught up in the tragedies of love, the only available access to tragedy that could be said to haunt the postlapsarian comic language we inhabit (cf. *EP* 14). Against this background, however, the Dante of the *Divine Comedy* can again be said to restore the properly comic dimension to love beyond the confines of the tragic. Yet, even on the threshold of a turn away from the tragic, Dante cannot fully escape its claims regarding language. There can be no return to a perfect state of happiness or love in Dante's world, because "his comic choice above all signifies the renunciation of the tragic claim to innocence and the acceptance of the comic fracture between nature and person, [and so] Dante must at the same time abandon the love poets'' attempt to return through perfect *joi* [joy] to an innocent, Edenic love" (*EP* 16). This, for Agamben, is where the nature of allegory, and of language, is revealed for what it is, as the expression of "the impossibility of the person," or of personhood itself we might say. Dante's persistent and unique use of allegory, in the context of his reinvigoration of the comedic possibilities opened to humanity through Christ's salvific act, therefore actually points toward the constant recreation of the human subject that takes place under this banner, again signaling for us those ceaseless acts of the recreation of the human being through language. "In this sense, the protagonist of the Comedy is the first 'person' of modern literature" (*EP* 20), though, we might also add, each stage of a new subject in history seems merely to repeat this logic of formulating a subjectivity anew, albeit from a different angle, and is therefore itself as dependent upon the formulation of the subject through language as any other attempt, whether tragic or comic.

Parody

Though Agamben seems to want to preserve the antitragic elements of comedy for contemporary Western thought through his reliance upon Dante and other Italian literary-poetic figures, as well as his oblique insistence upon the relevance of the Christian tradition (cf. *EP* 21), there is another side to this debate with language that Agamben will later find perhaps more convincing.[18] If the movement from tragedy to comedy forever marks the movement of the Christian event within our Western literary culture, then it is perhaps not surprising that Agamben has developed this train of thought further by clarifying the dimensions of our comic dwelling as being also those involving parody. As he tells us in an essay bearing the same name, "[m]odern love poetry is born under the ambiguous sign of parody" (*PR* 46), though parody, of course, can harbor several meanings, and not all of those meanings are here intended. Commonly conceived as an imitation of something which satirizes or exaggerates its source, parody also contains an ancient sense of being that which was separated from song (cf. *PR* 39–40). Hence, a rupture between language and music appears confirmed by the presence of parody, a "dwelling beside" song that seems to indicate something of the general unity that exists between parody and mystery.

Historically, parody initially created a space of "being beside" music, the space that was quickly given over to the creation of prose as we know it. Prose, then, as the parody of song, became a genre defined by its ability to preserve the sense of mystery around which it circles, the opposite (in a sense) of what we have come to consider as "fiction." That is, parody in effect says nothing about its object, but rather preserves its distance from it (*PR* 48). This is in stark contrast to those literatures which would otherwise "enchant" their readers by appearing to dangle the essence of mystery before them, rather than preserve its distance as parody is wont to do. As Agamben will state elsewhere, "[t]he fable had been able to separate itself from initiation rites only by abolishing the experience of the mystery which was at its centre, and transforming it into enchantment" (*IH* 141). Parody, due to its preservation of mystery, however, is thus "stubbornly suspended between reality and fiction, between word and thing" (*PR* 48).[19]

This is the lesson of parody's necessity, in fact, for in order to avoid being tasteless, as Agamben will put it, the closest one can come to representing mystery is through its parody (cf. *PR* 41). Extended beyond prose and into the realm of ritual, parody indeed becomes the basis for importing a different, nontragic, backdrop against which to view the human subject. Hence, its infiltration into theology and the basic practices of its tradition. Liturgy thus becomes a form of parody, if viewed in this way (*PR* 42). Though, as much as parody is able to enter into religious expressions, it also disrupts any genuine presentation of the mystery which is kept at a distance. By doing so, the intentions of parody are found to be none other than "to confuse and render indiscernible the threshold that separates the sacred and the profane, love and sexuality, the sublime and the base" (*PR* 43).[20] By accomplishing much more than Dante's elaboration of the "comic" project, then, the act of invoking parody becomes more essential to preserving mystery in the end than any religious effort to envelop mystery with the practices and pronouncements of a long and varied tradition. This is one of the major truths that Agamben's work on literary theory seems to be pointing toward, even beyond his musings in *The End of the Poem*. As he describes it here, "[l]ike language, life bears a split within itself (the analogy is not surprising, if we consider the theological equation between life and the word that profoundly marks the Christian world). The poet can live 'without the comforts of religion' . . . but not without those of parody" (*PR* 47–48).

There is a certain presentation of the world, its quality "as such," which poetry seems to point toward more "vitally" than those religious expressions which had previously sought to (re)present it.[21] Just as the presentation of "The Thing Itself" is so important to Agamben's project (cf. *P* 27–38; *IP* 123), the entire train of thought which I have been pursuing that would unite Agamben's theories on language and revelation within the genre of parody, a type of writing which is yet capable of preserving the (sacred) mystery which it lowers to a more common (profane) world, is hereby consolidated upon this point.[22] Indeed, a fuller understanding of parody opens up the metaphysical dimensions of literature, ones that had presumably lain dormant under the unpronounceable name of God (the *nomen innominabile* of the Tetragrammaton) until the "Christian" event revealed their reality (cf. *CC* 76–77). What in fact "the metaphysical vocation of parody," as Agamben terms it, reveals is a fracture within language itself, one that "presupposes a dual tension in being" that he has elsewhere taken up repeatedly as coinciding with the modern split in experience constitutive of contemporary subjectivities (cf. *IH* 15ff.). In this way, a contentless space of the "metaphysical" is conceived as a purely immanent sphere that is implicitly created through our inability to express the existence of language. The fact that language itself cannot "say" (or *name*) this space is what, in turn, gives rise to religious sentiment concerning mystery, or that which sits just beyond the reach of our expression.

It is as if we were always sitting beside the mystery we are seeking to discover, but cannot quite reach the threshold wherein we would encounter it in its radiant fullness. This, and nothing less, is why parody matters so much in terms of formulating our humanity. A renewed engagement with expressing a theory of our being, a fuller ontology as it were, is deliberately proclaimed by Agamben as caught up within this fundamental parodic gesture beyond the scope of the tragic. Just as metaphysics exists as an opening beside any sensible experience, parody demonstrates the (linguistic) reality of things existing beside themselves, the object itself "as such" lingering beside its name, or the words which designate it. It is in such measure that we constantly encounter the limits of language as parodic, and not without a certain humor being present (*PR* 49–50). Hence, in this context, it is poetry which again and again demonstrates for Agamben the sheer vitality of these aporias which are all we have to ground our existence. Rather than attempt to master them, the poetic celebrates the split itself, something which Dante singularized within his work and which threatens to overcome any act of mourning; to instead it points toward our dwelling in love if we allow it to do so (cf. *PR* 49).[23]

The traditional attempts to declare the existence of God, or to posit some sustainable metaphysics "beyond our world" (what is otherwise referred to as the "ontotheology" of Western thought), is here brought under critical scrutiny by Agamben through the utilization of parody. Rather than attempt to disprove God's existence, or to refute any mysterious "beyond" to our world, as some have done and as many more will undoubtedly continue to do, Agamben seeks fundamentally to alter the coordinates of how we have constructed those arguments in the first place. Thereby, he is able to state how parody is genuinely an expression of the failure of language to describe the "thing itself," and hence the impossibility of ever truly naming anything (PR 50). Only in this way can parody attest to "the only possible truth of language" (PR 50).

What are we thus to make of parody? How are we to understand the strong force of parody that reaches out to something deep within our humanity over and against its religious yearnings? Or are the basic tenets of religious faith really that detached from those parodic gestures which Agamben here focuses upon?

As a possible answer, Agamben suggests the ancient Greek point within their older comedies where the chorus, after all other actors had left the stage, turned to the crowd and faced them directly, as the more appropriate way to understand the direction in which parody is ultimately headed. *Parabasis*, as this technique was called, in fact suggests something of a solution to the problematic dwelling place of parody, for it is parabasis which brings the relationship of mystery and language to a sort of resolution: "In the gesture of parabasis, the representation is dissolved and actors and spectators, author and audience exchange roles. Here, the tension between stage and reality is relaxed and parody encounters what is perhaps its only resolution. Parabasis is an *Aufhebung* of parody—both a transgression and a completion" (PR 50). In the easing of boundaries that parody (as a form of comedy) had first called into question, such as between the audience and actor, or between the human and the divine, parabasis dissolves the representations we had come to rely upon so heavily in order to maintain the semblance of an intelligible order. Here is the presentation beyond representation that Agamben has been trying to disclose all along.

It is thus necessary to interrupt parody in order to establish a place for us to dwell. The implications of this understanding of the interruption of parody through parabasis seem to lead, for Agamben, to a space being opened up to the side of parody. This is a space wherein "nothing more than an exchange, simply a human conversation" may now take place (*PR* 51). It is, as he will later call it, an act of "profanation" in a certain sense because it is the suspension of the religious-parodic impulse that in turn allows the space of the "truly human" (beyond any "anthropological machinery", and hence even beyond what we typically conceive of as "humanity") to be encountered.

Though Agamben does not say as much in this context, the entrance of the divine into the human, as the core constitutive event which forever marked the Christian legacy, is fundamentally a resolution of the tensions opened up through the parody of the divine present within a monotheistic setting. The figure of Jesus could be seen, in this light, to perform the gesture of parabasis by turning from a traditional "transcendent" position as divine actor on a heavenly stage to the ordinary world of humanity which previously had sat as audience to the activities of the gods. The "lowering" of the divine into the human, however, is a parodic gesture that seems to be resolved through Christ's increased focus being placed directly in relation to a humanity which the Greek gods, for example, were content to keep at a distance.

The ultimate stakes of the task of profanation, a notion which Agamben will utilize as central to his entire project as a whole, are embedded within this understanding of parody and its advance over tragedy, a position which is perhaps not as far off from Christ's original intentions as Agamben's rhetoric might seem at times to otherwise indicate. In other words, if the religious is founded upon a parodic performance of our humanity, then the next inevitable step, as a threshold we have not yet crossed but to which Agamben leads us, is one of absolute profanation, a step away from what we have considered as the "religious" and back toward a more fundamental dwelling in our ownmost interiority that actually performs the truth which Christ potentially sought himself to illuminate. This is something which Agamben would not quite call our "humanity" as much as perhaps our "infancy" or a space of "pure potentiality," two related thematics, to be taken up later on, that seem to directly identify the coming political tasks for the creatures we have come to know as "human beings".

The implication of all this appears to be, at this stage of his argumentation at least, that religion can only sustain itself in our world today as a form of parabasis, that is, as a loosening of the boundaries that signification tries (in vain) to solidify. It should come as little surprise, then, that such a religion would be vastly different from what we have traditionally come to regard as being "religious" in the first place. Agamben's conceptualization would practically speaking involve nothing short of a radical revision of the traditional tasks and teachings of a majority of faiths, as well as a near total eclipse of political forms as we currently know them. This is to say that if Agamben is correctly discerning the truth behind the creatures that we are, we will have to delve deep into an imaginative world within ourselves in order to find the truth of our situatedness on this planet, something that we are perhaps only just beginning to acknowledge. What we might behold then, and for the first time indeed, would appear to be a realm of our potentiality that no singular religious outlook on life can ever hope to exhaust.

Chapter 2

The Eclipse of Humanity

The Vocation of the Human Being

Throughout the course of history, so much ink has been spilled trying to ascertain the precise nature of this animal we call the "human being," as well as the reason and purpose of its existence. Religion, for its part, has seemingly extended this discourse even further, providing a myriad of "calling" stories in which persons are called by God to "go forth" and achieve a unique identity which sets them apart from the rest of humanity. Without such narratives, religions would in fact be devoid of most of their prophets, saints, martyrs, mystics, and other such holy persons. These discourses, though varied and multiple, are often gathered under the heading of "vocation" narratives, for these calling stories actually demand a discernment of our precise vocation *as* an individual human being before the divine. Indeed, the word itself has a history within certain traditions, such as the Roman Catholic one, in referring precisely to those persons who take up a specific religious calling, becoming either a priest or a member of a particular religious order, for example. To this long and varied attempt at identifying what makes us unique, both as humans and as religious persons, Agamben adds his own perspective, one intended to do nothing less than realign the entire search for one's (always unique) identity, the essence of vocation itself.

Agamben's formulation of the human vocation, which exceeds being simply "religious" in any singular sense, is stated in his work in relation to our use of language, as well as religion in general. To begin with, it is important to understand that most traditional senses of one's vocation have been formed in league with humanity's indebtedness to the linguistic act of signification, *the* defining act of humanity as we have seen. Humans have historically "found" their vocations as one "finds" the right word to describe something, in the sense that a "right fit" is determined to take place in both cases. Language and religion once again overlap, it would seem, as the act of signification would seem to draw them together.

Agamben, for his part, has even gone so far as to recently refer to language as a "sacrament" of sorts, an accomplice in the processes of "anthropogenesis" that constitute the human being (cf. *SL* 66). This is a profound connection which already intimates something of the "sacred" link which he intends to draw between language and religion. A genealogy of oaths, such as that which he takes up in his recent book *The Sacrament of Language*, details how there is a force more primordial than either religion or law which engages in symbolic acts of violence, and which is, in essence, the force of signification itself (cf. *SL* 62–64). The *logos* which binds us to this historical task of signification consequently becomes the central principle whereby faith can be said to be guaranteed at all, and which the form of the oath seeks to solidify. This is in effect what will allow him to state that all monotheistic religions utilize the oath as the "essential content of the religious experience" (*SL* 102). Christianity, specifically, according to Agamben, immediately singles itself out as being a step beyond this general experience. In as many words, Christianity is "a divinization of *Logos*" itself (*SL* 102). Here, the reality of humans "putting themselves at play" in language becomes concretized as the major impulse behind all religious experiences, as central then to the experience of vocational aptitude itself. This adherence to "being-called" by one's religious experience is most emphatically expressed, for Agamben, in Christianity's doctrine of the incarnation, wherein all adherents of the faith "promise" themselves to the *logos*. As he summarizes matters here, humanity contrasts its language with its actions, and thereby establishes itself—as well as the realm of the sacred—something which animals themselves cannot do (*SL* 107).

Again, we are brought before the realization that the human being, in order to construct itself as a human being, must speak itself into existence, must pronounce the "I" in speech in order to make it their own (cf. *SL* 110). If philosophy were not the very act of calling this "I" into question, a religious veil would yet remain over the condition of the oath, the very thing which attempts to guarantee the self its (metaphysical, ontotheological) support. Characteristically, then, Agamben, in the name of philosophy, here offers a critique, not only of religious creeds and oaths, of the vocations which religious experiences have often placed upon various persons throughout history, but of signification itself, which has been, unjustly in his view, wedded to a certain interpretation of the Christian narrative. The *logos* has been aligned with signification, a transcendent act of naming bound to the active oath, and seemingly certified by the associated force of the name of God (*SL* 73). Hence, the certainty of one's faith is actually the certainty found in the strength of naming itself, of signification, or the name of God (*SL* 84), a certainty which Agamben seeks here to withdraw.

In essence, oaths, and the vocational direction which they give to those persons who make them (which here goes far beyond simply being aligned with religion, but extends to all spheres of social life), are a declining reminder of a time when religion reigned sovereign over its fabricated subjects, a time when a sacred ("sacramental") bond was woven between the human being and language (cf. *SL* 111). This was a time when humans were "called" into being as one is "called" into language, and therefore "called" into their various cultural vocations ordered by the religious symbolic worldview that signified it. It was an era when swearing an oath on an avowed sacred text meant something to the one taking an oath, something which seems to be slipping in force in our day.

In the era of the oath's decline, as much as of political emptiness, the time has come, in Agamben's eyes, to redirect our efforts at "profaning" our existence entirely—to free ourselves of the last vestiges of these violent metaphysical divisions brought forth through the linguistic act of signification. In this sense, he comes to find that the only thing we, as human beings, are "called" to be is ourselves, beyond any "sacred" calling as a defined historical experience, beyond any ideological or cultural encodings which have been placed upon us—indeed, to be the purely "naked" beings that we are, exposed to one another and without any signified essence being placed upon us. An apparently "posthuman" (or "prehuman" because "presignified"), creaturely being that does not conform to any produced "species" of the human being generated by the "anthropological machinery" thereby arises in his work.[1] This is what will enable him, at certain points in his work, to gesture toward our "infantile" stage of development as somehow being the goal for all of humanity (cf. *IH*; *IP* 95–98). In this formulation, there is definitely the recognition of a certain precariousness to our existence, one that is an exemplary illustration of the fragility of our creaturely being. It is also, however, a shift in perspective beyond what we normally conceive ourselves to be, beyond our typical vocations as it were.

For Agamben, ethics can be said to unfold anew from a realization of our true vocational calling. If there were some preordained sense of who we are, or who we are all called to be, there would be little sense in having an "ethics" at all (*CC* 43). Our freedom, then, is found within our lack of a specific vocation, what Leland de la Durantaye has referred to as a "decreation" of our created selves, a word which would seem to evoke the sheer radicality of what Agamben is proposing.[2] The differences that exist between each unsignified individual who comes to dwell in this world *without* a vocation as such thus constitutes the basis and rationale for ethics to exist in the first place. It is a difference that does not render each individual meaningless or as immersed in nothingness; rather it is the basis for our freedom as potentiality. It is this difference then which must subsequently be respected in its absolute precariousness, according to Agamben's reading of it.

In what can only appear as a most profound gesture of recognizing the unique pure potential of every human being, something which will sound more than just a bit theological at times, Agamben takes measure of the human vocation as nothing less than the recognition of existence itself, an affirmative "yes" he will later state, spoken into a void of nothing (cf. *CC* 103). Already at this early stage of our analysis, Agamben's indebtedness to a Spinozistic philosophy of affirming life begins to move out beyond what appears at times to be the nihilistic ("negative") furor of his arguments. This is a point well worth remembering throughout the next several chapters and is something which I will take up in the conclusion of this work with more deliberate focus. That is, it is very important to bear in mind the fact that, despite what appears to be a complete erasure of all things theological or linguistic, or even *meaningful*, there is yet an absolute affirmation of life lurking underneath it all that cannot be ignored. We may not have a specific, unique vocation that we are called to, he reminds us, but the absence of a particular calling is precisely the freedom to experience the unlimited potential of what we truly are.

In this manner, then, Agamben is reformulating our fundamental grounding in life as a sort of affirmation of our creaturely being rather than as the "human beings" which we have sought so hard over time to fabricate. That is, he is definitely, and defiantly, moving counter to those theological assertions that would posit all acts of generation as inherently corrupt or intrinsically sinful. Hence, he can pronounce in this context how ethics "has no room for repentance," at least if understood in this fashion. Indeed, the only way to be truly "ethical" is to simply *be* one's ownmost potentiality (*CC* 44). Though perhaps sounding like some perverse form of personal nihilism or the negating of one's own existence (our "actuality"), what he is actually attempting, however, is in reality a preservation of the uniqueness of our existence—an absolute respect for our differences that has more than a little overlap with other ethical projects of the last century.[3]

This is also a move for Agamben toward refusing an "actuality" of being which is itself overly indebted to the violent representations that have scored our political and historical landscapes and interactions. His challenge to the historical traditions of theology thereby expands upon this claim, rearticulating the way in which sin has generally been conceived—that is, as the refusal to enter into the pure actuality that God has often (mistakenly) been defined as being. The vision of God as the *Actus Purus* ("Pure Act") of the theologians, once the stronghold of ancient and medieval reasoning, has been intertwined with a definition of sovereignty which in turn produces a violent political power with which our world continues to struggle.[4] This is a conception of sovereignty that proceeds from a sovereign deity, one that Agamben himself will contest through his reading of the works of Saint Paul (cf. *TR*). That is, he will utilize parts of the theological tradition as critical voices aligned against any monolithic representation of a sovereign theology or sacrality. This reading would therefore serve as a correction of the manner in which theology has historically functioned to divide the world up through the sovereign vision it has of it, rendering all persons as part of a grand representational scheme that would see each member become either believer or pagan, friend or enemy, part of the good it seems to represent or the evil it seeks to destroy.

In so many words, Agamben revisions things entirely, profaning what was once sacred so that in effect we may begin to see how, in reality, the only sense of evil that can ever truly exist is one in which we repress our proper mode of being, our pure potentiality beyond any vocational "actuality" (*CC* 44). To grasp our pure potentiality that lies within our "infantile" being and thus to refuse any sovereign conceptions of a deity who condones those violent schemes of representation in our world is the task that we are repeatedly and insistently called to by Agamben. It is what will ultimately enable him elsewhere to

state that we are only called to the "revocation of every vocation" in an effort to achieve this state of dwelling in our
potentiality (*TR* 23–24). In the end, then, the state of original
sin is therefore nothing more than our feeling of a debt we
hold with regard to our own potential, a bad conscience that
originates when we enter into the realm of significations and
ignore our true vocation beyond all vocations.

The Nonmystical Darkness of Potentiality

It is no coincidence that Agamben turns to classic definitions of
God's existence in order to express a relationship between
God's existence and our inability to pronounce our own existence. Reformulating our sense of existence, our very identities
beyond all vocational callings, means that we must likewise
reformulate our understanding of God's existence beyond how
we have typically conceived it. For this reason, Agamben dips
far back into the history of philosophy, reaching all the way to
ancient Greece and Aristotle's significantly influential description of the divine as the cause of all causes, a definition which
has motivated countless theologians and philosophers alike over
the centuries. Indeed, this revaluation is most fully disclosed,
for Agamben, through focusing upon Aristotle's definition of
God as thought thinking thought, "that is, to a thinking that in
actuality thinks its own potentiality to think" (*HS* 47). A potentiality is thereby awakened within our reflective capacity, one
that seemingly arrives at the same time as the infantile primate
decides to cease following its genetic coding and becomes the
"human" species as it were (cf. *IP* 95–98). This potentiality is
one which is impossible to reflect upon exactly (as "thought
thinking thought") and yet it is one that could also be said to
ground all reflective activity as such. In a very literal sense then,
for Agamben, anthropology would precede philosophy, would
indicate the change within our creaturely being that would
make philosophy possible, a fact locatable within the acquisi-
tion of language itself. According to his conceptualization, this

insight runs parallel to our grounding of language in our inability to pronounce the existence of language, another deft attempt to locate and solidify our vocation beyond our creaturely being.[5]

Yet, several questions remain. For example, if potentiality is the blank slate, so to speak, upon which all representations are carved, how then does it ground our cultural, political, social, and religious norms? For that matter, how can potential even be said to exist in and of itself within a created being? Are we not actually existing human beings who live and breathe and *actually* do things? Or, more precisely, if potentiality lies at the center of our creaturely being, as our most proper characteristic, then what does it mean to pass over into actuality in any sense in the first place? Who or what could be said to inhabit such an actuality then?

Difficult as it might be to comprehend conceptually, for Agamben, potentiality exists as an autonomous entity that must be respected as such and not consistently considered as subordinate to actuality in any sense. He will therefore fiercely defend this interpretation of Aristotle's most fundamental philosophical claim by maintaining the integrity of an ability which is not yet exercised, an "autonomous existence of potentiality" that exists even when the individual does not exercise it (*HS* 44). Like the musician who maintains the ability to play even when not playing their instrument, in this way, potentiality can become (through "not-becoming") an infinite source of inspiration, the blank slate which grounds every representation, though it certainly does not have to pass over into a representational world (cf. *IP* 26).

This is where Agamben's most fundamental challenges to the political order will originate, since to exist in potentiality means to inhabit a world without representations, those steady bulwarks of what seems to be all social and political life. Potentiality is here envisioned as caught up in an existence of its own, and is only embraceable as such. It is bound up within a movement away from traditional notions of vocation and toward an inexhaustible wealth of being that was always present from the beginning, from our prelinguistic, creaturely dwelling. For this reason, he states: "The potentiality that exists is precisely the potentiality that can not pass over into actuality" (*HS* 45). In order for it to exist at all, it must therefore not pass over into its negation.

It is Herman Melville's figure of "Bartleby the Scrivner" who, in his insistence upon the preference not to, maintains a certain sense of "im-potentiality" that Agamben seeks to elaborate more fully (cf. *B*, translated in *P* 243–271; see also *CC* 35–37). Bartleby, of course, was the subject of Melville's short story bearing the same name, a copyist who refused to copy any longer, who in fact refused to inscribe the letter of the law any further in his office, and who is, as Agamben would have it, Melville's subtle commentary on the corrupt power of the will, the will-to-power which drives so much of the modern world.[6] Hence, rather than "I will not" being the declarative phrase of resistance uttered to his boss, Bartleby's "I prefer not to" is an emphatic distancing of himself from the entire machinery of actuality and its formulation of a decisive will, which is to be seen here as little more than a slightly veiled attempt to obtain power. According to Agamben, it is this figure of the nondescript Bartleby who in fact reveals an absolute contingency at the foundation of existence, whether humanity's or God's, because he disrupts the very processes of signification that had previously determined the boundaries of each. Hence also derives his subtitle for the essay: "On Contingency." This ineradicable contingency is what theologians have historically disdained in preference for a deity of "pure actuality," a deity whose every utterance revealed the power to make decisions, in fact to be sovereign—the *Actus Purus* found in Aquinas, for example.

According to Agamben, however, such gestures indeed run amiss of Aristotle's most fundamental point concerning the nature of potentiality. As Agamben reasserts in this context:

What Aristotle undertakes to consider in Book Theta of the *Metaphysics* is, in other words, not potentiality as a merely logical possibility but rather the effective modes of potentiality's existence. This is why, if potentiality is to have its own consistency and not always disappear immediately into actuality, it is necessary that potentiality be able *not* to pass over into actuality, that potentiality constitutively be the *potentiality not to* (do or be), or, as Aristotle says, that potentiality be also im-potentiality (*adynamia*). (*HS* 44–45)

The genius of Aristotle, according to Agamben, is precisely this insistence on the maintenance of a state of potentiality that does not pass into actuality, a state which both commentators and translators of Aristotle's work have seemingly neglected to give its due weight (cf. *HS* 45–46). Exhibiting a potentiality that is also its own impotentiality because it does not pass over into actuality, which would only serve as a negation of its potential, is Agamben's movement toward what could be described as a raw form of creative energy. Or perhaps it could be considered as a darkness beyond all darkest nights, the source spring from which both poets and mystics draw their illuminations. At the very least, it is the renunciation of any vocation which would threaten to limit this obscure but vital force within us.

Agamben will in fact make such claims, adducing that potentiality is ultimately what sustains all religious or mystical urgings in the end, though it has not necessarily been perceived for what it is. This is what Agamben himself hopes to rectify, the seeing of the things themselves, their true revelation beyond presupposition, even going so far as to claim that this is also what inspired Saint Paul to identify Jesus as a sort of Bartleby figure who refuses to copy the "dead letter" of the law before him, opting to save what was not, rather than redeem what was, hence to affirm our pure potentiality without its becoming any sort of actuality (*P* 269–271). In this way, Jesus' actions are perceived by Agamben as intending to lead us back to an original unity with God through a second creation that is an apocalyptic "decreation" of sorts, as already suggested, or what Agamben will elsewhere refer to as the ultimate act of profanation of these supposed sacred callings from a beyond (cf. *PR* 79).

It is for this reason that an overlap develops between the way in which he characterizes the realization of one's own potentiality as our true vocation (the reality of one's existence as a possibility or potentiality) and how he had earlier posited revelation as the realization of the existence of language itself. Understood thus, potentiality, by its very nature, demonstrates a connectedness between beings that results from a lack within our being, a failure to pass into actuality that is in reality a defining characteristic of who we are as human-speaking-beings. Language, then, can be seen as the attempt to articulate this lack at our core, an attempt which often flounders insofar as it circulates around our potentiality and is often partially utilized to try to avoid the realization that this lack is what makes us genuinely who we are. This lack is constitutive of our situation as a "creaturely" species, and should not be covered over by language or religion. As he puts it in another context, one where he also takes up Aristotle's basic distinction between *dynamis* (potentiality) and *energeia* (actuality),

> [p]otency—or knowledge—is the specifically human faculty of connectedness as lack; and language, in its split between language and speech, structurally contains this connectedness, is nothing other than this connectedness. Man does not merely know nor merely speak; he is neither *Homo sapiens* nor *Homo loquens*, but *Homo sapiens loquendi*, and this entwinement constitutes the way in which the West has understood itself and laid the foundation for both its knowledge and its skills. The unprecedented violence of human power has its deepest roots in this structure of language. (*IH* 7–8)

Violence thereby enters the picture through the human attempt to gain mastery (sovereignty) over this situation of a primordial lack at the center of who we are. We are willing to engage in violent acts if they can possibly preserve our identities as we have constituted (signified) them in their national, religious, ethnic, or personal forms.

If Agamben seems to be a bit preoccupied with establishing the correct reading of Aristotle's formulations on potentiality, it is not without good reason. In point of fact, it has been this precise (mis)reading of Aristotle's work which has led to the various (mis)uses of power by those historically "established" ruling figures such as the sovereign powers of this world or a God deemed to be nothing but "pure actuality" itself (the *Actus Purus* again). The problem, then, would seem to be that not only have we constructed a vocational sense of self upon a false sense of actuality, but equally we have built our social and political domains upon this foundation as well.

Agamben therefore cleverly depicts the struggle between potentiality and actuality as being parallel to the political tension between *constituting* power, or that power which founds the state, but which necessarily must remain outside the state (its "origins" as it were), and *constituted* power, or that power which comes to be through and within the state (its daily functioning) (*HS* 44; cf. also *RG* 149ff.). In this sense, our political "actualities," the typical day-to-day affairs of state, can be seen as being dependent upon the potential power which lies latent behind it, and which, in effect, grounds it. This is highlighted by Agamben in order to illustrate the profound linkage between those theories of our being, our ontological claims, and our most fundamental political insights, as well as the manner in which the connection between them could be said to be locateable within a theological framework (the "actuality"/*Pure Act* of a deity who could be said to ground any political claims to sovereignty).[7]

In his work on the *Homo Sacer*, then, the first major work of his to have a significant impact upon the English-speaking philosophical scene, and one which is centered upon Western definitions of sacrality in relation to the political, the articulation of this political paradox becomes in many ways a restatement of the fundamental metaphysical problem of the Western world since Aristotle. As he expresses the formulation, the relationship between constituting power and constituted power runs parallel to that between potentiality and act (*HS* 44). The difference between these forms of power is fundamental to our understanding of political systems, yet it is one that has consistently eluded a precise definition. It is this link that allows us to understand how sovereignty could be said to exist outside the political realm, how, in fact, hegemony is established in a certain sense precisely because potentiality has been historically perceived as subordinate to actuality (cf. *HS* 44). Nonetheless, and as his work on sovereignty will confirm, Agamben's ability to detect the essence of the "political" in the midst of what could be considered as the constitutive aporia of thought, the movement from potential to act, is what gives his work a particular rootedness in the metaphysical, encompassing those metaphysical formulas that once gave rise to the sovereign's divine mandate to rule.[8]

For Walter Benjamin before him, and as Agamben himself notes, it was a contrast of a form of violence that *posits* the state versus a violence that *preserves* the state which revealed this core dynamic of potentiality, something symbolized through the suspension of actuality that takes place in the workers' general strike (*HS* 40).[9] Perceiving the strike as a suspension which embodies the spirit of potentiality, a potentiality that is not "at work," but which yet harbors the *potential to* work, is the nonaction that Agamben will here repeat as essential to reformulating what we consider to be the political in the first place.[10] The suspension at stake here is therefore elsewhere characterized by Agamben as the potentiality symbolized in Bartleby's "I prefer not to" (cf. *CC* 35–37; *P* 243–271). Or as he will put it in this context, it is a potentiality capable of being its own impotentiality, that is, capable of suspending its own possibility (*HS* 45). It is thus the refusal to engage with the "will-to-power" which lies at the heart of the "dead law," or the Western political and economic projects as we have come to know them.

By sticking to the formulations of "actuality" put forth historically in both philosophical and political terms, for example, Agamben interweaves Aristotle's most basic metaphysical claims with the German political theorist Carl Schmitt's theory of sovereignty which he now sees as being implicated in this essential nexus between politics, ontology, and theology.[11] This is a nexus which demonstrates as well how the political is inseparable from the theological in terms of how humanity has perceived its sense of governance (cf. the central themes in *RG*, *SE*). This is likewise what will enable him to make the somewhat startling claim through his descriptions of potentiality that it was Aristotle who first gave birth to our modern conceptualizations of sovereignty as they are understood in the Western world (*HS* 46). This is so, of course, because, if Agamben's reading remains plausible, power is inseparable from the relationship between potentiality and actuality. If humanity has subsequently spent a large portion of its recent past in solidifying a link between actuality and sovereignty, then Agamben now seeks to overturn that singularly misguided connection by maintaining that, truly, and with an almost quasi-mystical tone, the force of a "pure potentiality" is actually greater than the actuality of political sovereignty. For, as he describes it elsewhere, in a phrase that comes to mirror (in more than one respect as we will eventually see) Saint Paul's declaration that he finds his strength in weakness, "[o]nly a power that is capable of both power and impotence, then, is the supreme power" (*CC* 36).[12]

Benjamin's earlier depiction of a "weak messianic force" moving through time to upend the dominant ("strong") ideological claims of "History" finds perhaps its most sustained extension here. This understanding likewise serves to explain the path that Agamben takes between expounding upon the sovereign, the "state of exception" (as developed through Schmitt's work) and the theological speculations of his

Homo Sacer project on the whole, something which might not always appear as immediately justifiable to all of his readers. It would also explain why he often detects this same originary potentiality at work in other philosophical movements, such as in Martin Heidegger's use of *Dasein* or Antonio Negri's political theories (cf. *O* 63–70; *HS* 43–44).[13] These connections in fact ultimately serve not only to critique existing political structures, but also to underline his direct critique of subjectivity as we have constructed it along these same "actual" lines, something which will continue to unfold throughout his work if taken as a whole. In the terms presented here, however, it takes the following form:

> For the sovereign ban, which applies to the exception in no longer applying, corresponds to the structure of potentiality, which maintains itself in relation to actuality precisely through its ability not to be. Potentiality (in its double appearance as potentiality to and as potentiality not to) is that through which Being founds itself *sovereignly*, which is to say, without anything preceding or determining it (*superiorem non recognoscens*) other than its own ability not to be. And an act is sovereign when it realizes itself by simply taking away its own potentiality not to be, letting itself be, giving itself to itself. (*HS* 46)

This is the ambiguity upon which sovereignty is founded, the ambiguity that is revealed most clearly in the abject figure of the *homo sacer*, the obverse creation of the sovereign figure who yet exposes the ruses of sovereign power, and for this reason *must* be killed (or excluded), though not sacrificed, that is, not brought into the realm of "sacrality" which the sovereign has created through the establishment of boundaries between the human and the divine as between the human and the animal.

The pronouncement of such an ambiguity at the heart of understanding sovereign power is essential to comprehending why Aristotle's statements on *dynamis/energeia* are so often misread, according to Agamben. It is what he calls the "constitutive ambiguity" of this Aristotelian theory. Hence, "if it is never clear . . . whether Book Theta of the *Metaphysics* in fact gives primacy to actuality or to potentiality, this is not because of a certain indecisiveness or, worse, contradiction in the philosopher's thought but because potentiality and actuality are simply the two faces of the sovereign self-grounding of Being" (*HS* 47). Sovereignty always exists as "double" in its self-expression, for in order to grant itself some sense of "actuality," being must suspend (ban/abandon) a part of itself in order to constitute its semblance of power or strength. The sovereign is the one capable of standing on the divide between potentiality and actuality, at the point where they are in fact indistinguishable, in order to declare the right to rule as an almost divine act of calling oneself into being (cf. *HS* 47). Hence, the historically attested divine (sovereign) mandate to rule can also now be seen for what it harbors underneath: the pinnacle of one's vocational sense of being-human, the ultimate effort made by each human individual to lift oneself out from among other animal species and to posit oneself *as* always, uniquely human.

On Sovereignty

The preceding reflections on potentiality were grounded in a recognition of the contingency of our existence, a contingency that many would like to forget exists as such. It is a contingency that many would like in fact to move beyond and replace with a decisive power that would stand over and against the threatening and apparent weakness of potentiality. Things appear much more "lasting" (even "eternal") when they are sovereignly taken to be a part of our "actual" living conditions, the "facts" of our existence. As one might suspect, a good deal of "natural law" throughout history has in fact taken root upon these same grounds. To be sovereign, then, is to make a choice to sever ourselves from our precarious animal existence and attempt to surpass those conditions through the establishment of a unique

vocation beyond what all other species seem capable of expressing with their being. As might be expected, of course, any
attempt to posit such a decisive "sovereign" power, if we follow
Agamben all the way down on this, fundamentally misreads the
truly imaginative, creative power locatable with the space of our
pure potentiality. This is a misreading which, as history testifies,
has essentially grounded most of our political, philosophical,
and theological activity, though if we allow ourselves to be
given over, as the creaturely human beings that we are, to a
condition of our simply "being-thus" beyond sovereign forms,
existing, that is, simply *as one is*, "absolutely exposed, absolutely
abandoned" (*CC* 39) within our world, then things might be
very different indeed. If we could only embrace the contingency of our world, instead of trying to overcome it, we might
find a peace which apparently often eludes our "species."

This characterization of a non-sovereign possibility for our
dwelling in this world would certainly seem to go hand-in-hand
with his pronouncement that the world thus understood is
"now and forever necessarily contingent or contingently necessary" (*CC* 40). The opposite of contingency is of course
necessity, a fact which Agamben immediately locates as politically identifiable within the only slightly varied notions of a
"state of exception" which has come to dominate contemporary political endeavors. This is so because actuality is aligned
with necessity, and, in truth, with those justifications for violence which typically accompany it. In this sense, we are able to
see how the contingency of potentiality is so often thrust aside
(or seemingly left behind as it were) in favor of a bid to establish the necessity for power, for sovereign rule and decisiveness,
"natural" laws, and thus ultimately, for the force and violence
seen as "necessary" to uphold these limits. For Agamben, there
is no doubt that Nazi Germany constitutes the exemplary contemporary model of the "exceptionalism" at the heart of
sovereign rule which he seeks to define, though it also creeps
up in his analysis of American imperialism among other
instances (*SE* 11–22; cf. *ME* 15–26, 44).[14] The link between

two such differing states, the Nazi German and the Democratic American, is not so absurd as it might otherwise at first appear to be; rather, their juxtaposition is illustrative of the "threshold of indeterminacy between democracy and absolutism" as he puts it (*SE* 3). This is what, in some sense, allows the suspension of law to take place at sites like Guantánamo Bay as well as in the Nazi German concentration camps of the last century (cf. *RA*).[15] Indeed, as specific instances of American imperialism have expressed, and as Nazi Germany made manifest, the state of exception has ceased to function as "exceptional" in any sense, and is rather now considered as the normal form of juridical rule (*HS* 168). This is so because, as he will make clear from the outset of his work devoted to analyzing the basic contours of the state of exception, "if the law employs the exception—that is the suspension of law itself—as its original means of referring to and encompassing life, then a theory of the state of exception is the preliminary condition for any definition of the relation that binds and, at the same time, abandons the living being to law" (*SE* 1). It would seem that our bondage to law is itself, then, bound to the drawing up of exclusions and the violences which proceed from such a rendering.

In this context, Schmitt once again plays a decisive role in helping to situate Agamben's analysis. By focusing upon this form of governance which has ruled historically almost entirely in a state of an emergency suspension of the law, Agamben takes steps toward once again illustrating the relationship between the state of exception and its theological underpinnings, even beyond Schmitt's lifelong attempts to formulate a type of "political theology" (cf. *RG* 19ff.).[16] In this regard, Agamben's use of both the twelfth-century Italian canonist Gratian and Thomas Aquinas are instrumental for these means, as they allow him to illustrate the close proximity between the theological and the political. Thereby, the state of exception can be perceived as not only a modern form of governance, that is, as a paradigmatic moment within the contemporary political experience (*SE* 7), but also as a theologically grounded conceptualization of the movement from potentiality to actuality, a bid for nothing less than sovereign power and as therefore bound up with our historical definitions of transcendence.[17] Theories of necessity, whether theologically or politically instituted, are essentially theories of exceptionality wherein "a particular case is released from the obligation to observe the law" (*SE* 25). This is what Agamben will subsequently etymologically link to theological formulations of dispensation, those formulations where a Church authority, for various reasons, suspends a believer's obligation to follow the "rules" of the Church.

The problem surrounding the implementation of a "state of exception," however, is that they are portrayed as politically *necessary*, as essential to maintaining the definition and boundaries of a given social ordering *as if* nothing else will do. What Agamben is trying to demonstrate, however, is that our potential to be so much more than what these narrow rules consign us to be dictates precisely that *something else* can in fact be done, even if we have not yet seen what this state of being might possibly be. Yet despite this being the case, humanity mainly refuses to relinquish its hold on the powers which have come to it, even though the questions surrounding the legitimacy of sovereign rule seem only to expand over time and without any possible lasting solutions being given. As he frames this quandary within a political–legal context:

> Hence the aporias that every attempt to define necessity is unable to resolve. If a measure taken out of necessity is already a juridical norm and not simply fact, why must it be ratified and approved by a law . . .? If it is already law, why does it not last if it is not approved by the legislative bodies? And if instead it is not law, but simply fact, why do the legal effects of its ratification begin not from the moment it is converted into law, but *ex tunc* [from then]? (*SE* 29)

In essence, what makes a political decision *necessary* in the first place? If the sovereign is defined as the one who makes a decision for the state of exception, as Schmitt once contended, and as Agamben seems ready to endorse, then what exactly makes such a decision necessary?[18]

The conundrums that arise through this reading of the problematic relationship between natural fact (*factum*) and law (*ius*) are only exacerbated by the nature of necessity itself, something which becomes extremely problematic in and of itself because it is rarely asked whether necessity itself *is necessary*. That is, our thoughts are not taken back to the split between potentiality and actuality which in fact gives birth to the various theories of necessity which have been used historically to posit both the existence of God and the legitimate rule of sovereign powers. Rather, we simply take for granted "the way things are" and the accompanying networks of power that signify our social and cultural realities. Hence, Agamben will refer to this situation as "the extreme aporia against which the entire theory of the state of necessity ultimately runs aground," that is, one which "concerns the very nature of necessity, which writers continue more or less unconsciously to think of as an objective situation" (*SE* 29). Assumed as being as necessary as the human subject of Western political thought, the state of exception and the rule of the sovereign reign unquestioned because they seem to better provide expansive answers to our most (undisclosed) pressing concerns.

Like those vague political and military strategies which claim to be aimed at taking "necessary measures" toward those opposed to a particular national or ideological agenda, and which are often accepted by a populace who need know nothing more than that these measures are indeed "necessary," the act of labeling something as necessary in the first place actually says more about political (sovereign) power than about the truth of the situation; it speaks of a fabricated actuality rather than the reality of our creaturely potentiality and the possibility for another, better existence beyond what lies before us. In other words, we would be justified, if Agamben's analysis holds, to continue asking who indeed decides on the nature of necessity itself, on its "objective" necessity for existing? Who is able to determine what is "of necessity" and what is not? It is in this regard that the decision of the sovereign has been historically posited as an attempt to provide definitive answers to these questions, though, as we have seen, this need *not* be the case. In the end, however, even the sovereign's decisions will be answers that cannot provide or maintain a permanent or just solution to the problems of our existence. Hence they only determine the realm of the political as being a realm that is in constant need of rearticulating and relegitimating its "right" to exist. Indeed, as Agamben puts it, "[i]t is as if the juridical order contained an essential fracture between the position of the norm and its application, which, in extreme situations, can be filled only by means of the state of exception, that is, by creating a zone in which application is suspended, but the law, as such, remains in force" (*SE* 31). A site of pure signification then emerges—the bare minimum, we might say, of sovereign rule. The fracture at the heart of all political-sovereign rule is thus only ever temporarily "effaced" by the creation of an exceptional state that in fact gives birth to the rule of law itself.

The decision of the sovereign, or the creation of the state of exception, is pivotal for the foundation of law, though what content is given to any historical embodiment of law is ultimately inconsequential, as radical as that might sound. From this viewpoint, what actually matters in terms of the social and cultural representations we often live by is rather that a decision is *capable* of being made, that is, that law is somehow born through the decree of the sovereign. More than somewhat ironically, what the law actually says is not as important as its sheer existence. As Agamben phrases it, "[n]ot only does necessity ultimately come down to a decision, but that on which it decides is, in truth, something undecidable in fact and law" (*SE* 30). Indeed, it is not as if law could actually become something permanent or beyond all historical conditions. With reference to the work of Schmitt again, Agamben relates how it is the sovereign alone who can call for a state of exception and who can in fact guarantee "its anchorage to the juridical order" (*SE* 35), and this is a sovereign being who is as historical (and as historically contingent) as the next sovereign will be. Despite this fact, however, the sovereign is perceivable as being both inside and outside the established juridical order, and is therefore the only one capable of making the exceptional decision to declare what is necessary for the rule of law to take effect. Society as a whole finds itself indebted to a system of sovereign articulations made so that the rule of law might govern our precarious existence at a simple remove from the animal world.

Again, the sovereign decision to move from the space of one's potentiality into a (political) sphere of actuality also implicates theology in its most declarative historical statements on the nature and being of God. Hence, one finds the occasional reference to phrases such as the "theo-political" or "political theology" as justly made pairings.[19] The manner in which we describe our very being, then, and nothing less, is caught up in these ontotheological underpinnings of political power and the decisive violence which often accompanies its reign. Agamben, for his part, will bring together this nexus of power, violence, and (ontotheological) metaphysics by defining pure violence as "the extreme political object, as the 'thing' of politics" which is "the counterpart to pure being, to pure existence as the ultimate metaphysical stakes" (*SE* 59). The attempt then to exit a state of potentiality and to thereby acquire an "actual" power within the world is thereby identified as "the strategy of the exception, which must ensure the relation between anomic violence and law" and which therefore "is the counterpart to the onto-theo-logical strategy aimed at capturing pure being in the meshes of *logos*" (*SE* 59–60). Or, as he will reword it, "[t]hat is to say, everything happens as if both law and *logos* needed an anomic (or alogical) zone of suspension in order to ground their reference to the world of life" (*SE* 60). In what could only have severe implications for Christianity's understanding of the *logos* (the "word" said by John's Gospel to be the Christ) and its relation to defining Christian identity, an empty space is thereby demarcated by Agamben as one being beyond the juridical sphere and in the realm of "pure being" (potentiality) beyond any representations of it.

This space of suspension around which all political activity revolves is in fact the space of pure potentiality, a void so monstrous that it must be disavowed through the violent institution of political actuality intended to cover up or obscure its existence. In this manner, the state of exception which the sovereign declares to exist comes to mimic the basic coordinates of a potentiality that exists beyond the rule of actuality (law). Instead of potentiality being allowed to remain as it is, permanently immersed in an infinite creative potential, however, it is "filled" as it were by decisions, judgments, and representations which attempt to "ground" being itself. This is the first step toward the act of signification which defines all political acts.

As Agamben will take up in a short work that bears the subtitle "Notes on Politics," signification results in a constitution of the political. It is its basis and ground, and yet it is also the result of the "fundamental biopolitical fracture" which accordingly characterizes humanity, with "biopolitics" here being a term used to describe the various forms which sovereignty has taken in the modern era. Biopolitics, in this sense, is little more than the force of sovereignty removed from a symbolic figurehead, such as kingship, and redirected into a myriad of effects produced upon our biological bodies.[20] Thus, as he puts it, sovereignty divides us still, as "[t]he concept of people always already contains within itself the fundamental biopolitical fracture. It is what cannot be included in the whole of which it is a part as well as what cannot belong to the whole in which it is always already included" (*ME* 32, deemphasized from the original). Exceptions and exclusions continue to define the space of political activity, just as the sovereign declares the "state of exception," and these processes, though evolving over time, in fact show little sign of receding. Politics is seemingly forever caught up in the continuous processes of having to rearticulate and rejustify its existence:

> Hence the contradictions and aporias that such a concept creates every time that it is invoked and brought into play on the political stage. It is what always already is, as well as what has yet to be realized; it is the pure source of identity and yet it has to redefine and purify itself continuously according to exclusion, language, blood, and territory. It is what has in its opposite pole the very essence that it itself lacks; its realization therefore coincides with its own abolition; it must negate itself through its opposite in order to be. (*ME* 32)

The precarious position of the political thus comes to define its existence, and in some sense at least to legitimate its often (inherently) violent means. The "People" of the *polis* are therefore wedded to the exclusion of certain forms of life (the "others," the "enemy," those "people" who are no part of the "us," or the always political "we").[21] In fact, these separations come to reflect the constitution of the human species itself in its "naked" form (as "bare life" or *zoē*) and as political existence (the "People" or *bios*). If these divisions can be said to haunt any substantial legacy of "the political" in our world, then they can also perhaps be said to reach their height, so to speak, in the last century, when the immense scale of political projects aimed at healing the fracture within our political "body" achieved a sort of zenith, a biopolitical plan to establish a People without fracture as an almost new form of the "species" we currently constitute (cf. *ME* 34).[22] Hence, the extreme focus that was made on racial purity and the rise of genocidal tactics intended to produce such a "healing" of the "People" should come as little surprise to us at this point, no matter how grotesque their reality became.

By viewing things thus, Agamben is able to concur with Hannah Arendt's assessment that the marginal political figures of today, such as immigrants and refugees, are the "new paradigm" of political thought, the subjects with which politics must begin its thinking.[23] Accordingly, he is also able to formulate an assessment of the historical-symbolic efficacy of the Jewish people within such a context (cf. *ME* 15–26). Like the refugee, the (symbolic) "Jew" signals the crisis in defining the boundaries of human rights, of where "bare life" begins and ends. This is the limit point where the "fiction of sovereignty," the imaginary link between birth and nation, is exposed as ultimately founded on a hollow center of potentiality that need not be covered over as such, even though it rigorously and violently is obscured, hidden or seemingly effaced, time and again (cf. *ME* 21). In this sense, and with Agamben's removal of all human vocations still before us, we are rather directed toward envisioning a world where we are all potentially those marginalized figures, such as the refugee or the "Jew" who are pushed to the edges of society. It is in this sense, that he will later assert how we are all now "homini sacri," or those persons excluded from society and forced to an exposure of our "bare life" (cf. *HS* 84).[24]

As an ontological being or thing, there is no nation. The nation, as it were, is only the imagined reality which must be presupposed in order for politics to be, or to exist in any sense, and its existence depends in fact upon the production of an excluded other. It is the natural outgrowth of a rationality that ceaselessly divides and classifies, categorizes and draws up boundaries between things, including the separation between "us" and "them" so essential to our sense of social identity. Yet it is a fictional reality, one that can easily be manipulated and which, for this reason, ceaselessly attempts to conceal this "fracture" at its core. This truth will have a deep resonance with his later statements on the essence and foundation of language, that is, on the imaginary existence of a "language" which defies all attempts to definitively articulate its being. As he expresses it, "We do not have, in fact, the slightest idea of what either a people or a language is" (*ME* 65). And so, for this reason, we are constantly driven to validate their (fictional, though "actual") existence.

By aligning our vision of the absolute arbitrariness of political identities (most often associated with the linkage of birth and nation in some form of citizenship) with the "necessity" of languages just as arbitrarily constructed, Agamben hopes to force new arenas of political interaction to emerge, ones not dependent upon a model of sovereign power. In this sense, he looks to break the nexus of language, people, and state that has dominated our history of political dwelling. This is a task that, for him, is as much philosophical as political, and as much theological as anything else. Indeed, the exclusions and divisions that have constituted the political sphere (a mentality often captured in the "us" versus "them" rubric), as well as the establishment of the human subject, are the same principles of identification that have historically determined the division of our world into sacred and profane—a categorization that has often eluded scholars seeking to give a more comprehensive account of contemporary political formations.[25] This, of course, is the general consensus that would rather see the world divided into the sacred and the secular, a worldview wherein religion is on the decline today and the secular appears to be the "wiser" choice for an evolving humanity.

Agamben's initiative, however, would rather be to efface this sacred/secular split, something which he sees as actually being two faces of the same coin (cf. SA 76–77), and to acknowledge a more primordial profane existence that in fact dissolves the divisions of thought which have continuously plagued humanity, including the traditional sacred/secular dichotomy. Indeed, this regression to a space before the sacred/secular division also takes us back to a place prior to the division between the immanent and the transcendent, as will become more apparent in what follows. Before seeing these last steps to their fruition, however, Agamben first sets his course to more fully expose the logic of sacrality in our world and its historically complicated relationship with the rituals and rites of sacrifice, something that has hovered as a specter over the entire legacy of Western political thought, and to which we now turn.

Chapter 3
The Sacred

Sacrality and Sacrifice: The Foundations of Political and Cultural Representation

There have been certain critical voices that have been quick to point out how Agamben's conceptualization of sovereignty appears to be rather monolithic and perhaps too all-encompassing. Judith Butler, for one, has questioned his movement beyond the work of both Hannah Arendt and Carl Schmitt precisely in relation to this characterization of sovereignty, opting instead for talk on multiple discourses of power rather than limit the discussion to sovereign power only.[1] Despite the fact that Agamben himself has subsequently appeared to shift his own perspective away from a focus upon notions of sovereignty and toward governmentality, or the rationality of governing in general (cf. *PR* 77; *RG* 408–409), however, he seems to detect something inherently theological in the models of sovereignty that he works with and which does not allow him to drift too far from the historical monotheistic traditions with which he deals.[2] In this sense, he perhaps retains a discourse on sovereignty such as we have seen it already precisely because it is the ontotheological tradition in the West that *has given rise to it* and has accordingly built its politics around it, utilizing its easy reductionisms in order to maintain the fabric of our representations. In this sense, then, perhaps Butler is correct in asserting that sovereignty appears as monolithic, though Agamben may also be right in demonstrating that this is precisely how sovereignty has historically functioned.

What Agamben's analysis of sovereignty highlights is the inseparable relationship between sovereignty and the religious structures of Western monotheism, a relationship which has been dominant for centuries over our Western political structures. By seeing things thus, the Heideggerian project of overcoming an ontotheology which is a "performance of language" (*SL* 88) and which has haunted Western thought since metaphysics was first formulated can be seen as the central task of Agamben's work, one that he attempts to merge with a more encompassing discourse on power which Butler, and Foucault before her, speak of often.[3]

Agamben does, however, at times seem to be referring to multiple sites of power, for example, when he tries to articulate the myriad attempts of humanity to generate itself through its use of "anthropological machinery," or what he will elsewhere refer to the "apparatuses" of society which take many forms (cf. *WA*). The anthropological machines which institute "humanity" come to depend upon their ability to construct a zone of indifference where there is a ceaseless articulation of an immaterial difference between the human and the animal, as we saw earlier. This "zone of indifference," however, is not a space filled with the content of our being; rather it is empty, without any content by which to uniquely identify humanity. Inasmuch as this fact might threaten to end our standard conceptions of what constitutes a human being, it also serves to bring some flexibility (or even *evolution*) to any supposed definition of what we in essence are. What is actually obtained is nothing more or less, we are told, than bare life itself, that essential kernel of our bodily life, or "creaturely" being, that Agamben is working hard to isolate over against any images of humanity that we have constructed.

Again, this construction is anything but *a*theological; it is rather immersed in a wide history of those varied (onto)theological attempts to posit human beings as divinely made creatures. This reality, in fact, is what often makes theological accounts of creation such hotspots of intellectual debate, for therein lies the much contested ground of what makes us "human" in the first place. For example, within his finely crafted arguments on the nature of the divide between human and animal made in *The Open*, Agamben has cause to reflect upon the theological implications of such a division, demonstrating that any reformulation of one boundary may also imply the reformulation of another, the divine-human (cf. *O* 21). Thus, in one of the boldest statements to come out of his work on the subject of theology, we find here that Agamben ultimately takes measure, not only of the manner in which the human being has traditionally been posited in relation to any sort of animality, but also of the (ontotheological) "machinery" which decides upon the nature of the divine (cf. *O* 91–92).

In essence, Agamben is dealing with what he refers to as a problem of "absolute foundations" that are ultimately themselves ungrounded. Rather than simply appeal to a postsecular "return to religion" or call for the complete abolition of religious tradition (two sides of the same coin to him), Agamben seeks rather to engage more deeply with the foundations of all religious ritual and thought, the foundations then of the human being itself. Thereby, he turns, in this context, to the mechanism of sacrifice as being historically intertwined with the establishment of communal and individual identities. The mechanism or apparatus of sacrifice was necessarily not only that which framed a sort of religious impulse within humanity, but that which also determined, as well as maintained, the boundary between the sacred and the profane. In its determination of this boundary, sacrifice served as an apparatus utilized to establish the very coordinates of our humanity over and against our animality, something which no doubt sheds great light upon the use of animals within sacrificial rites in particular. This is a matter which Agamben hastened to elaborate upon in his early work, where he makes clear how "[t]he fact that man, the animal possessing language, is, as such, ungrounded, the fact that he has no foundation except in his own action (in his own 'violence'), is such an ancient truth that it constitutes the basis for the oldest religious practice of humanity: sacrifice" (*LD* 104).

Already in *Language and Death*, written in 1982, that is, 13 years before he was to engage more fully with the figure of the *homo sacer* (his work bearing that title was not published until 1995), Agamben anticipates the fundamental trajectory behind this later line of inquiry:

> However one interprets the sacrificial function, the essential thing is that in every case, the action of the human community is grounded only in another action; or, as etymology shows, that every *facere* is *sacrum facere*. At the center of sacrifice is simply a determinate *action* that, as such, is separated and marked by exclusion; in this way it becomes *sacer* and is invested with a series of prohibitions and ritual prescriptive. Forbidden action, marked by sacredness, is not, however, simply excluded; rather it is now only accessible for certain people and according to determinate rules. In this way, it furnishes society and its ungrounded legislation with the fiction of a beginning: that which is excluded from the community is, in reality, that on which the entire life of the community is founded, and it is assumed by the society as an immemorial, and yet memorable, past. Every beginning is, in truth, an initiation, every *conditum* is an *abs-conditum*. (*LD* 104–105, emphasis in the original)

Remarking on the ambiguity and circularity of the concept of the "sacred," Agamben here defines the initial terrain wherein his later studies on the figure of the *homo sacer* will take root. Essentially, the "ungroundedness" of the human being, which is the basic platform from which humanity has sought to establish its distinction from its animality, becomes the source of an exclusive or divisive action intended to ground humanity in its representative (and subsequently *legal*) forms, and to remain as "that which, remaining unspeakable (*arreton*) and intransmissible in every action and in all human

language, destines man to community and to tradition" (*LD*
105). Sacrifice is implicated as part of, and essential to, the
operation of any anthropological machinery here under
examination; in many ways, *it is the anthropological apparatus par
excellence.* It is the rough attempt to give birth to the human
being through the intersecting coordinates of various historically established religious and political identities.

This "fiction of a beginning" that is undisclosed on some
level ("immemorial") and yet solidified as the foundation of a
particular community, is something which society attempts
to give to itself, an act which it then masks through the institution of a founding violence. Explaining the violent nature
of communal foundations, as they are often begun with a
seminal murder or sacrifice lying at their origins, Agamben
discerns in this founding violence the attempts of humanity
to posit itself as humanity, something inherently definitive of
what we consider violence to be as it were. Yet, despite the
reality of violence in our daily lives, we are told that

> [v]iolence is not something like an originary biological
> fact that man is forced to assume and regulate in his
> own praxis through sacrificial institution; rather it is
> the very ungroundedness of human action (which the
> sacrificial mythogeme hopes to cure) that constitutes
> the violent character (that is *contra naturam*, according to
> the Latin meaning of the word) of sacrifice. All human
> action, inasmuch as it is not naturally grounded but
> must construct its own foundation, is, according to the
> sacrificial mythogeme, violent. And it is this *sacred*
> violence that sacrifice presupposes in order to repeat it
> and regulate it within its own structure. (*LD* 105–106,
> emphasis in the original)

It would seem then that the mechanisms of the anthropological machinery which dictate specific representations of the
human being are caught up entirely within the violent logic
of sacrificial rites as ancient as the origins of what we have

come to call "humanity."[4] Hence, he can conclude that there is a certain "unnaturalness" to human violence, yet it is in a sense a foundational necessity, and therefore "[t]he foundation of violence is the violence of the foundation" (LD 106, emphasis in the original).

In this early effort by Agamben to overturn the logic of sacrificial violence, he isolates philosophy as capable of "absolving" human beings from their indebtedness to this cyclical logic, a point he will certainly not abandon later on in his work, but only reinforce. He makes it clear, however, that any attempt to think beyond this logic will most certainly appear as excluded from all of our common articulations (cf. LD 106). There is simply no space made within our representative logic for such an expression. And this would stand to reason, for if all representations proceed from our indebtedness to the tasks of signification and language, as well as their efforts to establish the human being, then any movement that tries to conceive of life beyond these violent ends is bound to exceed this otherwise shared logic or grammar. The question, however, remains as to how we are to express our common humanity beyond the unifying force of sacrifice and the logic of the excluded other (the one who is sacrificed in order to maintain the foundations of any conceivable "humanity"). This is the defining political task for the "coming community," we are told, and which Agamben clearly intends to situate later in relation to the excluded figure of the homo sacer. This is a task then that must insist on interrogating why Western politics as such has been founded on the exclusion of "bare life" (cf. HS 7). In essence, what Agamben is seeking to articulate is the foundational question of society and social relations as a whole, the relation between politics and life itself.

The Figure of "Bare Life," or the Homo Sacer

By extending beyond Schmitt's determination of all political boundaries as being based upon a division between friend and enemy, Agamben discerns rather that it is the contrast between bare life and political existence (*zoē* and *bios*, exclusion and inclusion) which constitutes politics in the West (cf. *HS* 8). Utilizing the distinction between the two Greek words for "life," *zoē* or life as being creaturely, its animality as it were, and *bios* or life as it is lived properly by an individual or group in relation to others, Agamben dictates how "the entry of *zoē* into the sphere of the *polis*—the politicization of bare life as such—constitutes the decisive event of modernity and signals a radical transformation of the political-philosophical categories of classical thought" (*HS* 4). Viewed from this angle, sacrifice would be some sort of attempt to leave behind, or at least suppress the animality within us which yet can never really leave us. It is a project thus doomed to fail from the start. It is also the movement that most dramatically signals a shift in the understanding of the role that theology plays in identifying what we understand as "humanity."

The realm of signification, or the differentiation between what is considered "inside" a given political sphere and what is "outside," is the act most traditionally associated with divine intentions. It has been the divine who most typically partitions the realms of existence (even the afterlife) into separate spaces for believers and unbelievers, the chosen and unchosen alike (and even those who fall "between the cracks," as many a medieval treatise on purgatory or limbo will demonstrate). In a very literal sense, the task of providing "natural" divisions, whether they be of race, gender, national, or ethnic derivation, has often become one so intermingled with religious pronouncements and identities that it becomes difficult indeed to perceive a sociocultural division apart from its theological or pseudotheological justifications.

Now, however, this traditionally sacred art of division is presented (or "revealed") by Agamben as a wholly human by-product, with everything from culture to politics to religion being predicated upon an exclusionary principle that ultimately gives birth to society as we know it. Society, therefore, by this estimation, becomes a grouping of people seemingly bereft of their animality, a fact which makes an encounter with more primitive peoples of the world often more than just a fascination for Western "civilized" peoples. Those encounters with "primitive" tribal people who live precariously, often indeed blurring the boundaries between animal and human, perhaps reveal in some sense the arbitrary boundary between "them" (the "primitives" or the animals) and "us" (the "civilized" or "proper" human beings), a boundary which Western society has yet fought rather vigorously to maintain.

Accordingly, Agamben can state how "[t]here is politics because man is the living being who, in language, separates and opposes himself to his own bare life and, at the same time, maintains himself in relation to that bare life in an inclusive exclusion" (HS 8).[5] As we have already seen, humanity attempts to move beyond its unstated potentiality and into a more "decisive" position, positing itself as human in order to reign sovereign over its animality. To do this, then, humankind must play the sovereign and consequently perform a certain violence upon itself (not to mention upon the animal world, or even upon the environment which gives us other abundant forms of organic life) through the implementation of the mechanism of sacrifice, an exclusion of persons, animals, or even parts of oneself that remain yet within, in order to establish and legitimate a sovereign form of human being (the "will-to-power" that Melville had once tried to counter through his character of Bartleby).

The *logos* now returns to the forefront of the discussion as it again appears to be the conceptual lynchpin used to formulate humanity. If Agamben's multiple assertions on the *logos* throughout his writings are to maintain their consistency (especially as they seem to permeate a good deal of his writing), then the *logos*, or the essence of language with which we identify, must have some function within this sacrificial logic. This is something no doubt at the center of understanding the Christian "incarnational" mystery and its relationship to the *logos*, though Agamben does not say as much in this particular context.[6] Any Christian undertones are therefore mainly implied, as when he states that "[t]he living being has *logos* by taking away and conserving its own voice in it, even as it dwells in the *polis* by letting its own bare life be excluded, as an exception, within it" (*HS* 8). And because this political *inclusion* is based on a sacrificial *exclusion*, the paradoxical situation results in a split sense of identity with an exception yet residing at the core of what constitutes the human being, like the dual natures of Christ being placed alongside each other in one person, an indicator indeed that Christianity seems to be aware of the permeability of these boundaries that the logic of sacrifice has sought to deny.

Hence, we are perhaps also poised to witness what many perceive as Christianity's original intention of putting an end to sacrifice once and for all through the hybrid figure of a Christ who renders the apparatuses which make those divisions null and void, a claim which Agamben's work seems also to point toward on multiple occasions. Accordingly, there is the occasional historical recourse to two senses of *logos*, one relative to his divinity and one expressed within the economy of salvation and incarnation (*RG* 104) both present in the same figure opposed to the anthropological machinery of any age. In this sense, then, politics would be far more than just a platform for the contesting of social identification; it is rather the arena for the disclosure of the "fundamental structure of Western metaphysics" at least inasmuch as it is concerned with the distinction between our "bare life" and the *logos* which seemingly animates it (*HS* 8). That is, the human being is what we have created in the space that appears between the "living being" that we physically are and the *logos* of symbolic utterances, of language itself (cf. *RA* 134).

This exclusion of the "bare life" that each of us in reality *cannot ever cease to be* will of course be repeated throughout history through these sacrificial rituals of exclusion that repeat and reiterate humanity's initial exclusion which it performs (via sacrificial methods) upon itself. Those figures of the excluded "bare life" which we are simultaneously attracted to and repulsed by therefore reappear in his work as those "creatures" who invoke a basic elemental shame every human being carries as a result of likewise performing those initial exclusionary measures upon which their humanity is built. The *Muselmann*, or the walking corpses of the Nazi concentration camps who were the objects of so much scorn and ridicule by both guards and prisoners, would seem to fit this description as they mark the threshold between the human and the inhuman (cf. *RA* 55ff.).[7] This fact, no doubt, is what will enable Agamben to state elsewhere that the emergence of concentration camps in the modern world demonstrates, albeit grotesquely, the disjunction between birth (bare life) and the nation-state (*HS* 175). They have become, moreover, the testing grounds for what constitutes a "human being" in the first place today and, even more frighteningly, *what does not*: they are therefore the *nomos* (law) of the modern world, he will say, "the space of this absolute impossibility of deciding between fact and law, rule and application, exception and rule, which nevertheless incessantly decides between them" (*HS* 173).[8] They are part of a larger process of determining the borders between the human and the animal, an experiment "which has ended up dragging the very possibility of this distinction to its ruin" (*O* 22). In short, the *Muselmann* is nothing more than a reincarnation of a more ancient figure who represents, not only the role which theology plays in formulating notions of the human being, but that originary exclusion at the heart of all identity constructions performed through the original sovereign decision.[9]

For Agamben, the memory of this originary exclusion performed in order to found the realm of the political is captured best by the figure of the *homo sacer*, or the "obscure figure of Roman law" that paradoxically "may be killed and yet not sacrificed" (*HS* 8). In this context, Agamben utilizes a genealogy of the term, from its earliest Roman usage to the present day, in order to demonstrate this fact. The *homo sacer* is portrayed throughout Roman literature as a figure represented by "the unpunishability of his killing and the ban on his sacrifice." And indeed this is a rather paradoxical if not simply contradictory proposition, the first such indicator that something is amiss within this classical legal formulation.

> In the light of what we know of the Roman juridical
> and religious order (both of the *ius divinum* and the *ius
> humanum*), the two traits seem hardly compatible: if
> *homo sacer* was impure . . . or the property of the
> gods . . . then why could anyone kill him without
> either contaminating himself or committing sacrilege?
> What is more, if *homo sacer* was truly the victim of a
> death sentence or an archaic sacrifice, why is it not *fas*
> [sacrificial] to put him to death in the prescribed forms
> of execution? What, then, is the life of *homo sacer*, if it is
> situated at the intersection of a capacity to be killed and
> yet not sacrificed, outside both human and divine law?
> (*HS* 73)

In no uncertain terms, Agamben states that, with the figure of the *homo sacer*, a limit concept is breached, one that actually serves to reveal the mechanisms at work in our definition of what is to be considered as "sacred" or "political" in the first place (*HS* 73–74).

In this way, he is able to construct a foundation for pursuing the limit concept of the *homo sacer* as part of "an originary political structure," one which is disclosed in a region that is prior to the typical distinctions made between the sacred and profane, what we have now come to recognize as a zone of our potentiality beyond the binary divisions of our world (cf. *HS* 74). Indeed, the figure of the *homo sacer* appears as vital to the conjunction of the realms inhabited by both the divine and the human, as well as the laws which could be said to govern these dimensions. Such a figure or model is exemplary for understanding the relationship posited between these two laws. In fact, this is why the figure of the *homo sacer* is said to be related directly to the figure of the sovereign, the obverse other who also straddles the boundaries between these two realms (cf. *HS* 82).

For Agamben, the divisions that characterize the political life of representations are fundamentally intertwined with the rule of the sovereign, an act posited by the "state of exception" itself, and his obverse image, that of the figure of "bare life," or the *homo sacer*. It is this last figure indeed who is a purely "metaphysical" creation, one who again demonstrates the close proximity between the basic (modern) tenets of political life and their theological legitimations. What sacrifice demonstrates is the subjugation of our bare life, or our animality, to the political order. This and nothing else is what constitutes that which we have come to call the sacred, and from which we have yet to depart in any real sense. Metaphysics is in fact established upon these grounds (cf. *HS* 8). As humanity in its creaturely being (*zoē*) is to language (the condition of entering into our *bios*), so is "bare life" to the *polis*. This is the essential sovereign act that constitutes our understanding of the body and its social worth. It is "the original activity of sovereign power" (*HS* 6, deemphasized from the original; cf. also *HS* 83).

For this reason, and in sharp contrast to hundreds of years of political and social theory, Agamben is willing to state that sovereign violence is not founded on some sort of pact between persons, the notoriously difficult to discern "social contract" at the heart of so many political justifications (e.g. Rousseau, Hobbes, and Locke). Rather, politics would seem to be an almost religious ritual of sorts, a continuous reenacting of the exclusive inclusion performed upon the self in order to constitute some sense of sovereign being in relation to the others (both persons and animals) surrounding this newly formed "humanity" (cf. *HS* 107). This is the profound implication of Agamben's "political theology" which will subsequently enable him to state that the entire history of political origins, from Hobbes to Rousseau needs to be reread, for the alleged "state of nature" subject to so much speculation is nothing other than a state of exception without true origin, a ceaseless act that we utilize in order to posit politics as we know it (*HS* 109). Any such notion of a "social contract" is therefore a reductive oversimplification when conceived as a founding event. For Agamben, what the sovereign sphere demonstrates is a profound capacity for ensnaring the bare, creaturely life of the human being and *excluding* it, that is, ignoring its animal reality, while yet simultaneously *including* it within the socially constructed nexus of political beings (cf. *HS* 83).

This constant duality of exclusion and inclusion is performed until the point where we begin to recognize that the production of excluded figures, those *homo sacer* figures of ancient Roman law, are not anomalies, but rather the founding members of our "humanity," or, as the subsequent *Muselmann* of the camps would seem to indicate, they are now the figures who threaten our very definition of "humanity" (cf. *HS* 185). They are essential to constructing our social fabric and sense of self(-subjectivity)—yet another reason why such "ordinary" citizens, like guards at a Nazi death camp, were capable of getting "caught up" in the most atrocious horrors of history.[10] This fact would also serve to explain why the *homo sacer* is able to be killed (hence "included") while simultaneously being removed from the dominating sacrificial logic (hence "excluded"). As Agamben puts it, "[j]ust as the law, in the sovereign exception, applies to the exceptional case in no longer applying and in withdrawing from it, so *homo sacer* belongs to God in the form of unsacrificeability and is included in the community in the form of being able to be killed" (*HS* 82). This will immediately lead Agamben to pronounce that "[l]ife that cannot be sacrificed and yet may be killed is sacred life" (*HS* 82, deemphasized from the original).

The existence of so many *homines sacri* today merely reiterates Agamben's point that politics is little more than a continuous reenactment of the original "exclusive inclusion" which renders humanity capable of positing itself as sovereign over its own animality. For this reason, every figure of the *homo sacer* is a distressing memory of our traumatic origins and so must be pushed to the margins of our social worlds, cruelly silenced as the animals that they are often perceived to be. The close proximity which the *homo sacer* maintains with the sovereign does little to lessen the violence which is performed upon these figures of our originary exclusion; in many ways, it only serves to heighten the brutality with which sovereign power acts upon the bodies it creates.

What Ultimately Constitutes the Sacred

The prohibition against sacrificing the *homo sacer* is therefore what most closely reveals the original nature of the sense of sacrality that is inseparably affiliated with how we have come to define humanity. The human being that sits midway between its animality, or "bare life," and its relation to *logos*, or language and the divine/sovereign act of signification, is the very figure which is consequently formed upon the border between the profane and the sacred. What we discover in this formulation, of course, is that our very understanding of what is considered as "sacred" in the first place is further illuminated by this relational structure that exists between the sovereign and the *homo sacer*, a structure which the sovereign in fact signifies as such. For this reason, Agamben will consider how the appearance of sovereignty as a defining mark of the human being was also simultaneously "an excrescence of the profane in the religious and of the religious in the profane," or that "which takes the form of a zone of indistinction between sacrifice and homicide" (*HS* 83). In so many words, this relationship between the sovereign and the *homo sacer* is what comes to define the sense of what has been sacred to humanity throughout time.

If our hypothesis is correct, sacredness is . . . the originary
form of the inclusion of bare life in the juridical order,
and the syntagm *homo sacer* names something like the
originary "political" relation, which is to say, bare life
insofar as it operates in an inclusive exclusion as the
referent of the sovereign decision. Life is sacred only
insofar as it is taken into the sovereign exception, and to
have exchanged a juridico-political phenomenon (*homo
sacer*'s capacity to be killed but not sacrificed) for a
genuinely religious phenomenon is the root of the
equivocations that have marked studies both of the sacred
and of sovereignty in our time. *Sacer esto* is not the
formula of a religious curse sanctioning the *unheimlich*, or
the simultaneously august and vile character of a thing: it
is instead the originary political formation of the
imposition of the sovereign bond. (*HS* 84–85)

Politics is therefore nothing less than a human situatedness
founded upon a notion of sacrality which, though religion
appears to many to be fading from popular acceptance in the
West, cannot ever be fully effaced from what constitutes the
basis for all personal and social identities formed in a sense
that conveys political meaning. It is this very same logic which
might assist us in understanding why the very problematic
conceptualizations of sacrifice that many would rather steer
clear of using in the modern world are not capable of immediately departing either.

This is a point that Agamben himself does recognize, as
"sacredness" is no longer defined directly in relation to sacrificial themes, and yet our sense of sacrality nonetheless continues
to be founded upon the legacy of the *homo sacer* entirely, though
without the precise nature of the relationship between our formulations and this ancient conceptualization being seen for
what it is (cf. *HS* 114). It is this all pervasiveness of the sacrificial
machinery in our contemporary world which continues to provide our varied definitions of what is considered to be sacred.

And it is this same notion of sacrifice which likewise renders every human being as potentially exposed to the "bare life" that is indissociable from our being, and this despite the myriad attempts to distance ourselves from it. This is what will enable Agamben to state that "[i]f today there is no longer any one clear figure of the sacred man, it is perhaps because we are all virtually *homines sacri*" (*HS* 114–115). In short, what we perceive as our humanity is the result of a complex process of exalting our sovereign being at the expense of our bare life, of relating ourselves to the *logos* in order to enter into politics and the various contestations of power. Religion, in short, thus functions as the historical mechanism most capable of constructing such subjectivities, thereby founding politics as a fundamental attempt to secure this expression of the human being. It functions in the zone of indiscernability which itself comes to be regarded as sacred ground, the site wherein the "homo sacer" is born (cf. *HS* 90).

These considerations are, of course, not confined to his analysis in *Homo Sacer*, but effectively become a central and recurring motif in Agamben's later works as well. This line of thought, for example, overlaps squarely with his focus placed upon the (political) task of profanation. In essence, the *homo sacer* is someone who is set apart from humanity, capable of living a profane existence among them. Yet the *homo sacer* is also a figure who once belonged to the gods and so therefore always carries something of the sacred within its being. Hence, the threat of violent death constantly hovers overhead: "As for his fate in the divine sphere, he cannot be sacrificed and is excluded from the cult because his life is already the property of the gods, and yet, insofar as it survives itself, so to speak, it introduces an incongruous remnant of profanity into the domain of the sacred" (*PR* 78). The *homo sacer* is nearly unbearable to behold because it is the figure which straddles the boundaries between the sacred and the profane; it is the figure which threatens, in an actual, physical sense, to undo the metaphysical boundaries which grant humanity its identity over and against its bare life.

The main problem that arises, it would seem, is that the *homo sacer* threatens to reveal the absolute arbitrariness of human existence, and thereby to expose the "machine of sacrifice" (the same "anthropological machinery" so frequently cited in *The Open*) that ceaselessly generates our conceptualizations of humanity somewhere between the animal and the divine (cf. *PR* 78–79). As I have therefore been illustrating throughout, this ancient Roman figure of the *homo sacer* is not an isolated historical figure. It is one that recurs in the concentration camps of Nazi Germany, it is one that can be seen on the margins of refugee camps today, and it is one that continues to haunt our complacent notions of what defines our humanity across the world in nearly every community. Indeed, even beyond what the *homo sacer* had once represented, these contemporary elaborations upon an ancient figure seem even to stretch beyond the *homo sacer* itself, undoing the very coordinates of humanity (cf. *HS* 181–188). For this reason, our era begins to experience a new antipathy to these figures, bringing words such as "genocide" and "camp" into our shared vocabulary. It would in fact be hard to imagine a "hate crime" or genocidal act that was *not* a reaction to this most basic principle common to our current political formulations.

As might be expected, for Agamben, this same articulation can be seen at the heart of what constitutes the theological project *tout court*, as Christ's situatedness between his humanity and his divinity, a precarious reworking, or deconstructing, of this same establishment of the human being in general. This would appear to be nothing short of a significant contrast between the *logos* of Greek thought, the *polis* and signification in general *and* Christ's embodiment of the *logos*, which in fact should completely redefine what the *logos* is capable of being. In short, Christ's assumption of the *logos* is a sacrifice of sacrifice itself, of the sacrificial logic once so indebted to the language of the *logos* and its ability to signify our symbolic reality. Agamben therefore considers the two natures of Christ as caught up within this same sacrificial logic that generates our conceptualizations of what it means to be human. Hence,

> [f]rom this perspective, it becomes easier to understand why, in the Christian religion, theologians, pontiffs, and emperors had to show such obsessive care and implacable seriousness in ensuring, as far as possible, the coherence and intelligibility of the notions of transubstantiation in the sacrifice of the mass and incarnation and *homousia* in the dogma of the trinity. What was at stake here was nothing less than the survival of a religious system that had involved God himself as the victim of the sacrifice and, in this way, introduced in him that separation which in paganism concerned only human things. (*PR* 79)

This introduction of a separation at the heart of the divine then appears to be a division within the boundaries between human and sacred, a division then of division itself that will elsewhere play such a decisive role for Agamben in rendering the anthropological machinery inoperative (cf. *TR* 45ff.). Understanding the difference between the act of signification, as well as the borders it defines, and the division of division itself, or that which renders signification inoperative, are crucial to maintain and yet almost excessively easy to distort, as history will testify. The introduction of a new division (even of division itself) produces the possibility that borders can be read and misread, that exclusions become inclusions, inclusions exclusions and that even the sacrifice of sacrifice itself be reappropriated for further sacrificial means.

Consequently, the Christian message that Agamben detects lurking in Christ's original sacrifice may in fact have been reappropriated by the Christian tradition itself and turned back into a justification for the anthropological machinery to operate. Indeed, as the history of theology relates, the presence of two distinct spheres of existence, the human and the divine, in one person can cause quite a problem for the operation of that particular machinery which constructs the human being. In essence, as Agamben so deftly puts it, this combination indeed "threatened to paralyze the sacrificial machine of Christianity" (*PR* 79). There would then be a theology historically at work here which is as metaphysical as it is ontological, as violent as it is political and yet, despite this reality, there may be *another* theology latent beneath it, one that runs counter to it, that deconstructs it from within and which promises to offer a complete rethinking of the Western theological project as a whole.

What theology eventually came to deploy among its efforts to maintain the integrity of the human being was the inventive doctrine of incarnation that, perhaps for the first time in history, attempted to seamlessly merge the two poles of a sacrificial machinery (cf. *RA* 129), and with immediate consequences:

> The doctrine of incarnation guaranteed that divine and human nature were both present without ambiguity in the same person, just as transubstantiation ensured that the species of bread and wine were transformed without remainder into the body of Christ. Nevertheless, in Christianity, with the entrance of God as the victim of sacrifice and with the strong presence of messianic tendencies that put the distinction between sacred and profane into crisis, the religious machine seems to reach a limit point or zone of undecidability, where the divine sphere is always in the process of collapsing into the human sphere and man always already passes over into the divine. (*PR* 79)

If Agamben's most basic claim that the historical project of what we call the metaphysical or the ontotheological is really what lies at the basis of all political, cultural, and social expressions, then the production of any "anthropological machinery" must be rigorously maintained and defended by a theological vision of humanity's boundaries in relation to the divine. Again, as the history of theology will testify, there have certainly been any number of theologians and church officials more than willing to violently signify our symbolic reality rather than jettison the sacrificial logic at the heart of our political, cultural, and religious representations.

Yet, the calling into question of the sacrificial machinery need not result in such a violent reduction of the creatures that we are—rather, a careful displacement of the sacrificial logic *is* possible, just as the division of all divisions can signal a passage beyond the act of drawing boundaries and borders. It is contained in the possibility of the human animal within wherein resides our pure potentiality for being and which the Christian message can be viewed as seeking to articulate. That is to say, perhaps there is a theological vision of Christ's actions that does not defend the anthropological machinery, but in fact dismantles it from within.

The Halo

Though he does not do so in this context, these remarks upon the unique intervention of Christian theological claims made with regard to the sacrificial machinery that far exceeds being the property of the Christian narrative alone should be read in conjunction with his comments on the existence of the halo as portrayed in Christian art (cf. *CC* 56 and 92; *IP* 34). For Agamben, the halo is a zone of indiscernability between possibility and reality, or potentiality and actuality, a mark of those "messianic tendencies" which enter into a present moment, or present *body* as it were. The halo is the "supple-mental possibility" for the holy being who has reached their end and otherwise "consumed all of its possibilities," who has divided all divisions and is thus the bare life beyond all sacri-ficial logic. The halo is in this sense to be understood as a purely immanent gift given to humanity.

In this fashion, the halo is a demonstration of the unique presence of Christianity within the sacrificial machinery, the sacrifice of sacrifice itself, a presence that cannot be easily ignored or suppressed, despite any significations or vocations that are bestowed upon individuals in this world. Indeed, it simply glows above whatever representations we give to holiness, such as the icons painted to honor the holy ones of the Christian tradition. The presence of a halo seemingly indicates that something unique has been presented beyond all representations. The "holy person" is marked with the halo as a (presented) sign without a (represented) sign, an absolutely singular ("whatever") being present to this world as if yet "beyond" it. The halo is an "imperceptible trembling of the finite," a "fusional act" of two worlds colliding, and for this reason, remains indeterminate. For this reason, its "beatitude" as he terms it, is "a potentiality that comes only after the act, of matter that does not remain beneath the form, but surrounds it with a halo" (*CC* 56). And with this image of the halo precariously conceived and hovering just over the image of Christ within the sacrificial logic of our world, we are able to discern the unique role which Christianity plays in our world, and this despite the fact that almost everything Agamben has dictated to us thus far would seem to dismantle the very mechanisms upon which an instituted religion such as Christianity today would seem to rely.

Despite his call for an absolute profanation of our world, Agamben seems to be detecting a movement of profanation within the Christian narrative that cannot be easily silenced or pushed aside. It is rather at the center of its message and, for that very reason, demonstrable from nearly every angle from which it is perceived. Profanation, in this sense, becomes the center of the Christian message, a paradoxical if not simply ironic formulation, though one that would seem to adhere to the conclusions which Agamben formulates. What once appeared so far away is now so close, and what was once unfamiliar is now familiar. The glorious divine presence and its joy unending are not something far away and unobtainable—they are right here, right now, if we could only see beyond the divisions we have arbitrarily created:

> The world of the happy and that of the unhappy, the
> world of the good and that of the evil contain the same
> states of things; with respect to their being-thus they
> are perfectly identical. The just person does not reside
> in another world. The one who is saved and the one
> who is lost have the same arms and legs. The glorious
> body cannot but be the mortal body itself. What
> changes are not the things but their limits. It is as if
> there hovered over them something like a halo, a glory.
> (*CC* 92; cf. the concept of "glory" as observed in *RG*)

Chapter 4

From Universal to Particular

The Beginning of the End of Sovereignty

If Agamben's claims to this point are to be registered as a damning critique of an ontotheological-political apparatus ("anthropological machinery") that continues to include us all through the exclusions it would have us perform to ourselves (and consequently to others) then, in light of this critique, what, we might ask, can put a stop to the violent forces of sovereignty that continue to permeate the apparatuses which ceaselessly generate our sense of humanity today? If the forces of sovereignty can be seen as an attempt to disavow the space of pure potentiality, which more properly defines our being, then any overcoming of sovereign violence must be linked to a return to such a space. This movement would entail the establishment of what he will refer to as a pure "means without ends" (cf. *ME*), or, quite simply, the "unmasking of mythico-juridical violence" at the hands of a "pure violence" we have yet to truly encounter at work in our world (*SE* 63; cf. *IH* 143–144). Attaining this state is tantamount to imagining a "figure of law after its nexus with violence and power has been deposed," though this of course would leave nothing but "a law that no longer has force or application" (*SE* 63). If law was previously defined by Agamben as a "force with significance" or meaning (*P* 168), then imagining law as existing without force, as an object discarded or without use, is a terribly difficult thing to imagine (let alone *achieve*) for a humanity that depends upon its usage daily.

Contemplating how such a thing might be possible is thus no easy task. It has led several commentators on Agamben's work to characterize his vision of the end of this anthropological machinery as simple "political nihilism," insofar as it appears to move beyond what we know and hold dear and into the vague shadowy realm of what cannot ever be pronounced as such.[1] In the context of a discussion involving Benjamin's advancement of a "pure (divine) violence," which was portrayed by him as manifest historically in the form of a strike, or a suspension of the actuality of working conditions (something similar to Agamben's insistence upon Bartleby the Scrivner's preference not to work), Agamben seeks to identify the manner in which such a violence could appear to counter any law posited by sovereign violence:

> What can be the meaning of a law that survives its
> deposition in such a way? The difficulty Benjamin faces
> here corresponds to a problem that can be formulated
> (and it was effectively formulated for the first time in
> primitive Christianity and then later in the Marxist
> tradition) in these terms: What becomes of the law after
> its messianic fulfillment? (This is the controversy that
> opposes Paul to the Jews of his time). (SE 63)[2]

The linkage is thereby established between potentiality, the messianic and the deactivation of law, a relationship which Agamben detects ranging from Pauline Christianity to Marxist discourse. The total vision that emerges here of a law rendered inactive by its messianic fulfillment is indeed the same vision that will sustain Agamben's work throughout his later lectures on Paul (cf. TR). It is what gives him the confidence to behold a future world wherein humanity will "play with law" just as children play with objects once destined for adult use, but are then discarded because no longer needed, a popular recurring image for him (cf. SE 64; PR 87; and the essay "In Playland: Reflections on History and Play" in IH 75–95. This is so because "[w]hat is found after the law is not a more proper and original use value that precedes law, but a new use that is born only after it" (*SE* 64). This is a new use that comes about as a result of a "studious play" with law that in fact frees it from its own value, that "disenchants" it as it were so that it can be brought to a new usage (cf. *SE* 88).

A dissolving of law after this messianic fulfillment has taken place is the stage wherein our pure potentiality could be said to reside, though not to "reign" as a sovereign power might otherwise do. Rather, it simply rests there in whatever form of being it is manifest as (in its existence *as such*), beyond judgment and beyond the hold of representations. Agamben can conclude that the force of the messianic will be the force of a deactivation of law, that which will render law inoperative and produce a path toward a new way of living beyond the political and social norms we had previously known (cf. *O* 85–87).

> The only truly political action, however, is that which severs the nexus between violence and law. And only beginning from the space thus opened will it be possible to pose the question of a possible use of law after the deactivation of the device that, in the state of exception, tied it to life. We will then have a "pure" law, in the sense in which Benjamin speaks of a "pure" language and a "pure" violence. To a word that does not bind, that neither commands nor prohibits anything, but says only itself, would correspond an action as pure means, which shows only itself, without any relation to an end. And, between the two, not a lost original state, but only the use and human praxis that the powers of law and myth had sought to capture in the state of exception. (*SE* 88)

It is hard to imagine such a "divine" violence severed from its historically religious roots. And Agamben does not seem eager to enact such a severing. Rather, he appears only to move closer to certain readings of the Judeo-Christian tradition which would seem to endorse his interpretation. And if this state is indeed what Christianity points toward with its essence, then it is captured nowhere more definitively than in the Judeo-Christian usage of the term "messianic," the very principle that, according to Agamben, can be said to undo the law and render it inoperative (cf. *RG* 253ff.; *P* 160–174). It should also therefore come as no surprise that he chose to devote a series of seminars between 1998 and 1999 (published as *The Time That Remains*) to Paul's letter to the Romans, and more specifically, to the implications of messianic thought in Paul's writings. This detailed study in fact enables Agamben to retain his proximity to theological discourse while simultaneously reenvisioning its heritage entirely.

The Weak Force of the Messianic

There are few religious terms that have received such heavy traffic in recent philosophical usage as "the messianic." From Walter Benjamin to Jacques Derrida and John Caputo, and from Slavoj Žižek to Judith Butler, the messianic has been conceived as a structure of religious thought now appears as detached from its religious roots.[3] It seems to have become a way for philosophers and cultural theorists to adhere to a universal ethical call for all of humanity without yet sacrificing their claims to particularity. It holds out the promise, then, of a claim to fidelity to the truth of a particular historical event, but also to make the logic of such a fidelity applicable to all. In short, the messianic has been "reborn" as that structural force which undoes all given norms from within, thus acting within any given representation in order to expose its shortcomings, not from *without*, as some presumed universal (objective) positions have often claimed, but from *within* the particularity of a given situation (its *subjective* dimension), thus evading the misleading ("objective") premises of attempting to present one narrative for all to subscribe to. For his part, Agamben has managed to consolidate this often jargon-filled discourse on the pursuit of a "messianic" force at work within history with the ongoing popular philosophical revival of the letters of Saint

Paul, which is where we find him uniting several strands of his own thought with the Christian legacy as a whole.[4]

As already indicated, Agamben is certainly seeking here to pass beyond the specificity of any particular religious (messianic) tradition and to arrive at the conditions of a messianism implicit in any historical formulation of a Messiah figure. That is, he wants to assess the logic of a messianic force at work within any given "messianic" event, whether that be found in the figure of Jesus Christ or the *homo sacer*. It is with this in mind that he addresses Paul's "Letter to the Romans" as the "fundamental messianic text for the Western tradition," hoping thereby to counter the various "anti-messianic" claims operating in both the Church and the Synagogue which would tend to downplay or neutralize Paul's messianic contentions (*TR* 1).[5] This alleged neutralization of a genuine messianic force on the part of organized religion is conceived as one that aims to suspend Paul's claims in general, and thus to continue the sacrificial logic we have already seen on display throughout the history of the Western religious landscape. Indeed, as Agamben conceives it historically, the attacks have come from two different directions, both Jewish and Christian, yet toward the same point, attempting to undermine Paul's Judaism and its messianic heritage. This is something noticeable, for Agamben, in the manner in which subsequent translations of Paul's letters have seemingly erased its messianic presence, replacing the Hebrew term "Messiah" (*mashiah*), for example, with the Greek calque "Christ" (*christos*) and thus effacing a great deal of its subsequent and essential meaning (*TR* 15). Eschewing any sense of combining *Iēsous Christos* into one proper name, Agamben chooses "Jesus Messiah," without an article between them, as the only possible translation of the phrase to be used in order to illustrate Paul's refusal to separate Jesus from his historical messianic task (cf. *TR* 16–17).

For Agamben, the Messiah is the figure who transforms all juridical or factical conditions without yet abolishing them, thus what makes him appear as such a controversial figure for organized (content-based) religions. The Messiah is rather said, by Agamben, to "hollow out" religions in order to prepare their end. By entering a zone of immanence which could be said to blur the division between immanence and transcendence, between this world and the "other" one, the messianic applies to any condition and yet it can be seen to revoke that very same condition, thus "radically" calling into question one's adherence to it (*TR* 23–25; cf. *P* 160–174). This is a "nullification" that is discernable in the pronouncements of Paul on circumcision, where it is at once an affirmation of the original bond with God and an assertion that it is nothing ("Circumcision is nothing").[6] In this sense, the messianic vocation has no content in and of itself: "it is nothing but the repetition of those same factical or juridical conditions *in which* or *as which* we are called" (*TR* 23, emphasis in the original). It is an adherence, then, to the state in which we appear as we already are—in apparent refutation of the standard vocational narratives where someone is called to another, more holy life.

In this contracted time, the "time that remains," Paul urges his listeners to consider a messianic vocation which is the "revocation of every vocation," to live in a particular vocation yet also to live "as not" within it (*TR* 23–24; cf. *RA* 159).[7] As a definitive position for the early Christian church, this stance indicated something essentially important for Christian identity; it was a position which sought to elucidate a proper relationship to the rule of law and governmental authority, something notoriously problematic within the history of interpreting Paul's letters specifically and regarding Christianity in general.[8] What does become clear, however, is that the messianic vocation evidenced in Paul's writings was the fulfillment of Judaic law, of all law in fact; it becomes that which moves through the law in order to bring it to its end: "In pushing each thing toward itself through the *as not*, the messianic does not simply cancel out this figure, but it makes it pass, it prepares its end. This is not another figure or another world: it is the passing of the figure of this world" (*TR* 25). As might be suspected, then, the end product of living within this singular vocation is not a representation like any other we might identify within our world; rather, it is portrayed by Agamben as the movement toward a generic potentiality of being, the "whatever being" that results from a recognition of the animality that lays latent within our humanity (cf. *TR* 26).

What the messianic force does as it moves through the given representations of our world is precisely to hollow them out, to eradicate their content and restore them to a place of pure potentiality beyond the reaches of any sovereign power. This is what he will see at work in Benjamin's insistence upon the messianic forces moving through history being "weak" in nature, that is, opposed to the "strong" forces gathered under the rubric of sovereign rule or law.[9] It is the messianic "division of division" itself which further subdivides the divisions already put in place by the anthropological machinery at work in our world, meaning in essence that the standard ontotheological boundaries between animal and human, as between human and divine, are themselves divided until their arbitrary nature is fully disclosed and their potential for violence averted in some sense. This is what would, then, appear to be a "divine violence" at work to counter the forms of "sovereign violence" fully on display in cultural terms.

Within the context of Paul's letters, as Agamben demonstrates, this movement is discernable in the division between the Jew and the non-Jew, a most salient example from the early church's history, and one which continually threatened to divide that very same church. Perhaps in response to such a misunderstanding of the Christian message which would actually attempt to establish itself upon the same violent premises of society's functioning (the installation of the division between "them" and "us"), Paul seeks to bring the early Christian community to peace with itself through a renewed clarity about Jesus Messiah's most basic messianic intention: to divide all divisions until none truly remain. As Agamben relates the rationale behind this formulation,

[t]he criteria for how this division works is both clear
(circumcised/foreskin) and exhaustive, for it divides all
"men" into two subsets, without leaving a remainder or
remnant. Paul cuts this division into two via a new
division, that of the flesh/breath. This partition does not
coincide with that of the Jew/non-Jew, but it is not
external to it either; instead, it divides the division itself.
(*TR* 49)

By delving deeper into the reality of the division between the
Jew/non-Jew, Paul asserts a radical new perspective on matters
by focusing on the constituent core of identity beyond the
representations of identity (i.e., circumcision, etc.) before him.
Consequently, the "true Jew" now becomes one in spirit, and
not necessarily in the flesh, rendering the ancient categorical
distinction, not superfluous, but opened up from within. Under
the effects of the "division of division," the original partition of
reality into an exhaustive "Jew/non-Jew" dichotomy is effaced,
rendering some Jews as being "not Jewish" and indeed some
non-Jews as being more Jewish in spirit than the Jews themselves (*TR* 50).

In essence, and as will determine Agamben's fundamental
rethinking of Western ontology in its entirety, the "division of
division" itself ultimately indicates that the representations we
depend so much upon for the comprehension of our world are
"not all" there is to reality. Echoing other philosophies of recent
memory devoted to exploring an ontology of the "not all,"
Agamben maintains that "the messianic division introduces a
remnant into the law's overall division of the people," one that
definitively states that "Jews and non-Jews are constitutively 'not
all'" there is to the constituted reality (*TR* 50; cf. *RA* 162–164).[10]
This same formulation is echoed throughout Paul's work (as in
1 Corinthians 9.20–23) as a recurring thematic: that the Christian should now live "as without law, not without the law of
God, but in the law of the Messiah," to which Agamben can only
add the logical conclusion that the person "who keeps himself in

the messianic law is not-not in the law" (*TR* 51). The Christian is to live as an exemplary form of life, not as included among humanity through a fundamental preceding exclusion, but rather excluded as different from the start and therefore included in a radical new universality of our creaturely being so to speak.

This Christian proclamation would then seemingly be beyond any sort of juridical religious intertwinement, and this was the hope for the messianic fulfillment which sprang from the roots of its Judaic tradition. It is thus also beyond the sacrificial machinery which has (sovereignly) dominated religious sentiment since the earliest forms of worship and sacrifice. Yet, as we are cautioned, "[i]f this remnant of potentiality is thus weak, if it cannot be accumulated in any form of knowledge or dogma, and if it cannot impose itself as a law, it does not follow that it is passive or inert" (*TR* 137). It is rather the case that "it acts in its own weakness, rendering the word of law inoperative, in de-creating and dismantling the states of fact or of law, making them freely available for use" (*TR* 137). This state of things, in fact, was what had earlier enabled Agamben to declare that, for this reason, and from a "juridico-political perspective," messianism functions as a state of exception without any form of sovereignty being associated with it. It exists in fact purely as a subversion of sovereign power (*HS* 57–58).

What we face, then, in the figure of the Messiah is the embodiment of a weak force moving throughout history, in contrast to its ideological-canonical representations, undoing the normative force of law. And if law became normative over time in establishing the foundations of all social formations, then it was Judaism which first formulated a religious tradition that grasped law's singular significance by simultaneously utilizing the language *of* law and thereby also assuming the aporias of representation which accompany it. That is, Judaism highlighted the internal limitations of law through its construction of a messianic form of thinking that threatened to undo law's operations. Thus, while citing the incorporation of the messianic concept within Judaism, Christianity, and Shiite Islam in this context, Agamben points toward the conceptualization of the Messiah that proliferates in these traditions, all of which understand the Messiah as signifying

> the fulfillment and the complete consummation of the Law. In monotheism, messianism thus constitutes not simply one category of religious experience among others but rather the limit concept of religious experience in general, the point in which religious experience passes beyond itself and calls itself into question insofar as it is law (hence the messianic aporias concerning the Law that are expressed in both Paul's Epistle to the Romans and the Sabbatian doctrine according to which the fulfillment of the Torah is its transgression). (*HS* 56; cf. *ME* 134–135)

By referring to a seventeenth-century Jewish messianic figure, Sabbati Zevi, who had once gained a loyal following only to convert in the end to Islam, thus shocking and confusing his many followers, Agamben is hoping to illustrate how the "transgression" of a (representational) law is in fact its fulfillment. Messianism is therefore perceived as a regression into the potentiality of our being that precedes any legal attempt to surpass it by entering into a realm of actuality that gives rise only to the reign of sovereignty as we have already seen. The messianic, then, is "forever near the word" of language's existence, Agamben tells us, yet it somehow also passes beyond language, regressing back toward the originary (non-presupposed) location of a prelinguistic existence (cf. *TR* 137). If anything, this is the "weakness" of the messianic that Benjamin, among others, had found so essential to challenging the ideological-canonical readings of history that seemed to be only bolstered by their "objective" representations of any given historical record. It is also, as Slavoj Žižek has pointed out, a replaying of the traditional Christian tensions between law and love (or grace) in Agamben's work.[11]

In order that the significance of this messianic force is not missed or underestimated, it is necessary to consider what the potential consequences of this regression "before" language, and hence prior to any given representation, might look like. From the outset, attention is immediately drawn to the manner in which the foundations of humanity's social order (its sovereign structure) are constructed upon this particular rationale. The messianic suspension of law's operations must likewise be accompanied by a fundamental change in the structure of human relations. The basis for this reading can be found as early as Agamben's vision of a "coming community" beyond the confines of a politics otherwise indebted to a logic of sovereignty (cf. the central thesis behind *CC*). It is this logic of sovereignty which functions as the essential presupposition of any political entity that Agamben is seeking to undo with his further meditations upon the messianic. In this sense, the messianic, with its closeness to the word, to *logos*, to language itself then conceived as the source of divinity that hovers just beyond humanity's established boundaries and yet is essential for comprehending humanity's identity, pushes language to its limits in an attempt to go beyond (or "before") it. The messianic accordingly seeks to undo the logic of sacrifice and signification by subverting the original relation of *logos* to humanity, that is, by having the former completely enter into the latter. This is what in reality lays open the possibility of a truer form of community, one no longer based on (linguistic) presuppositions, but rather that which embraces the limits of language as a "vision of language itself" (*P* 47).

To dwell therefore in a presuppositionless state is, for him, to exist without the political, social, or cultural representations that we typically utilize in order to identify ourselves. It is in fact to institute difference itself as the border that defines our separation from each other and subsequently to divide all divisions with an irreconcilable and irreplaceable difference that renders the initial divide itself superfluous. The messianic re(en)visioning of community, according to Agamben, goes beyond the compromise with law that the church has historically struck. For its part, the church only "manages" the messianic event through the use of indulgences or the "penitential remission of sins," and thus, in some sense, negates its powerful and radical import. In contrast, the pure messianic event does not compromise itself with the functioning of law; rather, "[t]he Messiah has no need for such a remission: the 'forgive us our trespasses as we forgive those who trespass against us' is nothing other than the anticipation of the messianic fulfillment of the law" (*ME* 135). What the Messiah invokes is a community beyond what the church as an institution has achieved, that is, what has not yet been achieved in history and what Agamben articulates as: "The task that messianism had assigned to modern politics—to think a human community that would not have (only) the figure of the law," a task we are told that "still awaits the minds that might undertake it" (*ME* 135–136).

This is of course beyond the manner in which institutions and their accompanying representations have been conceived throughout time, often involving scenarios wherein a sovereign God seemed to guarantee the significations that ordered our world. What Agamben envisions instead is a world bereft of this sovereign deity, one open to the differences of the created beings that we are and that can stand alone without any representation to reduce them to a base level of "cultural intelligibility." Ultimately, then, an ethics without theology is formed here, or at least an ethics which maintains the potential for becoming a different sort of theology, though it can never actually pass into a theology proper per se as we have known it ("traditional" theology). The person who becomes immersed in the messianic vocation therefore

no longer has similitudes at his disposal. He knows that
in messianic time the saved world coincides with
the world that is irretrievably lost, and that, to use
Bonhoeffer's words, he must now really live in a world
without God. This means that he may not disguise this

world's being-without-God in any way. The saving
God is the God who abandons him, and the fact of
representations . . . cannot pretend to save the appearance
of salvation. The messianic subject does not contemplate
the world as though it were saved. In Benjamin's words,
he contemplates salvation only to the extent that he
loses himself in what cannot be saved; this is how
difficult it is to dwell in the calling. (*TR* 42)

But dwelling in this calling, in this *chosenness* as it were is exactly
what the traditional monotheisms appear to be promoting in
their varied attempts to embrace a determined and decisive
notion of vocational being which itself is indebted to the anthropological machinery of our world, as we have already seen.

In stark contrast, the conception of the "remnant" becomes
as essential for Agamben as it appears to have been for Paul. It
is a term rooted in the Jewish prophetic tradition but which
now comes to define any people existing in a state of being
"not all." It is *not* a numeric association of an elected community, *nor* that which bridges "ruin and salvation," *nor* is it
identical to an Israel that survives some final apocalyptic
destruction. Rather, it is what Agamben calls "a consistency or
figure," one that Israel is supposed to take upon itself as a result
of encountering the messianic event of its election. It is what
institutes the division of division itself, a split occurring from
within which redefines all the historical markers of social identity. Accordingly, it is the remnant which refuses to align itself
with the standard divisions (significations) of our world, and in
this sense, it is an "instrument" of salvation *for* the world, what
"makes salvation possible" (*TR* 56). Existing as remnant then is
an "alternative" vocational calling which resides in the fracture
of any totalizing identity. It is a coming-to-be of the "not all"
that defines our socially constituted reality, the life of difference
lived among us. And it is a call that extends the "chosen" remnant's vocation far beyond any one particular people; it is a
radical universal vocation for all of humanity (cf. *TR* 55).

Dwelling in this calling, as Agamben will put it, is extremely difficult to do, as it is the exact reverse of how we normally conceive of a religious "calling" in the first place. It is difficult to complete because it means to assume an identity outside the boundaries of sovereignty which otherwise seem to guarantee some semblance of representation and thus ultimately of salvation itself. It is an embracing of the act that he will call "profanation," which is entirely unredeemable in and of itself and yet that which again makes salvation possible (*TR* 57). For this reason, it is apparently only presentable as being "out of place," or "out of joint" in relation to traditional religious frameworks which are complicit with ontotheological and politico-metaphysical frameworks. Yet, despite this absolute distance that the messianic must maintain from the rule of sovereignty, in its essence, it is the only way in which one can attain something like salvation. Consequently, the messianic "does not properly belong either to an eschatology of ruin or salvation, but rather, to use Benjamin's words, it belongs to an unredeemable, the perception of which allows us to reach salvation" (*TR* 56). Difficult, to say the least, then, because this certainly appears not to resemble what most religious persons contemplate when they hear the word "salvation."

As Agamben would have it, Paul's most definitive political legacy bequeathed to the Western world was made by fashioning a lasting sense of the remnant as forged in the heat of an historical messianic event, the only way to achieve a politics of the potential, that is, of a "weak" counterforce to the violence of social, cultural, and political representations that litter our world. In short, it is the source of all hope for the oppressed, an immanent upholding of creaturely life beyond the limitations imposed by sovereign powers, as he has been suggesting all along. And here, the messianic remnant, then, finally

is neither the all nor the part, neither the majority nor the minority. Instead, it is that which can never coincide with itself, as all or as part, that which infinitely remains or resists in each division, and, with all due respect to those who govern us, never allows us to be reduced to a majority or a minority. This remnant is the figure, or the substantiality assumed by a people in a decisive moment, and as such is the only real political subject. (*TR* 57)

And it is this "only real political subject" that Agamben has clamored for throughout the entirety of his career, offering glimpses and hints, but only fully being able to articulate its materialization through an analysis of Paul's messianic writings as part of the original Christian proclamation that Agamben now seems to champion as well. It is this "tiniest" seed of messianic hope which ultimately undoes the representations which have dominated Western political and religious thought since their inception and which a "theology of pure potentiality" might possibly bring to a halt.

The significance of these thoughts on reformulating the entire domain of politics as we know it can only be expressed after first realigning our most basic philosophical presuppositions, especially those concerning the nature of the relationship between potentiality and actuality, a debate that ranges all the way back to Aristotle and ancient Greek philosophy. What becomes manifestly clear in Agamben's more recent work, however, is that this same shift away from the necessity of actuality and toward the contingency of potentiality is accompanied by another paradigmatic shift in our understanding of philosophical conceptualizations, the relationship between the particular and the universal. "The impetus is now before us to rethink the relation of universal and particular in philosophical thought, as the messianic universal calling (its conditionality) does not add up to a universal position. It is rather the division of division itself, rendering universals in-operative, with no beginning or end, only the cut itself" (*TR* 52–53). There is a "universal calling" then which does not entail a "universal position" being established—but rather a respect for the singularity and particularity of each created thing that pushes these theological reflections back into the realm of the philosophical. In contrast to numerous contemporary philosophical approaches to the "messianic," it is Agamben who presumably has grasped the full complexity of this theological term.

An Ontology of Particularity

Walter Benjamin, a great inspiration for Agamben's work in respects almost too numerous to list, was very clear, in the first half of the last century, on his vision for the "coming philosophy" as he called it. And for as much as this vision was encased within his various philosophical and literary pursuits, it was also inseparably connected to the theological, as he made clear on various occasions.[12] In terms of what knowledge was to more closely resemble, he had this insight to offer: the era of the division between subjects and objects is nearly at its end. The real task, he would then say, was to find a middle ground of "total neutrality" between the two polarized labels that have dominated Western thought since the Enlightenment: "in other words, it is to discover the autonomous, innate sphere of knowledge in which this concept in no way continues to designate the relation between two metaphysical entities."[13] For Benjamin, as for Agamben who would later pursue this same trajectory of thought, both subject and object, even in their purely "immanent" expressions, are "metaphysical" concepts. They are caught up in the ontotheological, metaphysical traditions of the past several centuries, in which both subject and object are fabricated concepts attempting to transcend our immanent existence.[14] The division of our world into subject and object, then, is here portrayed by Benjamin as part of an overarching project by Western thinkers to unify the (nondichotomous) knowledges which would otherwise proliferate in our world, and which, if Benjamin was to have his way, would continue to defy such easy, and often dualistic, categorizations. In contrast, for Benjamin, experience is actually "the uniform and continuous multiplicity of knowledge" which arises outside all efforts to subsume the empirical world within a knowledge organized by the subject/object division.

Benjamin's project in this regard is explicitly picked up and prolonged by Agamben (cf. *IH* 15ff.). The binaries (dichotomies) which govern Western representations, such as the one that has become solidified as the division of all perceptions into subject and object, are the central targets which Agamben hopes to dismantle, especially their metaphysical foundations. Accordingly, he is able to gather a good deal of these previously established positions and critiques (which we have seen interlocked above) under the heading of what constitutes a "paradigm" in an essay devoted to exploring the theoretical implications of knowledge in general. Therefore, in "What is a Paradigm?," Agamben sketches how paradigms move only from the particular to the particular, rather than from the particular to the universal, or universal to the particular, as the binary logics of Western thought would otherwise have us understand the flow of knowledge (*SA* 9–32). What this means is that Western logic has dictated a system of thought that relies upon exclusivist propositions, those movements from particular to universal or vice versa that exclude certain elements that do not fit within a universalized framework (a thought which more than echoes what Agamben has already been saying regarding sacrifice and the figure of the *homo sacer*). This would perhaps be somewhat akin to learning the rules for a particular language's grammar, which almost inevitably leads to a discussion of the exceptions which do not fit under the general rule. We witness this phenomenon in the teaching of language, then, but also in medical diagnosis, ethnic or gendered classifications and even in our most basic interpretations which often lean toward making generalizations based on a few particular incidents in our everyday lives. It would not be a far stretch in fact to link such universalizing tendencies to the various economies of rumor, gossip, or hasty generalization that litter our world.

Paradigms, however, do not utilize the language of exceptionalism because they do not reduce particulars to a universal grid or matrix. Rather, they focus upon particular examples that are not taken up into a universal scheme—they are rather respected as the singularities which they are. In this sense, Agamben is trying to divert our patterns of thought away from making exceptions in order to form a norm and toward recognizing the uniqueness of each particular example before us. As he describes it, paradigms are singularities that function through the use of *examples* and not *exclusions* (*SA* 18). That is, rather than exclude a figure in order to establish a canonical economy of representations, the paradigm preserves the mystery at the heart of all singularities, those exemplary figures that stand alone as it were, without need of establishing themselves through the exclusion of an "other." Paradigms do not condense each particular into conformity with a universal set. In this fashion, "[t]he example constitutes a peculiar form of knowledge that does not proceed by articulating together the universal and the particular, but seems to dwell on the plane of the latter" (*SA* 19).

As he further makes clear, with paradigms, the movement of knowledge is radically altered from the manner in which we customarily utilize it. Rather than use either inductive or deductive methods, paradigms present another relation altogether, one that respects the singularity of the particularity in question entirely: "while induction proceeds from the particular to the universal and deduction from the universal to the particular, the paradigm is defined by a third and paradoxical type of movement, which goes from the particular to the particular" (*SA* 19). Paradigms, by definition, call into question the "dichotomous opposition" between particular and universal, an opposition that philosophical thought has come to (mistakenly) view as essential to forming the coordinates of all rational thought. The example can therefore be said to present "a singularity irreducible to any of the dichotomy's two terms," thereby causing all theories of knowledge to move from their reliance upon an exclusive logic to an analogical exemplarity (*SA* 19). In such fashion, analogy "intervenes" in those philosophical exercises of division that would constitute the framework of philosophical formulation as one of rigid dualism: particular/ universal; form/content; lawfulness/exemplarity (cf. *SA* 20). We are rather, in reality, caught up in a field of historical tensions which crisscross over each other, rendering identifications more than a bit complex, indeed causing them to be rather ethically unnecessary if the singularity of each exemplary life is to be respected in the fullness of its difference.

By striking the contrast thus, Agamben is poised to illustrate, in yet another setting, how the example escapes the antinomy between the universal and the particular by "showing" itself as a singularity (*CC* 10). The general features of any given being are thus prominently, though precariously, on display to the world, "exposed," as he will term it, to every other being. Agamben will devote a good deal of space within his remarks on the "coming community," which is beyond any contemporary understandings of the political, toward trying to explicate the exemplary nature of the "whatever being" that is neither "apathy nor promiscuity nor resignation." In effect, rather, "whatever beings" hold open the empty place of identity without yet constituting one as such according to a reductionistic logic of exclusion (*CC* 10–11). They are the implicit nature of the human creature severed from any ontotheological representations; they are in fact an instance of resolute creatureliness unveiled as the true nature of our being. They are life itself, then, as if viewed by the self from a distance, what Thomas Carl Wall describes as an experience of life "from which you have taken your distance because your life is always improbably older than you are and has already lived in the place of many lives, many first persons, all of whom remain unimaginable."[15]

Mirroring his claims that law (or rule) will eventually become something rendered inoperative or discarded, to be played with as if by children, Agamben is pointing to a new ethical understanding under the "rule" of the paradigm. And this is the clearest example we have yet seen in his work for what something beyond the exclusionary logic of sovereignty might actually look like. Paradigms become a gesture toward a world that allows the complexity within each particularity to be exposed as it is, *as such*, beyond all given social, cultural, political, or religious representations. Though this will undoubtedly appear as an aporia within knowledge (as we have formed it), it is actually an aporia that is determined by the limitations *of* our knowledge. It is an aporia that opens us up to new forms of encounter with the other or face before us (cf. *ME* 91–100). In this sense,

> [t]he aporia may be resolved only if we understand
> that a paradigm implies the total abandonment of the
> particular-general couple as the model of logical
> inference. The rule (if it is still possible to speak of rules
> here) is not a generality preexisting the singular cases
> and applicable to them, nor is it something resulting
> from the exhaustive enumeration of specific cases.
> Instead, it is the exhibition alone of the paradigmatic
> case that constitutes a rule, which as such cannot be
> applied or stated. (*SA* 21)

Again, the mystery is preserved, as the rule of the example cannot be stated. This is, of course, presented in strong opposition to the exclusions which are performed in order to found sovereign power as that which truly does little else than ceaselessly attempt to state its own being.

In contrast, Agamben can only point to religious models of counter-sovereign powers, at least insofar as they resist the exclusionary models through their reliance upon an exemplary-analogical one. For example, in this context, he discusses the manner in which certain monastic orders resisted the logic of sovereignty in an attempt to live more authentically in witness to Christ's example. What he discerns at work in these efforts is that "at least until Saint Benedict, the rule does not indicate a general norm but the living community (*koinos bios, cenobio*) that results from an example and in which the life of each monk tends at the limit to become paradigmatic—that is, to constitute itself as *forma vitae*" (*SA* 22). Here, a "form of life" is referred to as that which does not isolate or exclude its animality, that is, which does not draw out its "bare life" in order to reign sovereign over itself. And here we enter into what will seemingly occupy the final section of his *Homo Sacer* series, the "form of life" that can be lived as resistance to the normative political powers of sovereign rule.[16] It will be a form of life beyond the political, beyond the fundamental split within Western politics, and if Agamben is to be heard clearly on this count, what appears as the only way toward achieving any lasting sense of real happiness (cf. *ME* 8; *HS* 188).

These same reflections on the contrast between the exception and the example are what in fact had earlier motivated his work on the *homo sacer*, since that particular figure is a being conceived as the exception to the rule of the sovereign, an exception which yet belongs entirely to the rule of law (cf. *HS* 15–29). By shifting the focus away from the sovereign reign of the exception, a state which gives birth to (and is dependent upon) the creation of *homo sacer* figures, Agamben embraces the instance of the paradigm and its use of exemplary thought as an alternative model for disclosing that potentiality which resists being reduced to a given representation (and hence the arising of various "forms of life" lived in resistance to sovereign power). This point is what will allow him to state quite plainly that "[t]he empire of the rule, understood as the canon of scientificity, is thus replaced by that of the paradigm; the universal logic of the law is replaced by the specific and singular logic of the example" (*SA* 11–12). Therefore, and as will be repeated many times throughout his reflections on the contrast between exceptions and examples, he finds the example to be the "symmetrical opposite" of the exception: "whereas the exception is included through its exclusion, the example is excluded through the exhibition of its inclusion" (*SA* 24).[17] With this formulation, we are returned to the basic political distinction that

Agamben had earlier drawn between potentiality and actuality, or between constituting and constituted power.

Agamben's ethics of exposure also begins at this point, in grasping the fundamental bankruptcy that characterizes our modern condition and yet by initiating the task of comprehending each other only through the evident site of this failure. Only thus, it would seem, can we avoid the impinging (and approximate totalitarian) rule of sovereign powers today (or what he will later qualify as "biopolitical"). Instead of relying upon ethical frameworks that would pit subject against subject, Agamben is intent upon preserving the absolute singularity of the being who is ultimately beyond representation and thus can only expose its precarious being before the other.[18] "The paradigmatic relation does not merely occur between sensible objects or between these objects and a general rule; it occurs instead between a singularity (which thus becomes a paradigm) and its exposition (its intelligibility)" (*SA* 23).

In moving beyond the realm of representations, Agamben can only point toward the fragility of our being, our nakedness as it were, that is presented in its absolute singularity, an image that is neither "original" nor "copy," but rather each an *Urphänomen* (or "archetypal phenomenon") in itself, or what he defines as "the place where analogy lives in perfect equilibrium beyond the opposition between generality and particularity" (*SA* 30). In this fashion, we can see how all of Agamben's work has in some sense focused on utilizing the archaeological method to expose the relationship of paradigmatic examples which have "eluded the historian's gaze" (*SA* 31). Yet he is also developing something else here, a new manner by which to comprehend theology, or any sense of the theological beyond the ontotheological trappings he has worked so hard to eradicate. Perhaps, then, he is pushing toward another reading of theology altogether, an ontology of exemplarity, which is a theology of sorts because it points beyond this world as we know it to another one that is yet to come. This is what some interpreters have labeled Agamben's "Franciscan ontology," that which appears to be a special form of a "materialist Christianity" dependent upon his "weak" reading of our being, our "poverty" as it were.[19]

This would indeed seem to be how we are to read the development of an ontology in his work, something which has been relatively under-elaborated at times. For all the critiques he has offered of the Western ontotheological project, these are rarely accompanied by the presentation of a systematic ontology. For this reason, it is all the more significant that he states in this context that "[t]he intelligibility in question in the paradigm has an ontological character. It refers not to the cognitive relation between subject and object but to being. There is, then, a paradigmatic ontology" (*SA* 32). A paradigmatic ontology, one which attempts to respect the purity of our potentiality, appears to present itself here in order to safeguard its precarious creaturely treasure.

Agamben's methodology, harnessed in opposition to a history of political, cultural, and religious representations, has followed Michel Foucault's genealogical approach in exposing the ruses of Western thought all the way to its most fundamental assumptions, including the logic of thought itself, in order to establish a more positive presentation of our being, of a potentiality beyond representation.[20] This is likewise his challenge to the historical ontotheological visions of political sovereignty and its accompanying establishment of humanity, animality, and divinity alike, with each being allocated to their proper places. To move toward this type of creaturely ("whatever") being, this "form of life" lived in resistance to sovereign power, is, however, not a decisive act of a sovereign will. We would do well to recall in fact how the space of potentiality appears rather as a form of weakness to the sovereign powers of the world, its "Franciscan" quality. Instead of being caught up by those myriad myths of progress that have dominated so much of our historical landscape over the last couple of centuries, Agamben turns—perhaps rather startlingly—to the opposite of progression, that is, to a form of regression utilized in order to counter the violent forces of "progress" at work in our world. Hence, there arises in his work an intense focus upon the possibility of regressing to a space of pure potentiality that has historically been filled with juridical representations, but need not be so.

Chapter 5

First Regression

The Principle of Regression

If the coming political task of our age is to think beyond the political and toward new forms of being-together, Agamben's challenge to think beyond all forms of language, religion, and law appears as a perplexing challenge to be sure. Indeed, how are we to perceive any sort of prelinguistic, presignified realm of existence beyond the comfortable and conventional confines of political representation as we have come to know them? How would we recognize or talk about people or events, other than to place them in the categories and labels with which we are familiar, with which in fact we constitute the space that is considered "familiar" and of no little comfort to us? Agamben's challenge, then, seems to be as difficult as silencing our penchant for gossip, rumor, pigeonholing, or the reductionistic logic we often hold with regard to others. How on earth are we even to begin taking up a daunting task such as this? Though it is a rather counterintuitive proposition, to say the least, Agamben will suggest that the only option open to humanity is to "regress" to an infantile stage of being beyond these reductionistic phrasings, and that this movement is the key to forming a new being-together beyond the political, and, equally perhaps, the key to evolutionary "progress" on the whole, as I will try to make clear in what follows.

As should be clear by now, the task assigned to humanity by Agamben is nothing if not seemingly impossible. It is worth framing it as "impossible" because it is something beyond our definitions and knowledges, and therefore very literally impossible to conceive, though perhaps *not* impossible to eventually access. But, I am also struck by a parallel formulation once articulated in the Gospels: that, if we are to enter the Kingdom of God, we must, as Jesus once put it, become like one of these little ones, these children (even infants) in order to enter into a community beyond all earthly community as we have come to know it.[1] Though this parallel passage between Agamben's philosophical expressions and Jesus' enigmatic teachings may seem simply convenient at this point, I would claim that the equivalence between their thoughts, at least in this regard, is not coincidental, but rather that they are both intimating a similar movement beyond the representations of this world in which we are otherwise continuously mired. They are both pointing in fact to an "impossible" realm of existence that we are yet called to in a sense. If Agamben's statements on what appears to be a form of "political nihilism" seem overly difficult to conceptualize, as difficult as trying to depict what the "Kingdom of God" might actually be like, then perhaps there are good reasons for drawing the comparison in the first place. Perhaps some deeper truth lies dormant in our regression to an infancy we can hardly fathom, and to which we would like to respond, as once did Nicodemus: *how can we regress to our infancy? Are we to enter again into our mothers' wombs?*[2] Yet, indeed, if this were nothing but sheer nonsense, Christianity would most likely have evaporated a long time ago.

In a recent essay titled "Philosophical Archaeology," Agamben speaks openly about the methods he employs in conducting his research. Following Foucault rather closely in what he also terms a genealogical approach, or "something of an archaeology," he is quick to cite the work of Freud as influential upon this method's unfolding, particularly Freud's insightful notion of regression.[3] How does regression function as an archaeological tool? For Freud, indeed, regression was what signaled a backward sliding toward past habitual action, to a time in fact before we were split into a binary division between the conscious and the unconscious. It was the psychoanalyst's task to get those persons being analyzed to gently regress to a place in their mind prior to their already accepted (and entrenched) worldviews in order to map how their world of symbolic meaning came to be. What makes this concept so philosophically meaningful in the context of a genealogical inquiry is that, in Agamben's hands, it is the cornerstone upon which any attempt to formulate a movement beyond the entrenched dichotomies of rational thought is constructed. It is the means by which to go beyond the universal/particular, or conscious/ unconscious binary oppositions that have thus far dominated Western representational logic.

Through his utilization of the concept of regression, Agamben seeks to "go back" as it were, not to the latent unconscious, and not to the traumatic memories that we hold deep within, but to the source of this dividing action itself (*SA* 98).[4] Regression therefore embodies an attempt to ask, in essence, why we, as subjects, are so rationally dependent upon these dichotomies, or, in essence, why we are so eager and insistent to label and divide the objects we encounter within our world. What Agamben hopes to achieve by inspecting these processes is no less than to resolve the aporias which haunt Western, rational thought, not to mention religious practice. He is actively seeking to undo the false dichotomies of all representations, such as between the particular and the universal, or between historiography and history, which are reproduced or staged, so to speak, by the conscious/unconscious division itself. Ultimately, he intends to demonstrate how there is no primordially religious human (*homo religious*) underneath it all—there is simply a blank space which must be accepted as it is (cf. *RG* 286).

In psychoanalytic terms, the movement of regression that is being disclosed here is one that does not simply try to locate the coordinates for those deep, traumatic memories which people spend so much money, time, and effort trying to return to and hopefully resolve. Positing the "solution" to one's profound emotional problems as little more than the act of identifying a repressed memory is simply a caricature of how psychoanalysis "works," and one which, according to Agamben, misconstrues how regression functions as an archaeological tool. And so, he muses, what happens when we engage with regression, allow it to take its course and reach that source, when we actually arrive, not at the historical origin(s) some might rather have us look for, but at the origin of the formative split that itself constitutes our being-human? This split, of course, is what Agamben has been after from the start, and it is therefore the fracture upon which our humanity is "founded" over and against "the others" (i.e., animals, God, other races, nations, genders, etc.).

First off, we are told, "[i]t should by now be obvious that our way of representing the moment before the split is governed by the split itself" (*SA* 99). This state of things, as we might expect, makes discerning the nature of our selves quite problematic. As a consequence, any conceptualization beyond this split often becomes entangled in trying to depict some primary "state of happiness," "a kind of golden age devoid of repressions and perfectly conscious of and master of itself" (*SA* 99), a state therefore akin to the various political formulations of a "state of nature," as we saw above. But this is not what Agamben is wanting to point toward; rather, he envisions something quite different, something as seemingly ephemeral as it is significant. Regression points to nothing less than the present moment, something much more inaccessible than most subjects might like to admit. For Agamben, regression leads to a fuller present, one that includes both a presence and an absence of sorts: "before or beyond the split, in the disappearance of the categories governing its representation, there is nothing but the sudden, dazzling disclosure of the moment of arising, the revelation of the present as something that we were not able to live or think" (*SA* 99). This is a present beyond those (sovereign) decisions we have made for ourselves, to be, look, or act in a certain manner based on the traumatic kernel which we hope psychoanalysis will help us uncover. It is the bringing of all the "noise" that we believe constitutes "us" to a certain point of silence, more than simply somewhat akin to Benjamin's notion of bringing the progress of history (its "dialectics") to a standstill.[5]

Yet, if regression is not a matter of realizing a repressed, unconscious desire which we persistently cling to, as Freud had thought, then what exactly constitutes the uniqueness of the regressive archaeological method? The answer would seem to be that regression holds out the possibility of returning to a "subject" that exists *before* the (other) subject of our metaphysical claims—an originary subject not founded upon unlivable traumas or the exclusion of others or even parts of oneself, but rather, an exposure of the self that holds out the potential for a new subjectivity beyond what we have heretofore conceived, a "creaturely being" indeed *beyond* subjecthood entirely. Such a "subject," to Agamben's mind, can only be thought through an act of regression which serves to "displace" and "deconstruct" the currently reigning (sovereign) subject; hence, it is

> a matter of conjuring up its phantasm [the phantasm of the subject], through meticulous genealogical inquiry, in order to work on it, deconstruct it, and detail it to the point where it gradually erodes, losing its originary status. In other words, archaeological regression is elusive: it does not seek, as in Freud, to restore a previous stage, but to decompose, displace, and ultimately bypass it in order to go back not to its content but to the modalities, circumstances, and moments in which the split, by means of repression, constituted it as origin. (*SA* 102–103)

It is a new adaptation of what constitutes "regression" then, one intended to redefine the archaeological project as Foucault described it some years earlier.[6] It is a regression which brings us to the present, in a creative, imaginative exposure of our being. It is also an act of embracing an existence without content, a constitutive principle which we have already seen at work in Agamben's other writings. Citing Foucault as his inspiration in this movement beyond Freud, Agamben here in fact clarifies how "[t]his dimension beyond images and phantasms toward which the movement of the imagination is directed is not the obsessive repetition of a trauma or of a primal scene, but the initial moment of existence when 'the originary constitution of the world is accomplished'" (*SA* 105).

The mimicking of a creation language is here not coincidental to his theological explorations elsewhere. Indeed, theologically, as Agamben will illustrate with the three monotheistic faiths serving as his examples, this regressive method enables us to conclude that salvation in fact *precedes* creation, making creation intelligible as such (cf. *N* 9ff.). Redemption and creation "are not simply separate but rather persist in a single place, where the work of salvation acts as a kind of a priori that is immanent in the work of creation and makes it possible" (*SA* 108). Therefore, he concludes, "to go backward through the course of history, as the archaeologist does, amounts to going back through the work of creation in order to give it back to the salvation from which it originates" (*SA* 108). Regression grants us the method by which to comprehend the entirety of what lies before us in the present, not necessarily as providing the fantasy-laden backdrop by which we comprehend all symbolic orderings (which is contained in the dichotomous split of our knowledge), but rather as that which clears away the symbolic representations that hinder our being-creaturely. This is done in order that the present might appear as completely open, as a "pure potentiality" before us within which we are capable of dwelling. In other words, everything that we are, everything we thought constituted the subjectivity upon which we relied (our "created" being as it were), is eroded, displaced, destabilized, and deconstructed until all that is left is a sparkling moment of our exposure in the light of day. It is a self completely within the present moment, as if finally brought to a day of reckoning, a day of judgment as well, a day in which redemption is completed and shown to be prior to the creation of the subject in the first place. For this reason, these theological musings upon the Last Day or the Day of Days, are not idle talk, but rather at the center of understanding and articulating this momentous insight, as Agamben will attempt to further illuminate.

The Day of Judgment

In a short essay quite simply titled "Judgment Day," Agamben contemplates how Christian theology has struggled to find an adequate solution to the practical problems surrounding a general resurrection of the flesh. As theologians have often wondered throughout history, how indeed will the believers come to life once again on the Last Day? Will they be old or young? Will they still carry those physical defects or blemishes that once characterized their daily living, or, perhaps far worse, that defined the moment of their death?

In short, he tells us, Christian theologians were never fully able to resolve these problems (cf. *PR* 26; *N* 147ff.). Rather than attempt to formulate some vague answers to these questions, however, and once again, Agamben tries to alter the angle from which we are viewing the question. By contemplating the eschatological dimensions of photography, he hopes in this brief context to demonstrate how the visual medium of the photograph seeks to capture each human gesture as might be seen on something like a "last day." Hence, the frozen image, forever transfixed in time, becomes the ever-present judgment looking at us from its singular distance. Under the photographer's lens, there is nothing but the fleeting present moment, a concern for the image which is forever relegated to the past the instant after the shutter closes. Yet, in its attempt at being absolutely contemporaneous, the photograph somehow testifies to all the "lost names" of history, bringing each haunting image before the viewer's gaze and disrupting any attempt to form a cohesive viewpoint. There is thus a "new angel of the apocalypse—the angel of photography" who holds a new Book of Life in its hands "at the end of all days, that is, every day" (*PR* 27).

The medium of photography is significant here because it manages to capture something essential in Agamben's formulation of an ethics beyond the law and normativity it is usually filled with. This is, for him, the realm of gestures, captured in the photograph as if extended in that singular pose for all of eternity. Gesture is, for Agamben, and as Deborah Levitt describes it, "an exhibition, a process of making visible, a revelation device, and what it makes visible is the *medium*, the *milieu* of human beings."[7] Though she immediately qualifies this expression of our potential situatedness in the realm of gesture, "[s]uch a *milieu* refers not only to the medium that human beings are *in*, but equally to the medium that human being *is*." It is what survives after the constructed image of the "human being" that the anthropological machinery created has been rendered inoperative. In this manner, then, "bare life" itself lives on in pure gesture, "like creatures bathed in the light of the Last Day, surviving the ruin of their formal garment and their conceptual meaning" (*P* 80). As in the photograph with no caption, only the basic, even enigmatic, gesture is presented through the visual image before us, revealing something of us beyond the limits of expression.

As can be heard echoing throughout this suggestively rich passage, Agamben is referring to a realm of gesture beyond its historical-theological guise, to "a wholly profane mystery in which human beings, liberating themselves from all sacredness, communicate to each other their lack of secrets as their most proper gesture" (*P* 85). It is then a mark of profanation, an experience "of mediality as the ethical dimension of human beings."[8] And this characterization of gesture, we might say, is a new form of politics or politics in its purest form, as a "means without ends" which thereby avoids becoming a mimetically scripted attempt at forming some sort of totalitarian schema, whether that be a political or theological configuration of a sovereign form. This is the case because gesture, in Agamben's words, "breaks with the false alternative between ends and means that paralyzes morality and presents instead means that, *as such*, evade the orbit of mediality without becoming, for this reason, ends" (*ME* 57, emphasis in the original). Politics, in this sense, is capable of becoming a "sphere of the full, absolute gesturality of human beings," that is, philosophy, though it, of course, has not yet been fully realized (*P* 85).

This seeming reduction of the Last Day to the *every* day before us certainly appears to foreshorten the lasting theological significance of God's judgment, at least from a historical point of view. Here, Agamben, however, once again utilizes the theological heritage in order to justify his reading. It is therefore in the writings of the early church, specifically in Origen (whom he cites without reference), that Agamben finds a suitable alternative. As he puts it in the context of theological debates concerning what form the resurrected body (the "glorious body") would take, "Origen cut short these endless discussions by claiming that the resurrection concerns the form of the body, its *eidos* ['image' or 'form'], rather than the body itself" (*PR* 26–27). This is the "incorruptible" core of our existence, that which Origen tried to isolate when he spoke of the *eidos* beyond corporeal substance in which manner we would return after our judgment. This type of reasoning is what subsequently allows Agamben to assume the glorious body back into its earthly existence, as all speculation on our resurrected forms was really a discussion about the earthly bodies we actually inhabit. In essence, then, the real issue for him was how we are to understand our relationship to form itself and not one concerning the body. Photography, in this light, becomes a sort of "prophecy of the glorious body" rooted in its attempt to capture the absolute contemporaneousness wherein we reside, a fleeting moment of pure form before us, something he elsewhere links to the poet's task of "being contemporary."[9]

There is a resonance here in Agamben's depiction of the "last day" with the redemption of the past as found in the work of Walter Benjamin, for whom the "angel of history" was to figure so prominently as a melancholic image that confronted the ruins left behind by (historical) progress.[10] For

Benjamin, the freezing of a past image was the only way to achieve a present moment beyond the past's hold on us, a "now-time" (*Jetztzeit*) that liberates us from our oppression to those ideological scripts that dominate our reading of history and which is the time of the messiah (cf. *WA* 52–53). In a discussion concerning Benjamin's conceptions of both history and redemption, Agamben states that "to redeem the past is not to restore its true dignity, to transmit it anew as an inheritance for future generations" (*P* 153). A true redemption of the past rather can only bring matters to a close, not perpetuate them further. This in fact is a reality only conceivable as such on something like a Day of Judgment. As he continues, "what is at issue is an interruption of tradition in which the past is fulfilled and thereby brought to its end once and for all. For humanity, as for the individual human, to redeem the past is to put an end to it, to cast upon it a gaze that fulfills it" (*P* 153). This is a task both to "shake off the past and bring it into the hands of humanity," what Agamben unhesitatingly calls an "unusual" task (*P* 153). There is an upending of the hold of traditional historical representations lurking here as well as an invitation to live in the present which cannot be manipulated for particular ideological or religious ends, a grasping of the form beyond its content (its body) which renders all historical representations superfluous.

This act of realizing the present moment, it should also be said, is no minor gesture. Rather, its significance can be felt in the way in which humanity has struggled to posit itself as humanity, to erect those (ontotheological) boundaries that would grant it its "humanity," its name as it were. Despite this fact, however, it would seem that the best that humanity can now achieve (in terms of self-definition), according to Agamben, is a sort of "suspended" living, one that neither touches the core of our reality as human being nor proposes a solution to the deadlock between the past and the present. In other words, the charted course of modernity is a damned prospect from the start: just barely self-aware enough to suspend what has been, but not self-aware enough to make things any better. Everything in fact seems bound for a course of destruction, as Benjamin had already foreseen, due to be lost in the accompanying debris that seems to dissolve any chance for a final redemption.

This is a problem as theological as it is historical, and the difference between them is not always so clear. The only reality to be grasped in this world, then, is one of an inherent alienation for the subject who struggles to comprehend and grasp the symbols at hand.[11] Accordingly, Agamben's commentary on Benjamin's most fundamental historical image unfolds as such:

> The redemption that the angel of art offers to the past, summoning it to appear outside its real context on the day of aesthetic Last Judgment, is, then, nothing other than its death (or rather, its inability to die) in the museum of aesthetics. And the angel's melancholy is the consciousness that he has adopted alienation as his world; it is the nostalgia of a reality that he can possess only by making it unreal. (*MC* 110)

The integrity of experience once present to us in its fullness, as undivided and in some sense "pure," is now forever separated from itself, causing each possession (as part of a collection, like museum pieces suspended from any real use) to remain in an ethereal state only. Each concrete reality exists as ultimately inexperienceable. As with his comments elsewhere on the poetic (*IH* 15ff.; *S* xvii; *LD* 74ff.), Agamben here depicts the aesthetic project as one that is fundamentally intertwined with the plight of the modern autonomous subject insofar as this subject must, in a sense, utilize art in order to inhabit its world, even if it is an "unreal" world in many respects. This is, in fact, the best that humanity can expect to achieve for itself.

Yet, this is no small achievement either. Theology indeed runs aground in the face of this political task, one rooted entirely in the possibilities of our humanity. And so, only by moving away from the economy of theology, can we truly embrace our being "without humanity" as such: "Like the freed convict in Kafka's *Penal Colony*, who has survived the destruction of the machine that was to have executed him, these beings have left the world of guilt and justice behind them: The light that rains down on them is that irreparable light of the dawn following the *novissima dies* of judgment. But the life that begins on earth after the last day is simply human life," a life then without the standard conceptualizations of humanity accompanying it and thus without its traditional divine supports as well (*CC* 6–7; cf. *RG* 422).

Again, the image of the "last day" emerges in Agamben's framework as the threshold against which all other spans of time are measured; it becomes the indelible line existing between a humanity indebted to its most basic metaphysical gestures, and a humanity that has freed itself from their guises. This formulation of human life as being "simply human life," then, is an allowance for the revelation of our own true nature, something which Agamben had been driving toward in his work on animality, clarifying the boundaries that are said to divide the blessed life of animals from our own. Through this clarification, then, humanity might be able to gain access to its true nature, something it has otherwise sought to avoid: "Here darkness and light, matter and spirit, animal life and *logos* (the articulation of which in the anthropological machine produced the human) are separated forever. But not in order to close themselves in a more impenetrable mystery; rather, to liberate their own truer nature" (*O* 90). The true impetus here is to regress, to return, and thereby to reconnect, with our animality, with the foundations of our "creaturely" being that we are seemingly forever divided against, and thus constantly engaged in having to articulate and defend our humanity over and against this "more natural" state.

What Agamben seeks to articulate and defend then is a "new humanity" that belongs neither to a pure animality (which is characterized as having a poverty of world) nor to a purely rational humanity. It is a characterization that also avoids becoming a Nietzschean *Übermensch* ("overman," in the sense of "superman") because it is a regressive *in*-fancy to our origins and not a surpassing of our humanity to a state above or over it. Though it may in some sense resemble (or be) a form of nihilism, it in fact constitutes the opposite of Nietzsche's claims. Agamben is rather trying to formulate a state of being beyond the mythical-religious (anthropological) machinery, beyond the political and cultural representations that have so shaped and dominated our identities historically. A new zone of dwelling is now possible for humanity to enter: a space *beyond* because *behind* or *before* humanity's origins

> [i]t is not easy to think this figure—whether new or very ancient—of the life that shines in the "saved night" of nature's (and, in particular, human nature's) eternal, unsavable survival after it has definitively bid farewell to the *logos* and to its own history. It is no longer human, because it has perfectly forgotten every rational element, every project for mastering its animal life; but if animality had been defined precisely by its poverty in world and by its obscure expectation of a revelation and a salvation, then this life cannot be called animal either. It surely "does not see the open," in the sense that it does not appropriate it as an instrument of mastery and knowledge; but neither does it remain simply closed in its own captivation. The *agnoia*, the nonknowledge which has descended upon it, does not entail the loss of every relation to its own concealment. Rather, this life remains serenely in relation with its own proper nature . . . as a zone of nonknowledge. (O 90–91)

In this fashion, Agamben aims to restore humanity to its intended present moment, not one in which the human subject, as the centerpiece of Western, rational thought, would reign over all of creation, but rather, a present wherein the human animal might reappear in its originary environment.

This appearing would thus constitute something of a healing experience for the fracture at the heart of Western thought, an act of forgiveness unlike any other ever experienced because it would be a reconciliation of humanity with its animality (and perhaps even divinity). It would therefore also avoid mirroring those treacherous political projects of the last century which sought to "heal" the very same fracture through the complete exclusion of its perceived "animality," the genocidal actions taken toward those persons who had been marked as forms of "bare life." Though perhaps sounding rather mystical as it were, for Agamben, entering into a zone of nonknowledge between the human and the animal is an entrance into a realm beyond knowledge as we have constructed it—beyond the dichotomous logics that have governed our representational thoughts. It is a regression to the blank slate of pure potentiality that becomes an offering of a type of forgiveness to us. Indeed, the *tabula rasa*, or "blank slate," the lack of form that is one's pure potentiality, returns, but this time as the ultimate source of what the great religions perhaps hold dearest, as the source of true forgiveness itself (cf. *IP* 32–34). By suggesting the etymological origin of *ignoscere* as "to forgive" and not as "not to know," Agamben renders this "nonknowledge," or ignorance, which the image of the blank slate tries to capture, as itself the source of all acts of forgiveness: "To articulate a zone of nonknowledge—or better, of a-knowledge—means in this sense not simply to let something be, but to leave something outside of being, to render it unsavable" (*O* 91). To let something *be* outside of how we have traditionally conceived of *being*, outside the sovereign decisions of the anthropological machine to establish the *human* in its *being*, this is the realm of forgiveness, a state of existence outside of being as we have constituted it thus far.

If we can say that the Day of Judgment is most typically conceived as a day involving famines, earthquakes, war, and a general pestilence, then the images of it we might conjure are mainly those of destruction and destitution, and the Lord God walking through the midst of the rubble, judging all in consideration of what they have done in their lifetime. In Agamben's estimation, however, all of this symbolic content fails to perceive the true nature of the "Last Day" that religion tries (often in vain) to capture—that of an essential threshold of our humanity now broached in relation to our animality. Though this gesture "beyond being" certainly might appear as the nihilistic end of all ontological forms, what I have been suggesting throughout is that Agamben's most fundamental insight concerning our potentiality is to suggest an ontological form beyond the violent logics of our world. Whether or not this gesture appears as a form of nihilism or of a purer religious expression seems often to miss the point: that they may be in fact the same thing.

Nihilism and the Lack of Content

Though nihilism has often received a bad reputation for the primacy accorded to "nothing" over "something," it has historically often been the case that even the most avowed nihilists, such as Nietzsche, were merely repackaging "something" as "nothing," even if this meant reintroducing forms of religious thought masked as the "death of God."[12] One might go so far as to conjecture that Agamben's reading of the Christian legacy is just that: Christianity boldly announces the death of God and of all representations tied to such a deity's supposed transcendence *so that* another kingdom might come upon our world, one founded without any sovereign legacy supporting it.[13] It would be what Dominick LaCapra has indicated as a possible Christian legacy in Agamben's work, or as he puts it: "The formula here—whether paradox or one of the oldest of Christian *doxa*—seems to be that only by descending to the depths can one ascend to the paradisiacal heights of revelatory language."[14] If this is a nihilistic vision, then perhaps it can yet also be wedded to an affirmation of life through our (artistic) efforts that Agamben sifts out from among the ruins.

In his first book, *The Man without Content*, Agamben begins to construct an elaborate and profound relationship between the "destiny of art" and "the rise of nihilism" that will shape the course of his future research avenues and which bears repeating in this context. Their interaction, and mutual development, is portrayed as the "fundamental movement of the history of the West" (*MC* 27). The connection is so essential to our way of seeing the world, it might be argued, that we often miss what all the fuss is about, and therefore lack the vision to see why the connection between nihilism and the "destiny of art" has provided a good share of the "bizarre" art forms we now witness in our world today. From Warhol's pop art to Duchamp's *Fountain* (which is, to most, what appears as little more than a urinal with a signature on it), from Pollock's abstract expressionism to the average video installation in a modern art museum, there are so many potential reasons for the modern museum-viewer to be more than a bit confused as to the presence of what might at first glance appear to be something "other-than" art. In the midst of this potential for confusion, perhaps Agamben's comments can help shed some much needed light on the role of art (as essential to the search for establishing meaning) in an increasingly nihilistic (postreligious) world.

From the outset, the main problem of art today would seem to lie in a loss of traditional meaning; that is, art seems to have lost its "positive" (historically, often religious) content. All that remains, most typically, is something of the "negative," or its shadow. In a remark on the critical reception of art, and yet which is also a statement that typifies his basic stance on the nature of all artistic content, Agamben asserts that: "Our appreciation of art begins necessarily with the forgetting of art," or more succinctly, "critical judgment thinks art as art" (*MC* 43). This is generally the case, we are told, because "[w]hat has been negated [by the critic of art] is resumed into the judgment as its only real content, and what has been affirmed is covered by this shadow" (*MC* 43). If we are to understand this correctly, it would seem that the ability of art to underscore its own meaning has receded upon the horizon, leaving only the formidable absence of any meaning to connote the sense that it would otherwise convey. As he further defines our context of art:

> The extreme object-centeredness of contemporary art, through its holes, stains, slits, and nonpictoral materials, tends increasingly to identify the work of art with the non-artistic product. Thus, becoming aware of its shadow, art immediately receives in itself its own negation, and in bridging the gap that used to separate it from criticism, itself becomes the *logos* of art and of its shadow, that is critical reflection on art. (*MC* 50)

Art thus ceases to point toward the "loftier" eternal values that it once sought to express; hence, also, the decline in more "eternal" forms of art such as sculpture. Instead, we are immersed in the "transient" art forms such as film and "pop art" where the commercialized object moves into the space where our potentiality should rather be exposed.[15] The common, everyday objects, or the artists themselves (as in certain forms of "performance art"), are allowed to become art as it were, to be picked from among the ruins of civilization like Duchamp's urinal and made art precisely because they are labeled *as* art. Seemingly anything can thus be picked up and framed as art insofar as it can be utilized by an artist as illustrating the ("negative") void of meaning which cannot be communicated directly.

The truth of this statement would seem to be almost palpable in our modern world. The artist today is nearly given over entirely to constructing representations of "nothingness" itself, leaving us caught up in a negativity of art that we can hardly make out for ourselves, often in fact confusing this negativity with the positive content of times past (cf. *MC* 43ff.). Criticism accordingly now runs the risk, according to Agamben, of letting itself be eclipsed and of not allowing new forms of art to arise, ones otherwise immersed in more original, initial (perhaps even *infantile*) processes. This problematic nature of contemporary art, represented here as the "decline of all contents" (a thought which should be familiar to the reader by now), renders the artist as one who faces a choice between desperately clinging to its violent actions as forms of "new content" or to become the "man without content, who has no other identity than a perpetual emerging out of the nothingness of expression and no other ground than this incomprehensible station on this side of himself" (*MC* 55).[16] And it is here, at the juncture of art and the formation of the "man without content" that Agamben's work finds its emblematic figure: the human being who exists without content, who often, though in vain, strives unceasingly to prevent this characteristic emptiness from being exposed to public view.

Art becomes, in this sense, a "negation that negates itself, a *self-annihilating nothing*" and thus can also be said to somehow "eternally survive itself" (*MC* 56). That is, it survives itself at the cost of liquidating its "positive" content, which is the near total emptying of its traditional, metaphysical (religious) content. Indeed, though Agamben does not engage with any historical-theological speculations in this context, as he often will in his later works, it is nonetheless clear where he envisions these remarks concluding. The contemporary state of this nihilistic furor in art can only result in the loss of the divine:

> Artistic subjectivity without content is now the pure force of negation that everywhere and at all times affirms only itself as absolute freedom that mirrors itself in pure self-consciousness. And, just as every content goes under in it, so the concrete space of the work disappears in it, the space in which once man's action and the world both found their reality in the image of the divine, and in which man's dwelling on earth used to take its diametrical measurement. In the pure self-supporting of the creative-formal principle, the sphere of the divine becomes opaque and withdraws, and it is in the experience of art that man becomes conscious, in

the most radical way, of the event in which Hegel had already seen the most essential trait of unhappy consciousness, the event announced by Nietzsche's madman: "God is dead." (MC 56–57)

The "death of God" becomes then the conclusion which the loss of meaning in art has been moving toward. Art, for its part, has become the "pure potentiality of negation," a fact which thereby allows a certain sense of nihilism to reign over the traditional forms of value or meaning.[17]

In an age where the great Western religions are seemingly in decline within a more "mainstream" culture, I am tempted to see Agamben's critique as more than a bit apt. As it appears, the ruins of theology brought about by modernity's suspension of traditional forms of meaning and captured perhaps best by Nietzsche's pronouncement that "God is dead" (wherein he also implies that we are the ones who killed him), mirror the ruins of cathedrals, monasteries, convents, or at least their emptiness, which is perhaps another way to stress their "ruin."[18] What we witness today, then, with regard to these ruins, is their mass conversion: cathedrals turned into meeting rooms, or into apartments or hotels, or even into museums for the purposes of mass tourism. This nihilistic fire has seemingly burnt up the meaning which people once found in the art and architecture of Western religion. But, it is important to stress, new forms of cultural meaning do continue to creep up and grant significance to what lies before us, new forms that can be explored and possibly embraced.

And so, rather than simply lament this state that we find ourselves in, this image of a purifying fire would seem to gel cohesively with one of Agamben's recurring themes, the principle that "it is only in the burning house that the fundamental architectural problem becomes visible for the first time" (MC 115). Perhaps the "fundamental problems" which nihilism exposes can give rise to new forms of meaning. Perhaps, that is, art can find another way to express itself in the midst of so much loss and decay of traditional forms, as it is only through the ruins, the skeletal remains, then, that we might see what was at stake in the first place, what mattered and is still perhaps of decisive importance for us today. Elsewhere, invoking the same analogy of the house ravaged by fire, Agamben reviews this task of aesthetics by calling it a "destruction of destruction," a movement which involves "the destruction of the mode of transmission" itself (*IH* 161). As would befit the structure I am here pursuing, this movement of double destruction would seem to confirm the essential regression at hand that coincides with his pronouncements elsewhere on the "division of division itself" as we have seen. Only a regression such as this could reveal the structure that now stands disclosed upon the horizon without any "positive" content undergirding it. The ruined structure is what Agamben is apparently after: the pure form beneath the content.

This quest can be seen, for example, in his numerous attempts to rid theology of its "positive" content, its doctrines or dogmas. More recently, he had made clear how tradition, and here the undertones of "religious tradition" are as manifest as they are in his other writings, serves to "block access to history" and must be "cleared away" just like the "ghosts of the unconscious" (*SA* 106–107). For Agamben, the (archaeological, genealogical) method is the important thing, and it is this method which reveals the structures of human experience for what they are, without any content (i.e., doctrine) per se.

Religions, in his estimation, have historically attempted to illustrate the significance of this methodology throughout the centuries, but have explicitly failed to come fully to terms with it, thus miring themselves deeper and deeper into content-filled propositions that in fact threaten the true nucleus that underlies the entirety of their existence. This nucleus is what Agamben is after time and again, that is, their messianic core which those institutions dependent upon an exclusionary logic have in fact tried to silence. In his estimation, they have tacked content onto that which should remain contentless, and they have obscured the goal of living in a present moment beyond the given cultural, social, and political representations. If we are now strolling through their ruins, there is perhaps then some cause for rejoicing, if Agamben is to be fully understood on this point. As he emphasizes in this alternation of meaning, and again utilizing the Christian context as his primary example,

> [t]here is no such thing as a content of faith, and to profess the word of faith does not mean formulating true propositions on God and the world. To believe in Jesus Messiah does not mean believing in something about him . . . and the attempts of the Councils to formulate the content of faith in *symbola* can only be taken as a sublime irony. (*TR* 136)

This is so, we are told, because the "word of faith," as he calls it, is a "pure power of saying" that cannot simply be labeled as a content-based proposition. It indeed exceeds any attempt to do just that. Rather, as he makes clear, this pure power "exists as an absolute nearness of the word" (*TR* 136). In what will later appear as the pure ("weak") force of this power, its messianic heritage, Agamben champions the claims of a contentless faith by drawing a line between its activity and that of law: "The act itself of a pure potentiality of saying, a word that always remains close to itself, cannot be a signifying word that utters true opinions on the state of things, or a juridical performative that posits itself as fact" (*TR* 136). Law, as the alterable norms established through a world of sovereign significations, is rendered inoperative by a force that appears to have little strength to undo it and yet, somehow, does. For this reason, Paul's adherence to a messianic power can only be described as a form of "weakness" (*TR* 136).

Thus, it is through a careful, genealogical deconstruction and displacement of the theological tradition, an act that would appear to mirror his understanding of what any "nearness to the word of faith" should be, that Agamben hopes to reveal how our "ontological anchoring" is no more than "a field of essentially historical tensions" which can be disclosed by this methodological inquiry of regression (*SA* 111). Hence, the focus upon ruins is neither a convenient image, nor simply a metaphor for what religion, in the Western world, currently resembles. Rather, it is only by comprehending the nature of ruins in general, and religious ruins as foremost among them, that we can adequately regress to our origin.

For the Romantics, ruins were a kind of focal point, a nostalgic reenvisioning of the past. For Freud, they were as so many symbols littered among our unconsciousness, speaking to us in our dreams.[19] For Benjamin, as for Agamben, ruins are rather that which provide the material for the present moment, that which is itself present through a transience of almost eternal significance, even if it is something we have forgotten. The entire scope of this genealogical project of regression would appear to dictate as much. This is a project of digging among the ruins which provide more insight to our present reality than any "epic history" ("grand narratives") that we were once given could.[20] By delving into the ruins before us, we might then be able to see how the basis for understanding Agamben's work, not to mention the relationship between his work and the various discourses of theology, lies in a conjunction of the possibility for a "coming theology" alongside the ruins of a theology eclipsed. Only in this manner, by considering their relationship, could something like theology be thought again, or thought always again from its beginning.

Samuel Beckett, in the context of contemplating the viewpoint of some soldiers within occupied France during the Second World War, spoke of how they may yet come to see their actions as "a vision and sense of a time-honoured conception of humanity in ruins," but also, and, this is where the emphasis must lie, as "perhaps even an inkling of the terms in which our condition is to be thought again."[21] For apparently, only in the ruins of civilization, in its destruction as it were, can the "human condition" be thought through again—perhaps as if for the first time.

From this, one can (re)turn to Agamben's contemplation of the "urgent" task of the destruction of aesthetics as we know it, the job of clearing away that which is taken for granted in our day and age. From this vantage point, we can see perhaps how

> [t]he question, however, is whether the time is ripe for such a *destruction*, or whether instead the consequence of such an act would not be the loss of any possible horizon for the understanding of the work of art and the creation of an abyss in front of it that could only be crossed with a radical leap. But perhaps just such a loss and such an abyss are what we most need if we want the work of art to reacquire its original stature. And if it is true that the fundamental architectural problem becomes visible only in the house ravaged by fire, then perhaps we are today in a privileged position to understand the authentic significance of the Western aesthetic project. (*MC* 6)

As with Beckett's conception of how we might begin to formulate our condition after a period of its destruction, so too does Agamben perceive the near total liquidation of our Western aesthetic project. The pronouncement of the "death of God" within this same context becomes an acutely felt abandonment of humanity within a realm of profane dwelling that *is* our world, yet an abandonment that might actually signal a new comprehension of what "humanity" is.

Profanation

The contemporary Western religious context is filled with those traditional (and often polarizing) contrasts which are not easily dissolved, such as that between the believer and unbeliever. These are contrasts which more than simply mimic Schmitt's basic friend/enemy distinction said to lie behind all political structures.[22] If we are able to see Agamben's claims as he intends, then they are in fact cut from the same cloth. Theology, within this framework, would indeed seem to be a sort of discourse that serves to indicate the assumed boundaries that these contrasts will be capable of enforcing, making theology explicitly then a discourse on power and the cultural divisions within our world, making it thus political as it were.

There are certainly theological movements indebted to moving all believers toward more "orthodox" positions in the face of a looming secularization, an attempt perhaps to embrace religion in a "postsecular" guise seemingly beyond these contrasts (though obviously still wedded to its terms).[23] No matter how these arguments are formulated, there is still a lingering sense that the basic contrast of forces is between the sacred and the secular, believers and atheists, and that culture is basically determined in accordance with these divisions. What Agamben offers us in this debate is an interesting attempt at resolving this impasse through a dynamic alteration of the very terms which define it. This is to say, and as I have been outlining throughout, that perhaps there is something within the theological (if we can regress to it) that goes even further than the secular in eradicating the presence of a (false) sacrality. That is, ironically, perhaps only a properly conceived theology can truly present us with the realm of the profane existing beyond that of the merely secular.[24]

This possibility would certainly seem to cohere with Agamben's distaste for what passes as constitutive of the secular. Indeed, the secular is for him merely another way of expressing a false sense of sacrality, one that is simply repressed under the many layers of culture we inhabit. Secularization, for its part, is only "a form of repression" of the sacred, as he describes it, or the signature of the theological which the secular yet still points toward (*PR* 77; *SA* 76–77; *RG* 21). As the sacred goes "underground," it is therefore retained in new "secular" forms, yet its basic economy is discernable nonetheless (cf. *RG* 20ff.), in much the same way, it might be suggested, as sovereignty has remained active by acquiring new forms within the modern era (such as the biopolitical). Perhaps detectable in the nonreligious ritualistic trends of modern culture (e.g., mass sporting events, major holidays), secularization mimics traditional religious forces, according to Agamben, by "simply moving them from one place to another" (*PR* 77). Following the insight offered by Schmitt, Agamben is further able to state how "the political secularization of theological concepts (the transcendence of God as a paradigm of sovereign power) does nothing but displace the heavenly monarchy onto an earthly monarchy, leaving its power intact" (*PR* 77). The structure of a functional "sacrality" thereby remains within the secular, despite its being displaced onto purely "political" concepts.

The contrast therefore between secularization and profanation in political terms is quite relevant. As Agamben makes abundantly clear, both secularization and profanation are political operations, though with differing purposes. Secularization, for its part, secures a transcendent guarantor for political sovereignty by referring politics back to its sacred source despite its apparent distance from it (*PR* 77). In essence, today's condition, he will again claim, is one dominated by the spectacle (of original sin), a state which actually prevents the profanation of objects for everyday use as we are still, despite claims to the contrary, bound to its religious form. The "secular" can therefore be viewed as a condition or state of dwelling that denies humanity its true (profane) dwelling in its authentic ("creaturely") state of being. The slow turning of our society into one dominated by the spectacle, or the "museification" of our world (i.e., everything being brought into the realm of the quasi-sacred museum, forever suspended from any real use in our world), maintains the structure of religious separation only, thus illustrating an empty sacred gesture as the end product of our unchecked capitalist intentions (cf. *PR* 81ff.).

The combination of a critique of capitalism and the processes of secularization seems to be in many ways a single thread running throughout Agamben's reflections upon the

coming political task now before humanity. His remarks on the
theological understanding of the body and its subsequent transformation into a modern commodified form as taken up in
The Coming Community appear then to more clearly direct his
attention toward the political task of profanation, a theme he
had not yet taken up as explicitly at the time. By turning our
attention toward this early strand of thought, however, I would
simply like to demonstrate how his critique of capitalist representations of the body and the "secret solidarity" maintained
with its theological supports actually demands that an act of
profanation appear as the only genuine action capable of disrupting the violence of these given cultural and economic
representations.

This is not to indicate that the critique of the commodification of the body is a simple one, or indeed that it will lead
to an easy judgment concerning the forms it takes or their
effects upon individuals subjected to its images. In fact, as he
tells us, as soon as capitalist forces began to commodify the
human body (something he locates in the early twentieth
century), there seemed to be two sides to its commodification, a negative, but also a positive perspective (*CC* 47). As if
from the outset, then, the commodification of the body, its
use and dissemination as an object for marketing and advertising, not to mention social objectification or pornography,
was to be seemingly torn from within, split between its all-
too-obvious negative aspects (the "objectification" of the
"subject") and the faintest traces of something "positive" yet
within it as well. As Agamben develops this train of thought
further, the commodification of the body, though subject to
the apparent degradations of "becoming-object," was at the
same time exposed to a new type of existence, one free
("redeemed") from the "stigma of ineffability" that had so
dominated it for centuries (cf. *CC* 48). As with photography,
something of the pure form was presented through the body's
commodification which had been concealed by its various

(ontotheological) historical representations. Hence, the body began to "break away" from its bonds to metaphysical presumptions and biological destiny, and began to appear in its singular being, in its *flesh* so to speak, and therefore as "entirely illuminated" (*CC* 48).

Previously, and as history tells us all too well, the body had been indissociable from those religious images that had subsequently become culturally normative. As Agamben illustrates, the biblical account of humanity's creation "in the image and likeness" of God consequently "bound it in this way to an invisible archetype, and founded with it the paradoxical concept of an absolutely immaterial resemblance" (*CC* 48). The body, as such, had little chance to express itself apart from the images that culturally constituted its intelligibility, that is, apart from the typical gendered (and at times racial or ethnic) norms which accompanied it. What was now changing was that, for the first time, the image was becoming detached from the body, allowing the body a freedom it had never been furnished with before. It was an emancipation that sought to free the body from any theological images underpinning its existence and to grant it a social legitimacy.

In this respect, the commodification of the body was accompanied by a potentially insurmountable obstacle of objectification, but it also served in some sense at least to release our bodies to an expression of themselves in "whatever" form, that is, beyond the religious images that had previously signified their meaning. It is therefore within this framework of historical understanding that Agamben can state, "[n]either generic nor individual, neither an image of the divinity nor an animal form, the body now became something truly *whatever*" (*CC* 48). Hence, the decline in the art of portraiture, which sought to capture something of the "unity" of the human figure in relation to the divine, to "immortalize" the human being as it were. Now, rather, we are immersed in the world of the photographic lens and its attempts to capture the "whateverness" of being (cf. *CC* 49), those gestures he has referenced on so many occasions.[25] The nihilistic furor of art that has only been embraceable in the modern period as such is nothing more than the outworking of an original emancipatory desire that is found to lie at the base of all artistic production (cf. *MC* 35, 100).

Despite this potential for emancipation, however, the body was still caught up in the semblance of its theological representations, betraying its "secret solidarity" with these theological images, as he will put it (*CC* 48). This is so because the commodity is not able to entirely free itself from the realm of sacred semblances and their ascribed meanings which yet maintain a (veiled) hold over our cultural representations. And so, though commodification detaches the body from its previous theological inscriptions, it nonetheless "preserves the resemblance," thus allowing theology to continue its sovereign hold over us (*CC* 48). In contrast, however, the "whatever" form of the body is just that, a form to be respected in its absolute singularity, without content or metaphysical support. Hence, he can state that "[w]hatever is a resemblance without archetype—in other words, an Idea" (*CC* 48). And though Agamben does not say as much in this context, the commodification of the body, in its preeminent position within the spectacle of society brought upon us by the force of capitalist production, would seem to be inextricably intertwined with the parallel forces of secularization which manage to maintain the semblance of theology without the weight of tradition and its accompanying dogma appearing alongside it.

And yet, even with all these manifold efforts to technologize the body being made in our world today (such as those found in advertising or in the commodification of the body), these efforts can only modify the cultural *images* of the body and not the small, precarious body that lurks behind its image. It is *this* body, our naked life as it were, that Agamben seeks to isolate and defend through his later remarks on "bare life" (cf. *HS*). The protection of this ("creaturely") "bare life" behind the images that circulate culturally can only be achieved through an act which unites the body to its image over and beyond the theological images which have historically been forced upon the body. The "whatever" body must be freed from its enslavement to resemblance and (metaphysical) representation (*CC* 50). Profanation, to be sure, is the subsequent attempt needing to be made in order to achieve this, to wrest away what is our "creaturely" existence subsisting beneath the spectacle of capitalist consumerist media.

Profanation accordingly "neutralizes" that which it profanes rather than repress it (*PR* 77). It takes an object intended for use in the sacred sphere and removes it from that economy, transposing it into the realm of the profane, and thereby deactivating it: "Once profaned, that which was unavailable and separate loses its aura and is returned to use" (*PR* 77). To "consecrate" something is to remove it from everyday usage and to make it sacred, to remove it "from the free use and commerce of men" (its economic sense) (*PR* 73). To "profane" an object, then, is quite simply to return the sacred item to the economic sphere of human living, to put it *in* our world as something with a practical use. As he puts it, "[t]he thing that is returned to the common use of men is pure, profane, free of sacred names. But use does not appear here as something natural: rather, one arrives at it only by means of profanation" (*PR* 73–74). It is an act that requires the utmost effort as it even appears to be unnatural and against the grain of how we have constructed our world. The only thing comparable (and not coincidentally, I would add) would be the difficult path of religious commitment which tries to direct individuals toward and through a "better," though difficult to enter, narrow gate, as Jesus phrased it.[26]

Secularization, for its part, however, remains opposed to such an effort and would seem to be little more than a conglomerated effort to maintain the "spectacle of society" in its commodified form. Indeed, as we are told in his much later essay on profanation, "[t]he apparatuses of the media aim precisely at neutralizing this profanatory power of language as pure means, at preventing language from disclosing the possibility of a new use, a new experience of the word" (PR 88). Mirroring the reflections he had earlier offered in *The Coming Community*, Agamben resituates the antagonism between image and body into the tensions present between secularization and profanation.

As it stands, though there is perhaps something radical lurking within the original event of faith, or that which Jesus, Paul, and the early Christians seemed to comprehend moving through their actions, the church subsequently aligned itself with the social-cultural spectacle of secularization and political (sovereign) power, thereby negating the possibility for any authentic, genuine faith to arise. Agamben's critique of institutional religion does indeed seem to stem from this basic proposition: "Already the church, after the first two centuries of hoping and waiting, conceived of its function as essentially one of neutralizing the new experience of the word that Paul, placing it at the center of the messianic announcement, had called *pistis*, faith" (PR 88). Recovering this sense of faith, then, would appear to be a main task of Agamben's throughout much of his writing, even though the term itself is infrequently used.

With this understanding, and though Agamben does not clearly identify it as such, there again seems to be another sense of the religious opening up to us, one that does not conform to the polarized scheme of sacred/secular, but rather overlaps entirely with the profane realm we inhabit. This is assuredly to present a religious "faith" that sees itself as an attempt to collapse all of these binary, polarizing divisions which sustain a "false" sacrality in order to uncover a true kernel of faith beyond, because *before*, these sovereign articulations. Religion was originally an act of separating, and thus what makes the act of division itself appear as the essential trait of "being religious." Traditionally, sacrifice functioned as the apparatus of transition between the two realms, cordoning off all movement between the profane and the sacred. This reading is what in fact will cause Agamben to identifying the etymological origins of "religion" as residing in *relegere* (a scrupulousness and attention to boundaries) and not in *religare* (to unite the human and divine) (*PR* 74). Yet the task of profanation, he will reiterate time and again, is not simply to eradicate all religious boundaries between the sacred and the profane; rather profanation is concerned with putting those already existing boundaries to a "new use," to play with them as a form of pure means without ends (*PR* 87).

As Benjamin Morgan has pointed out, Agamben's use of "play," visible from his early work, such as in *Infancy and History*, to his *Homo Sacer* project, is seemingly displaced by a focus upon Christian love as the fulfillment of the law in *The Time That Remains*.[27] Yet the term returns here in *Profanations* and does not seem to signal anything other than a possibility for relationships to expand beyond their juridical (representational) limitations, something which Christian love seems thus to point toward as well. Agamben's recovery of the writings of Saint Paul thus seems to fit within this recovery of an originary "faith" beyond the sacred/secular separation with which we are familiar. Though it will undoubtedly sound paradoxical, his reading of Saint Paul will only confirm that, for Agamben, the task of profanation is nearly identical to Paul's understanding of the messianic vocation (cf. *TR* 23ff.). Though this is also, of course, an interpretation that would completely redefine the theological meaning of redemption in our world today.

Indeed, redemption subsequently appears in this context as the "pure means" of profanation which Agamben has been seeking. Understood as the profaning of objects and as a restoration to their purely human use, redemption can be identified as part of the "coming community," and thus as part of the vague political, philosophical, and theological task that he heralds as being always yet "to come," a task for "future generations." This is the difficult practice of dwelling in a "state without state" that can only resemble an act of belonging without a shared representation other than our generic humanity (cf. *CC* 86). Yet to picture a world without our normal means of representation is no doubt a difficult task. It can only come about through a regression beyond (and so *before*) the constituted subjects of representative thought. This would be, as he has stated elsewhere, to halt the anthropological machinery that dictates contemporary forms of human life and to form new relationships between humanity and nature, as between nature and history (cf. *O* 81–84).

Contrary to Paul's linkage of nature and redemption ("creature and redeemed humanity"), however, the work of Benjamin is cited by Agamben as establishing the image of a "saved night" which offers humanity back its "closedness and muteness," or what Agamben will elsewhere characterize as its "infancy" (cf. *O* 81; *IH*). Recalling the manner in which certain infants have been said to be eternally "abandoned" to a blissful, blessed life in limbo, Agamben contemplates how Benjamin's vision of the "saved night" plays upon a similar understanding of what it means to be locatable "beyond" salvation as it has been traditionally conceived, that is, how we could possibly dwell in a space no longer in need of a theological image to give meaning to the body as we have perceived it. Rather, this is a dwelling in the natural body that we have been given, severed from its theological heritage in a resolute act of profanation.

> The "saved night" is the name of this nature that has been given back to itself, whose character, according to another of Benjamin's fragments, is transience and whose rhythm is beatitude. The salvation that is at issue here does not concern something that has been lost and must be found again, something that has been forgotten and must be remembered; it concerns, rather, the lost and the forgotten as such—that is, something unsavable. The saved night is a relationship with something unsavable. For this reason, man—insofar as he is "at some stages"

also nature—appears as a field traversed by two distinct
tensions, by two different redemptions. (*O* 81–82)

And this gloss should help us understand what Agamben means
when he elsewhere expresses the act of redemption as "not an
event in which what was profane becomes sacred and what
was lost is found again. Redemption is, on the contrary, the
irreparable loss of the lost, the definitive profanity of the profane. But, precisely for this reason, they now reach their
end—the advent of a limit" (*CC* 102). Once again, we reach
the critical threshold of indiscernability, the site of our "sinful"
significations, but also, if we can attain it, the location of our
potential redemption.

This redemption, however, does not entail that we *do* anything, but rather that we only cease to do what we have already
been more than busy doing thus far. What it singularly requires
is that we stop creating the representations of ourselves and our
bodies that continue to plague us and to weigh us down as so
much unnecessary baggage. We are thereby called instead to let
things appear as they already are, in "whatever" form they
present themselves. This is to invoke a state that, in effect,
removes salvation—as traditionally characterized—from us
entirely. There is nothing to be saved, then, because we have
regressed "beyond" salvation—we have been profaned.

We can have hope only in what is without remedy. That
things are thus and thus—this is still in the world. But
that this is irreparable, that this *thus* is without remedy,
that we can contemplate it as such—this is the only
passage outside the world. (The innermost character of
salvation is that we are saved only at the point when we
no longer want to be. At this point, there is salvation—
but not for us.) (*CC* 102)

And this would seem to characterize his sense of redemption
entirely.

Redemption is an act which would restore to humanity its "proper place" as creaturely being, as caught up in its nature and returned (profaned) to its more originary heritage as a form of "bare life." Accordingly, a new relationship between humanity and nature is disclosed beyond those theological constructs which humanity has long toiled with under the various guises of religious tradition. As Agamben unfolds this further still, he conjectures that what Benjamin intended to illustrate was something completely different from the representations we have heretofore known; what is needed is a world in which humanity ceases to attempt to master nature, though this does not entail nature in turn mastering humanity or some synthesis of the two models formed into a third.

> Rather, according to the Benjaminian model of a "dialectic at a standstill," what is decisive here is only the "between," the interval or, we might say, the play between the two terms, their immediate constellation in a non-coincidence. The anthropological machine no longer articulates nature and man in order to produce the human through the suspension and capture of the inhuman. The machine is, so to speak, stopped; it is "at a standstill," and, in the reciprocal suspension of the two terms, something for which we perhaps have no name and which is neither animal nor man settles in between nature and humanity and holds itself in the mastered relation, in the saved night. (O 83)

The saved night, then, appears as a "going beyond" of human nature, as an end to the mystery that constitutes our human condition. It is the contemplation of "a human nature rendered perfectly inoperative—the inactivity and *desœuvrement* of the human and of the animal as the supreme and unsavable figure of life" (O 87). This is the profaning gesture that Agamben marks as the place of the human "creaturely" being, a purely immanent form in relation to the conditions of what constitutes a theologically grounded (transcendent) "human nature" in the first place.

There is little doubt that this is a dramatic challenge to theology as a historical attempt to define humanity's relationship to the divine image (*imago dei*). It should also, however, serve to provoke theology to seek to articulate a more adequate conceptualization of the human being in relation to nature, its own animality (or "creaturely being"), and the divine image that supposedly guides its most basic expressions. This, perhaps more than anything else, grants a tremendous significance to Agamben's ongoing relationship with theology.

Chapter 6

Second Regression

The Biological

What I would like now to demonstrate is that the methodological rigor in Agamben's work, the push toward regression that was so essential in his consideration of Freud's work, is completely enmeshed with his formulations concerning the origin(s) of the human being as an evolved species, as we will shortly see. By following this course of thought, I additionally hope to make clear that the notion of regression at use here is not a coincidental term in Agamben's work that appears from time to time (as it otherwise might seem to), but is one significant for articulating the truth of our human nature, not just philosophically, but biologically as well. This insight is what Agamben has tried on various occasions to discuss under the rubric of the term "infancy," a term which automatically conjures up a biological stage of our human development. I will begin then with his understanding of our biological origins before connecting those particular insights to the overarching framework of his work. I do this with the intention of demonstrating how his use of regression actually tilts the biological back toward the ethical, which becomes, in the end, for him, the only possible way to encounter the divine in our world.

In his book *The Idea of Prose*, Agamben tells the story of a Mexican freshwater salamander known as the axolotl (*Ambystoma mexicanum*) that maintains many traits normally only associated with the larval (infantile) stages of its species. If given the correct hormones at a certain stage of its development, it would in fact mature into a type of speckled salamander (*Ambystoma tygrinum*).

No longer considered as a singular species, the axolotl continues to marvel scientists as a peculiar case of "stubborn infantilism," or what appears as an "evolutionary regression" to most. For Agamben, however, what it truly represents is a "new key to the understanding of human evolution" (*IP* 95).

Rather than see this as a backwards step along the evolutionary road, Agamben will maintain that this is the only way in which to understand the fundamental trajectory upon which humanity has constituted itself and upon which it must now continue. Human beings, he theoretically posits, evolved from a young primate and not from a mature, adult form of the species (though, it should be noted, he offers here no scientific basis for these conclusions). They were seemingly "captured in language" as it were, and the human being thus emerged (cf. *WA* 14).

In essence, human beings appear to be a regression of the species, not a progressive evolution of the mature member of a species, as is sometimes casually assumed. Following Agamben, "[t]his would explain those morphological characteristics of man, ranging from the position of the occipital orifice to the form of the auricle of the ear, and from his hairless skin to the structure of his hands and feet, which do not correspond to those of adult anthropoids, but to those of the foetus" (*IP* 96). Illustrating our unique infantile traits, then, is Agamben's manner of determining how "Characteristics which in primates are transitory became final in man, thereby in some way giving rise, in flesh and blood, to a kind of eternal child" (*IP* 96). It is therefore the plasticity of the young, along with their innate abilities and curiosities, which defines the separation between primate and human. Humans have somehow, throughout the course of evolutionary "progress," remained the curious infantile primate that we once presumably were.

In short, here is how the difference between animal and human can best be expressed. Animals follow a code, or a law, that is prescribed by their genes and unquestioned by the animal itself who in fact has no reason to question that which only needs attending to. The "neotenic infant," however, according to Agamben, is precisely a halt in the process of maturing, a stoppage that gives rise to an attentiveness for the "unwritten" and the "arbitrary," to that in fact which is outside the pre-scribed genetic codes of the mature members of the species (*IP* 96). Essentially, then

> [t]he neotenic infant . . . would find himself in the condition of being able to pay attention precisely to what has not been written, to somatic possibilities that are arbitrary and uncodified; in his infantile totipotency, he would be ecstatically overwhelmed, cast out of himself, not like other living beings into a specific adventure or environment, but for the first time into a *world*. (*IP* 96)

Our world is therefore created, according to Agamben's evolutionary regressive schema, through our abstraction from the genetic code, a separation which also allows human beings to be captured by a state of wonder, the fundamental curiosity which grounds our reflective capacities. It is no surprise to Agamben, then, that, as a point of fact, it is children who are the most adept at acquiring language, not the mature members of the species. Humanity, as this "neotenic infant" which generates its own ability to "stay infantile," finds itself posited over and again within a (symbolic) world precisely in such a way, through the sheer "taking-place" of language which infants encounter.

Reflection comes about as a response to this peculiar, and highly precarious state of existence. Indeed, this state is what gives rise to the origins of language itself insofar as the "neotenic infant" is not confined by a genetic code, but rather is free to "name" things beyond their genetic predispositions, somewhat like Adam in the Garden of Eden. As Agamben describes it, the neotenic infant would be particularly attuned to hear the voice of being itself, and thus

> [h]is voice still free from any genetic prescription, and having absolutely nothing to say or express, sole animal

of his kind, he could, like Adam, *name* things in his language. In naming, man is tied to infancy, he is for ever linked to an openness that transcends every specific destiny and every genetic calling. (*IP* 96–97)

Language, culture, politics, and religion all subsequently arise from this strange removal from the call of our genetic coding. Our "original sin" it would seem was nothing more than ceasing to follow the genetic code; this is the truth which we have not been able, and will *never* be able, to atone for. It is a paradoxical situation: our separation from our genetic calling simultaneously gives rise to a reflective capacity, and yet leaves us with an acute sense of alienation from our common animal species, so acute that we attempt to atone for it through our "second nature"—that is, our linguistic being. We invent vocational callings, hence, as a way to try and atone for this initial separation, as a fleeting chance to perhaps reacquire something of what we had once lost. If we follow this logic to its end, religion would therefore appear as the supreme attempt on the part of humanity to (symbolically, linguistically) atone for this separation from our genetic calling. Consequently, we are able to see how the attentiveness to boundaries and borders with which religion continues to preoccupy itself is in fact rooted in humanity's original division from its genetic coding. Religious "desire" would, by this count, be little more than a replaying of our traumatic separation from our animality on a grand scale, all in an effort to "atone" for something that appears nearly now beyond our control.

Humanity's ability to think the "unthought," that is, what genetic coding cannot "think," is what sets it apart from the rest of our planet's animals. The "unthought" or "unlivable" within the present, perhaps best characterized as a sense of childlike wonder at the simplicity of whatever it brings, whatever *life* brings, thus leads us to a level of reflection in which humanity's alienation is capable of being thematized. As such, a form of redemption might yet be possible through an act of embracing our animality in contrast to the all-too-familiar (rationally constructed) human subject. And so, even in this context of evolutionary speculation, Agamben returns to his primary themes of language, salvation, and a movement beyond the "human-being":

> In fact, if something distinguishes the human tradition
> from that of the genetic code, it is precisely the fact that
> it wants to save not only the saveable (the essential
> characteristics of the species), but what in any case
> cannot be saved; that which is, on the contrary, always
> already lost; or better, that which has never been
> possessed as a specific property, but which is, precisely
> because of this, unforgettable: the being, the openness of
> the infantile soma, to which only the world, only
> language, is adequate. (*IP* 97–98)

Agamben's remarks on redemption now begin to come into a much sharper focus. That which cannot be saved, namely, that which cannot be passed on genetically, is precisely what appears to set us apart from all other creatures: an infantile wonder which truly lies at the center of all cultural acts of representation and transmission. Hence arises the singular significance of language, of transmitting it, and of learning it as an indoctrination into this constitutive difference of humanity from the animal world.

In effect, the processes of cultural representation and transmission are bound up in our various cultural traditions and their myriad attempts to resurrect the past in order to, in essence, occlude the present nature of what can be transmitted, that is, our genetic heritage, our animality. Religion, in this sense, has historically been most concerned with those aspects of humanity which are not part of this transmission: morality then, or what appears to regulate our "animal instincts." This, in turn, opens upon a genealogy of morals and religion, one in which Agamben is preceded by both Foucault and Nietzsche.[1]

This is a genealogy that intends to expose the historical tensions that constitute the human subject and are yet concealed by the traditions that would otherwise depict a unified (religious, ideological) subject. This quest to produce similar subjects is what in fact has condemned religions to a preoccupation with the past and an incessant activity of re-creating a singular historic (past) event that would guarantee the religious subject's unity, through adherence to a *logos* or order that we identify with through language (hence, our use of oaths as well as creeds) (cf. *SL* 16ff.). It is also the trap of Western, rational thought, we are told, wherein all efforts are aimed solely at preserving a universal conception of the subject. On this point, then, religion and rationality converge to sustain our "flesh" beyond its genetic calling: "What idea and essence want to save is the phenomenon, the irrepeatable that has been, and the most fitting purpose of logos is not the conservation of the species, but the resurrection of the flesh" (*IP* 98).

The temptation to which many have succumbed has often been found in the multiple efforts to transcend our creaturely life, which has the "conservation of the species" as its goal, and to focus on a "resurrection of the flesh," which would yet maintain the subjectivity of the rational subject, and in many ways serve only to secure one's comfort in remaining within the boundaries created for them by language. On this point, Agamben likewise reveals Freud's limitation, as it was through Freud's discovery of an unconscious core within us that is both shaped by a traumatic past and governs our present that the figure of a divided subject was reaffirmed. Instead of capitulating to this scenario, however, Agamben rather sees a way beyond the "resurrection of the flesh" (as well as the need for a recollection of an historical trauma) and toward an embracing of the body before me, the face exposed to me, in its nudity and in its profound creaturely being. Only thus could politics therefore become what it has not yet been, the task of bringing humans away from their particular traditions and toward adopting the universal task given over to humanity: to recognize the quest for language itself as fundamentally intertwined with its alienation from its own animality, as therefore the original sinful act, but also as the only thing which could resemble our search for love as we have constructed it over the centuries (i.e., the poet's amorous search). Moving beyond language, then, as Agamben will attempt to point toward, and as he will envision as locatable in the silence of the faces we each stand before, is the only way to truly embrace our prelinguistic infancy, and only thus does politics become infused with an ontological and ethical imperative for the present moment.[2] What this looks like, however, still remains to be seen.

Infancy

How is one to think of a space prior to the origin of language, to a state apparently beyond the spectacle exposed through our "original sin"? How are we to comprehend the genesis of our linguistic being without simply referring to an undisclosed (and unlocatable) Edenic narrative? Or, as Nicodemus puts it in the gospels, "How can a man be born when he is old? Can he enter the second time into his mother's womb, and be born?"[3] To commence this task of thinking it is necessary to return, with Agamben, to our individual linguistic origins, to those earliest moments of our infant years where we learned to dwell entirely prior to our capacity for language. This is a place as linguistically flexible as it is fragile, where we were as capable of forgetting language as we were of learning it. Following Agamben, it is a stage within this movement toward our infancy as a form of regression that we are after—a backward movement to our origins which need not reveal an historical source per se, but rather a truth about how our linguistic being is structured. This, he will assert, should be enough to assuage the concerns contained in the questioning of our origins, of what role language plays in our formation, and of what presence, if any, religion has in this formulation of the human animal.

In *Infancy and History*, for example, Agamben sketches out an early indicator of what difference lies between the messianic and the mythical, a distinction which will become central to his later work on the messianic in general. As he succinctly renders it, "[f]or in the messianic night, the creature's gesture is loosed of any magical–juridical–divinatory density, and becomes simply human and profane" (*IH* 143). In essence, the task of the Messiah is to profane things in relation to the principle of infancy. Though there are contemporary theological movements that would rather see a postsecular "re-enchantment" of our world, such as we find in those proponents of "Radical Orthodoxy," for example, Agamben utilizes the image of the crib, and of an infancy that accompanies it, to liberate humanity from any sense of enchantment:

> At the centre of the crib's figurative intent is not a
> mythic event or, even less, a spatio-temporal happening
> (that is, a chronological event), but a cairological event. It
> is in its essence a representation of the historicity which
> takes place in the world through the messianic birth.
> Thus in the sumptuous, endless proliferation of figures
> and episodes, in which the original sacred scene is
> well-nigh forgotten and the eye tires of searching for it,
> all distinctions between the sacred and the profane fall
> ways, and the two spheres are bridged in history. (*IH* 145)

This, of course, is now already recognizable to us as the emancipatory act of profanation which I have already attempted to sketch above. It is the act wherein the division between sacred and profane itself falls away, leaving only a creaturely dwelling of individuals "abandoned" to themselves.

We are given over here to an almost theological conceptualization of "infancy," a term which Agamben locates at the limits of language as an "invisible articulation" which "governs the interpretation of the sign in Western thought" (*S* 157; cf. *IH* 4–11). Thus its significance as pivotal in defining the experience of humanity is not to be overlooked. Indeed, it provides itself as a fitting foil to the traditional notions of experience which reside beside the boundary of death. As such, "[t]raditional experience . . . remains faithful to this separation of experience and science, human knowledge and divine knowledge. It is in fact the experience of the boundary between these two spheres. This boundary is death" (*IH* 21). A formulation of our infancy, however, pushes beyond the traditional boundary of death in order to arrive at (by stepping backwards or regressing toward) the pure potentiality captured before this traditional religious separation of language, that is, to think the existence of language itself. It is a step then toward the zone of indistinction that casts off the typical constructions of the "adult" human being.

But rather than imagining this step toward indistinction as something only achievable for infants, practically speaking, it is rather this focus on the threshold of our linguistic being that indicates how infancy is more akin to a reminder of our continued and co-originary animality. As William Watkin has described it, "infancy is to be found within the human at all stages as both remnant of the animal and potential for the post-human."[4] It is a wordless existence that lies latent within every utterance and, as such, it "coexists with language."[5] Infancy, as Jesus' injunction to his followers to "become like one of these little ones" seems to indicate, is a state which must somehow, within a potential form of understanding, be possible for the "adult." (It is, of course, no coincidence that the typical language used to describe a new convert to the Christian faith is one of being "born again," as if finally and mystically restored to one's infancy, no matter how preposterous it may literally sound.)

The imagery of an infancy given over eternally to itself is precisely what Agamben is able to articulate through the traditional theological explanations given for the existence of limbo. In this regard, the concept of limbo is more than an occasional gloss for Agamben. It assumes the role of a central image for understanding the unique prominence of our infancy beyond either guilt or redemption. Quite simply, he defines it as such: "As is well known, limbo is the place not of innocents but rather of those who have no other guilt than natural guilt, of those infants who could not have been submitted to the punishment of language" (*EP* 132). The entrance of language (and this is what religion points toward) can be seen (historically) to supplant this more natural guilt with the superimposition of language: "The baptism of the Verb cancels this natural guilt, but it cancels it only through another, more atrocious punishment" (*EP* 132). In this sense, "language is death" for Agamben, the death of an infancy that is otherwise overcome.

Yet, from another angle, how could one expect to live interminably within a state of sustained infancy? Agamben's references to the possibility of discovering an insight here just as significant as the evolutionary progression from primate to human certainly seem to imply that he believes such a state can be attained, though it perhaps has not yet appeared (cf. *P* 45–46), a bold claim to be sure. The regression from being a mature member of the primate species to an infantile (human) form would already seem to indicate something along these lines, something he wishes to push further. As he ponders in his book *The Open*, "[p]erhaps there is still a way in which living beings can sit at the messianic banquet of the righteous without taking on a historical task and without setting the anthropological machine into action" (*O* 92). There is a separation brought about by the anthropological machinery which theology has maintained even unto the afterlife, as evidenced by its continuous focus over the years on the various divisions imposed by God upon believers (even those in need of further purification) and unbelievers (including both the innocent and the heretics) alike. But it is a separation that Agamben wishes to push entirely to its limits and only from there to work beyond.

For Agamben, it is precisely a state of being "in-between" these divisions, such as that found dwelling in the state of limbo, which become paradigmatic cases for thinking beyond (or *before*) the divisions themselves. In essence, his vision of our humanity as rooted entirely in its infancy is the presentation of the potential for a world beyond these separations that normally apply to our conceptions of existence. This would moreover be a state of natural guilt (in being severed from one's genetic calling) that would evoke an accompanying "natural blessedness" captured in the various historical representations of limbo.

Utilizing the writings of Thomas Aquinas as his starting point, Agamben in fact captures the essence of how the unbaptized infants do not undergo an afflictive punishment in limbo, and therefore experience no pain as such (*CC* 5). They are ignorant of being deprived of anything in fact because their knowledge remains natural, not having been blessed with a supernatural understanding. They therefore enjoy a "natural perfection" that upholds the justness of God, and which, in this case, involves suspending the usual notion of blessedness ascribed only to those residing in heaven. For it is apparently within limbo as well that a sort of "natural blessed" state is allowed to exist, though it is one—and this is the supreme irony of its existence—that does not involve the presence of God. For Agamben, this exception to the ordinary configurations of the afterlife is one that indeed subverts the typical division of believer and nonbeliever. It is nothing short of a major blow struck against those various political representations that have extended their logic into the hereafter and which are henceforth in need of some retraction.

In limbo, God's forgetfulness is revealed as an "impotent" measure, of no effect upon those who have already, as if naturally, forgotten God. In a very direct sense, the inhabitants of limbo are filled with a joy that cannot be taken from them, a joy that Agamben is not hesitant to appropriate for a humanity which he sees as abandoned by God, one that is indeed called to dwell in its profane state:

> The greatest punishment—the lack of vision of God—
> thus turns into a natural joy: Irremediably lost, they persist
> without pain in divine abandon. God has not forgotten
> them, but rather they have always already forgotten God;

and in the face of their forgetfulness, God's forgetting is
impotent. Like letters with no addressee, these uprisen
beings remain without a destination. Neither blessed like
the elected, nor hopeless like the damned, they are
infused with a joy with no outlet. (*CC* 5–6)

It is within this setting as well that Agamben urges us to embrace
the task of profanation which theology in fact points to with its
paradoxical and contradictory formulations, and thus to be, like
the inhabitants of limbo, forgetful of God even if God is not
forgetful of us. In this sense, there is nothing to be saved from
and nothing to save—there is only the embracing of a purely
human life beyond signification and judgment. This is both to
reconceive salvation, in its explicitly political dimensions, and
to diverge entirely from traditional notions of soteriology as a
whole. Theology is indeed what enables him to conclude that
an "unsavable life" is one wherein there is nothing to save. And
this truth seemingly undoes the Christian economy of salvation as it has up till now functioned (*CC* 6; cf. *RG* 309). This
insight is therefore a reality that theology actually uncovers for
itself, and, in Agamben's eyes, despite its claims to the contrary.
This disclosure serves to bring the theological project, at least
as it has been historically conceived, once again to a standstill.

Like those ignorantly blissful figures in limbo whom Agamben
has had cause to reflect upon on occasion, he here posits a sort
of "blessed life" which is yet to be considered as "unsavable," as
one beyond the spheres of redemption which theology has traditionally conceived: it is, as he elsewhere states, "the idea of this
natural life that is unsavable and that has been completely abandoned by every spiritual element—and yet, because of the 'great
ignorance,' is nonetheless perfectly blessed" (*O* 90). This is why
Agamben immediately points in this context to a description of
"letting be" as the supreme category of Heidegger's thoughts
on being (*O* 91). For Heidegger, this became a state of letting
animal nature simply be, "beyond both being and the nothing."[6]
As Agamben articulates it, "[b]ut what is thus left to be outside

153

of being is not thereby negated or taken away; it is not, for this reason, inexistent. It is an existing, real thing that has gone beyond the difference between being and beings" (*O* 91–92). An "existent," as he will elsewhere designate it (cf. *CC* 100), is a designation that describes those souls who abide eternally in limbo as a "letting be" in which they can exist joyfully even if abandoned by God.

As simple, though as profound, as it might sound, all that we are left with is all that we are. We are exposed to one another as if on the Last Day, naked to the other who is as precarious as any one of us. From our irremediable particularity, we are able, then, to approach the formation of an ethics beyond ontotheological proposition, that is, beyond the resultant moralities intended to do little more than maintain the boundaries of the anthropological machinery. We are poised, then, to move toward beholding the divinity which could be said to reside in the myriad faces that present themselves naked before us.

Beyond Representation: Envisioning the "Whatever" Singularity in Love

Perhaps this focus upon the exposure ("nakedness") of our being will help clarify why the apostle Paul continues to appeal to Agamben, for it is Saint Paul who appears most forcefully to grind all representations to a halt through an entrance into what could only surface as a kind of cultural death. For this is the apostle who considered all representations to be *as nothing*, and who considered the ultimate act of fidelity to the *logos* to be an embraceable death in imitation of this loss.[7] According to Agamben, who will take up these themes most emphatically, perhaps what Saint Paul was actually advancing was an historically genuine profundity for religious and philosophical thought, an embracing of the nihilistic tendencies that would see all political representations ground to a halt, their dialectics being brought to a standstill in time.

Second Regression

In a small and perhaps oddly conjoined section of *The Coming Community*, one which focuses upon both the Talmudic reading of the difference between Eden and Gehenna as well as upon the Christian community of Badaliya founded by Louis Massignon in the mid-twentieth century, Agamben takes up the interesting thematic of love. As he relates the story, it was Massignon who developed a theology of substitutability, of one person taking the place of another, for the sake of their salvation. This is at once an act of isolating oneself from oneself (as much as from others), yet in order to provide an ultimate form of hospitality, and ultimately, a space for love to enter. Agamben conceives of this theology of substitution as a horizon for human togetherness "beyond representation," as the gesture of "exiling oneself to the other as he or she is in order to offer Christ hospitality in the other's own soul, in the other's own taking-place" (*CC* 24). It is this fundamental act which is the "destruction of the wall dividing Eden from Gehenna." If such an act were possible, indeed it would seem to be an "unconditioned substitutability, without either representation or possible description" and "an absolutely unrepresentable community" could be said to result from it (*CC* 24–25). Much is contained in this tiny fragment of thought which we will need some time to further unpack.

The first focal point should be to notice, as Agamben does, that this form of substitution presents what could only be described as a "whatever" community, "whatever" because it is truly "whichever," that which is unrepresentable and external to a more or less violent logic that would otherwise seek to bring it under the rubrics of political participation. This is to suggest that the taking-place of whatever being is an infinitely substitutable event, one in which the "event" of the singular being is shared with every other, though not reducible to the same identification. Recognition of this fact is a form of "hospitality" that remains undefined, and therefore truly hospitable beyond any prescribed regulations (*CC* 24). It is a "whatever" being that is allowed to exist as it is at the summit of all

155

conceivable hospitalities. Agamben subsequently presents the "whatever" being as commensurable with the being of Saint Paul's believer who is seemingly beyond the binary codes of worldly representation in some sense ("neither Jew nor Greek, slave nor free, male nor female").[8]

But there is a second point to be noted as well, one that goes beyond the simple formation of a new "whatever" community and toward the basis for welcoming love in our world. As the concept of faith illustrates in Saint Paul's writings for Agamben, the recognition of the "whatever" being is what makes loving them accessible in the first place. As he puts it, love becomes the experience of "taking-place in a whatever singularity" (CC 25). To allow such a place of pure open hospitality to exist within someone is the very act which also allows a substitution to take place, and this openness to an infinite series of substitutabilities is what enables love to take place, what enables us in fact to enter into "whatever" form of creaturely being resides before us. As he will make even clearer, the strict division between the general and the particular is collapsed through the presence of love itself, something which can also be said to "transcend" the boundaries of the particular as found in language precisely through its "indifference" to the boundaries themselves. Thus, the face (of the beloved, of the other, of the stranger that we all are) is what opens the doors wider toward a reception of the self behind and beyond any socially determined representations.[9]

To see things thus would be to embed the conception of "whatever singularity" within love itself, to hold the example (and not the exception) as that which dissolves the antinomy between universal and particular, and thereby to comprehend the always already autobiographical attachment to the "whatever" being that grounds any subsequent philosophical reflection (CC 2–3). Indeed, this is the only possible way to return all dichotomous understandings of philosophical discourse (otherwise divided between particularity and universality) to their groundedness in love. As Agamben will formulate it, love can embrace the particularities affiliated with each individual, though it is not bound to them (*CC* 3). Love is the experience of the "taking-place in a whatever singularity," which is not necessarily a comfortable experience that we undergo. Rather, as Julian Wolfreys has pointed out, it is an "unnatural" feeling, one that is as "uncanny" as it is foreign.[10] It is what Agamben, in a short paragraph titled "The Idea of Love," defines as living "in intimacy with a stranger, not in order to make him known, but rather to keep him strange, remote" (*IP* 61). To be in love is to be "forever exposed" and yet, at the same time, "sealed off."

The affinities established here between the history of religious thought (as found in Saint Paul's writings, the Church Fathers and medieval theologians, even the path from art to myth) are not coincidental to developing a broad context in which to outline the contours of love. Rather, these affinities are essential; they are the particularities within history itself, as it were, that sustain and give weight to Agamben's claims. Hence, in this context, where the discussion quickly drifts to questions of political engagement, God suddenly returns to the forefront. Yet it is a sudden emergence of a new "God," one, however, that has been here somehow all along, continuously present in "whatever" face before us. It is the "pure potentiality" before us that is God, a pseudopantheistic (or perhaps pan*en*theistic) model of articulating God's ability to love in and through the form of "whatever" singularity appears before us.

This, in turn, leads to the appropriation of specific historical religious propositions utilized in order to reinforce and further develop Agamben's position. For example, it can be found in the "multiple common place," one "which the Talmud presents as the place of the neighbor that each person inevitably receives," and that ultimately is "nothing but the coming to itself of each singularity, its being whatever—in other words, such as it is" (*CC* 25). This being "such as it is" is what sparks the transition in Agamben's thought, once again, toward the suspension of all representational being (in its actuality) in favor of a "pure potentiality" which would rather instill love as essential for our movement toward our own "infancy," or birth, the reassessment of which likewise implicates the "being" of God: "Creation—or existence—is not the victorious struggle of a power to be against a power to not-be; it is rather the impotence of God with respect to his own impotence, his allowing—being able to *not* not-be—a contingency to be. Or rather: It is the birth in God of love" (*CC* 33). What follows from this is that love can only be paradigmatically presented, in its absolute, irreducible singularity. It cannot be universalized, but instead only moves from particular person to particular person.

The particularity of love, then, would seem to dictate that each particular person or face before us calls forth their own "whatever" being which both defies any generalized representation and is as such the very condition of its capacity to be loved. It is in the face of this encounter that we are exposed— one of the great reasons why the experience of falling "in love" proceeds to cause one to feel absolutely vulnerable before the other. Our very condition as creaturely beings develops then through our exposure to another beyond any predicates which otherwise define us (*CC* 97–98). That is to say, these particulars *do* define us before another, though not as violent reductions of who we are into prefabricated representations—rather, they are the conditions of our exposure, the markers that we claim for ourselves, that we own so to speak. It is a subtle difference at times between this form of exposure and the forms of representation within our world that Agamben opposes so vehemently, and this is perhaps why he immediately remarks in parenthesis afterward that "suchness" is the category of thought that "remains unthought in every quality" (*CC* 98). It is the pure immanence of the thing to itself that conditions the particularities which we find lovable. It is the existent or whatever being's unique particulars that genuinely attract us, *not* the simplified, and simplifying representations that would reduce someone to a type or a character set within some epic narrative.

To comprehend the nature of our particularities, in all of their difference and fullness of presentation, means then to comprehend that what makes us lovable is also what makes us vulnerable, a paradox which actually results in the "torturous" presentation of our selves: "How you are—your face—is your torture and your source. And each being is and must be its mode of being, its manner of rising forth: being *such* as it is (*CC* 98). Whatever singularity of creature presents itself before us is capable of being loved as it is—in full possession of those qualities that are presented to the other, rather than submitting to those qualities which are ascribed to us beyond our ability to accept or reject them, that is, as given representations.

The Quasi-Mystical Encounter with the Face

Since the mystical (as traditionally, transcendently received from within the history of theology) is, strictly speaking, denied to us by the total immanence of our existence, we are thrust into an immanence that can yet reveal something about the quasi-mystical in its everydayness.[11] This "mystical" nature that is purely immanent can be found most directly in Agamben's formulations of the face, a rare treatment of a subject that concludes with an even rarer imperative voice otherwise absent from his writings. With the absence of the mystical, a state exterior to our humanity, the focus shifts rather to the subdivision within our being, that between the exterior and the interior. In other words, the split between exterior and interior is projected onto a split between the mystical-transcendent and the immanent. By focusing on the face as the exterior point of reference, Agamben simultaneously resituates and recreates the tensions between these realms as essential to understanding the entrance of the ethical into our world.

Beholding the face as a pure presence before us, its "pure communicability" (akin perhaps to a pure "transmissability") elicits an "exigency of history," or a demand from the past, that Agamben seeks to transform into an ethics of the face (cf. *ME* 91–100). He is able to develop this ethics as such because it is only the face that is "capable of taking the abyss of its own communicability upon itself and of exposing it without fear or complacency" (*ME* 96). And this is the imperative that lingers just long enough to form an impression of itself as a discourse of values (ethics) based upon the concept of "character": "As soon as the face realizes that communicability is all that it is and hence that it has nothing to express—thus withdrawing silently behind itself, inside its own mute identity—it turns into a grimace, which is what one calls character" (*ME* 97). Agamben speaks here of a "character" in relation to its manifestation in the face, in the ability to present the face beyond any representational schemes, a "nakedness" as it were of the face itself. "Character is the constitutive reticence that human beings retain in the word; but what one has to take possession of here is only a nonlatency, a pure visibility: simply a visage" (*ME* 97). And as he goes on to say, "[t]he face is not something that transcends the visage: it is the exposition of the visage in all its nudity, it is a victory over character—it is word" (*ME* 97). A word, then, of pure expression beyond all linguistic forms, a point, which, as we will shortly see, he shares in common with Spinoza's understanding of the "Word of God."

The face is (pure) language itself, the pure word that humanity has been searching for and longing to cite in contestation of an unjust (authoritarian) sovereign rule of representations within the present. It is what history has been searching for and what Benjamin's "dialectical materialism" sought to retrieve from the ruins of civilization. It is the summit of that which all character points toward and which must courageously be presented in its "nudity" before another face. This is what Agamben will refer to as the quasi-mystical, quasi-sacred "exposition" of the face:

Everything for human beings is divided between proper and improper, true and false, possible and real: this is because they are or have to be only a face. Every appearance that manifests human beings thus becomes for them improper and factitious, and makes them confront the task of turning truth into their *own proper* truth. But truth itself is not something of which we can take possession,

nor does it have any object other than appearance and
the improper: it is simply their comprehension, their
exposition. (*ME* 97, emphasis in the original)

The face is therefore the truth presented beyond representations, beyond the limitations constitutive of the human being
"as construct." Over and beyond this, its exposition is also the
pure showing of the face that language is unable to present in
linguistic terms. The face can only present this reality by exposing itself, by showing itself as it were. This is also, of course, a
presentation that runs contrary to any totalitarian political
forms which would advocate a "will to total self-possession,"
something which a proper (vulnerable) presentation of the self
would ultimately seek to destabilize. This is so because "[t]he
face is not a *simulacrum*, in the sense that it is something dis-
simulating or hiding the truth: the face is the *simultas*, the
being-together of the manifold visages constituting it, in which
none of the visages is truer than any of the others" (*ME* 99).

The face is a heterogeneous "presence," posited solely through
its externality, the "being-outside" of the multiple underlying
desires that constitute the self. Therefore the "truth of the face"
is to be found in grasping "not the resemblance but rather the
simultaneity of the visages, that is, the restless power that
keeps them together and constitutes their being-in-common"
(*ME* 99). Only thus is the face "recognizable" as such. Yet it is
also an externality which demonstrates a certain indifference to
the internal/external boundary in the first place:

My face is my *outside*: a point of indifference with
respect to all of my properties, with respect to what is
properly one's own and what is common, to what is
internal and what is external. In the face, I exist with all
of my properties (my being brown, tall, pale, proud,
emotional . . .); but this happens without any of these
properties essentially identifying me or belonging to me.
The face is the threshold of de-propriation and of

> de-identification of all manners and of all qualities—a
> threshold in which only the latter become purely
> communicable. And only where I find a face do I
> encounter an exteriority and does an *outside* happen to
> me. (*ME* 99, emphasis in the original)

The face thereby becomes a point of pure exposition that is devoid of all representational content, the only form of a religious event which Agamben seems to find acceptable: it is an encounter with the face of the other and the presentation of your face without pretext that opens the door to any possible sense of divinity. It is perhaps also then the messianic bridge between art and myth that promises to unite our fractured human selves (cf. *MC* 114–115). The outside as exteriority, as that which is sought in our infancy as the site of pure language, is broached in the face. It is our only chance to grasp the purity of an existence that the religious impulse points toward.

It is within this context that, for Agamben, the divine returns to the discussion, as "the face of God" is "the *simultas* of human faces: it is 'our effigy' that Dante saw in the 'living light' of paradise" (*ME* 99). Indeed, this is where God is most present—in the encounter of visages, a recognition of which would constitute a sort of liturgical act for Agamben. Here, a form of implied pantheism or panentheism is presented as the only model of reality wherein God becomes the conglomeration of faces in the simultaneity of their appearance, perhaps merging then with Agamben's pronouncement elsewhere that the world *is* God (cf. *CC* 90).

By resituating the divine as such, Agamben is not only looking beyond "resemblance" as the dominant principle governing over the field of representations; he is also pursuing the pure word spoken in the exposure of the face, *through* the face, and thus toward a rethinking of the role of theology tout court. Agamben's confrontation with the *logos*, which has come to dominate Western representational claims since its emergence in Greek thought, and its subsequent appropriation by

Christianity, can be found here. It is an initiative to let the truth of a proposition speak and not simply the authority which is supposedly lurking behind the utterance of any given cultural citation.

For Agamben, being beyond representation means being beyond someone's ability to cite and perform what has presented itself, and beyond the varied notions of sovereignty associated with it.[12] In truth, the face is what our cultural citations, enacted through the varied representations we created, ultimately strive to become, to embody as it were, like the "whatever" nature of the infant's face that searches for something wholly beyond any sense of authority, what can come to define itself rather as a relation of love (cf. CC 106). The face is the citation sought among the ruins of history that can yet give life to the fractured human self and which can provide that long sought after sense of "transcendence in immanence" that religions have subsequently distorted and monopolized. Hence the appropriation of citationality by a gender-theorist such as Judith Butler is not as remote from this context as it might seem at first glance. It is this stress upon the body called forward through language into history that she is seeking to recover as well, and to love as it were, in all its embodiable forms, a celebration of a "whatever" being that demands to be loved as much as addressed, not subjected to a series of violent (normative) representational frameworks which strive for hegemonic positions under the rule of a sovereign power (CC 19–20).[13]

Agamben's development of Benjamin's theory of citationality therefore also contains a hope that human nature will detach itself from cultural significations and political representations and enter into an unforeseen world that can only be conceived as theological insofar as it is "atheological." For Agamben, "here language . . . returns to that which never was and to that which it never left, and thus it takes the simple form of a habit" (LD 97). It is a profanation of our world, he might suggest, that reveals a deeper layer of the purely immanent, and possibly pantheistic or panentheistic belief at variance with much of

Western theology, though there are signs today, especially from feminist and interreligious perspectives, that such a form of immanentism is the sole manner in which theology can retain its continued pertinence.[14] This is not, however, a reality which Agamben constructs solely in order to undermine the Western theological tradition. Rather, since Agamben is attempting to be faithful to the logic of the messianic he has discovered in the work of both Benjamin and Saint Paul, faithful then to a destabilizing force working from within, it is now the Western theological tradition itself that provides the tools for its own dismantling. It is a "deconstruction" of theology, to be sure, but one that may in fact, if Agamben's reading of Saint Paul is in any sense accurate, resonate deeply with the claims once made by Jesus Messiah.

For deconstructionists, such as John Caputo, the Kingdom of God that Jesus proclaimed indeed comes to resemble such a "weak messianic" claim of truth made upon humanity, a rejection of worldly sovereignty and an attempt to go beyond the traditional religious structures that encompass an institutionalized ecclesiology.[15] For his part, in performing such a philosophy (or genealogy) of theology, Agamben does seem at present to share (at least in part, and despite his divergence from any Derridean lines of thought in Caputo's reflections, for example) in such movements, providing a vast and challenging reworking of centuries of theological speculation and concrete religious doctrine in an attempt to embrace that most fundamental of God's creative acts (and one said to be in God's own image): the creaturely being before us, which need not even be human, that is, whatever face we happen upon. If the Kingdom of God, then, is composed of those very same faces, each calling out to be respected as divine in the midst of their exposure, then perhaps for all of his apparent distance from theological discourse, Agamben lies much closer to it than even he might admit.

Conclusion

Regression of the Divine

One Last Significant Regression

If the existence of language is the inexpressible fact which all of our words strive to express, and if language is that phenomenon which our animal-being finds so entirely perplexing, the source of an alienation wrought through our separation from the animal world, then what are we to make of Agamben's claim that we now find ourselves ready to pronounce this fact into our world? Are we in fact those creators who speak a *logos* into the profane world surrounding us? What are we to make of the languages we actually do speak, of the languages we inhabit and that grant us the entirety of our (symbolic) world? How are we to respond to a life, *our* life, devoid of its traditional moorings in which the aporias of language once had such a fundamental role to play? Indeed, every linguistic formulation, from the logics of sovereignty to the binary divisions of representational thought, from the highest speculations on God's attributes to every expression of human subjectivity, rests upon this foundation which Agamben is daring enough to call into question.

If we lie now in the ruins of theology, it is because this cleansing fire (with its accompanying nihilistic furor) has decimated the content of all its propositions, doctrines, and dogmas, every one. Yet, as Agamben is fond of reminding us, a building is only able to reveal its true structure after everything which surrounds its skeletal frame has been removed, as in the case of a fire. This, and nothing less, is what he will term a "revelation" (cf. *P* 39–47). And if everything he has been circulating around has pointed to this moment of revelation, the revelation of the centrality of language as such, then it is this: language points toward existence itself, even if it seems at times to negate it, and, more specifically, it points toward the potentiality within existence that cannot *not* be. There is therefore a potentiality to *not* not-be lodged within it (*CC* 105). And a "potentiality to *not* not-be" of course, is an affirmative proposition, not a nihilistic vision.[1] Religion (as myth) creeps back into the scenario here being sketched, for, as Agamben will elsewhere tell us, nihilism is the trajectory of a modern aesthetic that cannot cross over into the realm of myth (cf. *MC* 114–115). Only something like the messianic can therefore attempt to bridge the gap between aesthetics and myth, which is nothing other than a poetic disclosure of our potentiality, one that reveals the fracture within our nature as human subjects. It is this "poetic" task, as he will often call it, which allows us to enter a community beyond the representations that sovereignly signify a violent reality.

In the face of such an alternative, we must poetically affirm our bare animal existence. This is the imperative declaration that Agamben lays before his reader. It is a radical affirmation of our existence, of the thusness of creation, an affirmation that is a new language of creation, a "yes" into the void before us: "So be it" (*CC* 103). "Yes" is the name of language, "said to the world" as a fundamental affirmation of our being, the most content we could truly ever claim to have (*CC* 104). It is an affirmation that cannot be said *in* language as it is beyond our being-as-subjects. It is rather where an "incorruptible" core of our existence resides within our creaturely being, that which, as Agamben tells us, the ancient theologian Origen intended when he spoke of the *eidos* beyond corporeal substance in which we would return in a general resurrection after our judgment on the Last Day.

It would now seem in fact that Agamben has spoken the judgment, and that he has indeed pointed to the form in which we can now return, ending so many centuries of discussion on what form our bodies would take after the resurrection. To take but one historical example: Agamben might be able to finally discern "whether in the resurrection the soul will be reunited to the same identical body."[2] Not to be mistaken, the question is really one of the relation between immanence (the material flesh) and transcendence (the soul). If viewed from Agamben's eyes, we can now see how the question itself is in need of rewording, as the transcendent is no longer that which reigns over everything, but is rather the sheer taking-place of every created thing (CC 14–15). It is a matter of perspective, he continues, for where we are capable of recognizing the irreparable nature of the world, its contingency and yet its beauty, there alone is it transcendent (CC 106). There is only flesh before us, there will always be only flesh, and it is not resurrected, but exposed before us. What this is about, as we have already seen, is the conservation of the species and not the resurrection of the flesh.

If we can indeed reenvision the world before us, we could perhaps then see it for what it is: the divine convergence of the multitude of visages before us, the "whatever" face that in simply "being-thus" elicits a call for love, he will tell us, that insofar as it is "irreparable" is love (CC 106). How then are we to reformulate our vision of a God who is said to be nothing but love? Following Spinoza rather closely, Agamben once again has an answer: God (or the good) is seemingly that which does not "take place" in and of itself; rather, God is made manifest in the "taking-place" of each entity, "their innermost exteriority" (CC 15). Hence, the existent properties of each thing are divine, he will state; that things are is the good we seek after. The situatedness of every thing is what transcends and, if it is willing, exposes each thing for what it is. Evil, by this count, of course, would simply be the act of reducing the wonder of each singularity's existence to the "facts" of reality, as if each thing could simply fit within a given representational scheme. To see things thus, however, would be to miss the transcendence within the "taking-place" of things. Good, on the other hand, is a recognition that this transcendence is not elsewhere, beyond us, but is actually in the existence of the (literal) matter at hand. In so many words, the divine touch of non-transcendent matter can be seen as the regression of God (or of the soul, or of the transcendent) into the material world, a permanent ongoing kenosis that could not truly be anything else, and that is perhaps closest to some forms of pantheistic or panentheistic belief. This is the regression that instigates every other regression, the one we reach in the end that frames our every move from the beginning. It is the redemption that precedes creation (cf. *SA* 107; *N* 9ff.). And it is the regression of God as a potentially transcendent sovereign deity into God as an immanent weak force moving throughout all matter. Hence, "[t]he world—insofar as it is absolutely, irreparably profane—is God" (*CC* 90). This is the essential revelation that would seem to animate Agamben's thought.

The Immanence of God

As I have tried to note throughout, though all-too-briefly perhaps, Agamben has had a wealth of influence placed within his work by such notable figures as Walter Benjamin, Martin Heidegger, Michel Foucault, Carl Schmitt, Guy Debord, Georges Bataille, and Hannah Arendt, to name just a few. It appears in many ways that the majority of commentary on Agamben's work has centered mainly around his affiliation with these thinkers' thoughts, as well as his critical-productive relationships with such contemporary figures as Jacques Derrida, Jean-Luc Nancy, and Antonio Negri. What I would like to focus upon, however, is what I perceive as the "missing link" within Agamben scholarship, a link that has seemed to dictate a subtle, but strong, undercurrent of thought which is only just now beginning to surface dramatically within his more recent thoughts on the theological: the Spinoza-Deleuzian nexus.

The connection, of course, has not gone completely unnoticed. Indeed, Agamben currently holds the "Baruch Spinoza" chair at the European Graduate School. Antonio Negri, for one, has continued to point toward the overtones and reverberations of both Spinoza and Deleuze in Agamben's work, most notably in his works *State of Exception* and *The Reign and the Glory*.[3] What Negri sees in Agamben's work is a particular path toward a materialist metaphysics created by the "hollowing out" of traditional (ontotheological) forms of power, as we have seen. And as he describes the situation in an article devoted to assessing Agamben's work, "primitive Christianity or early communism went through and out the other side of imperial power and enslavement, destroying them by hollowing them out and dematerializing them from within," and such is what Agamben's messianic claims, as we have seen, are all about.[4] The utilization of such messianic forces for materialist (profane) ends is what subsequently allows Negri to conclude that "Agamben's analysis shows how immanence can be both realist and revolutionary."[5]

This suggestion of the proximity between Agamben and Spinoza–Deleuze is not however to suggest that their characterizations or implementations of a plane of immanence overlap entirely.[6] Yet the similarities continue to mount as they likewise provide illumination for the path which Agamben's work continues to take, especially as he draws closer and closer to what potentially constitutes the theological. For example, the two notions of the *logos*, one immanent to our human economies and one transcendent to it, which have haunted Agamben's work from the outset, are given an interesting twist, as they function similarly in Spinoza's understanding of scripture, or the "Word of God." This is something which Deleuze, for instance, picks up in Spinoza's thought and develops in a manner similar to Agamben's formulations.

In a section dealing with Spinoza's conception of revelation and its relation to expression in a book devoted to Spinoza's thought, Deleuze notes how the "Word of God" can be divided into two "very different" senses: "an expressive Word, which has no need of words or signs, but only of God's essence and man's understanding; and an impressed, imperative Word, operating through sign and commandment."[7] The latter sense leads to a requirement of submission to the historically issued religious commandments; it is the domain of scripture, creeds, and dogma, and also then of our mistaken impressions of the divine. In this realm, the divine cannot be reached and no accurate presentations of the divine being can be given. The former, however, seems to point beyond all forms of representation and to an immediate presentation or expression of God as nature, "*Deus, sive Natura*" ("God, or Nature"), a distinction which some have contended truly lies at the heart of all philosophical thought.[8] This would indeed seem to present a univocity of being which is a sheer affirmation of our immanent life, what would otherwise be a form of pantheism or panentheism (as Spinoza's thought has often been called) except that it does not necessarily recognize belief in a deity separable from nature itself.[9] It is a pure form of immanence, something which Deleuze himself will come to address toward the end of his own life in his essay "Immanence: A Life . . . ."[10]

Agamben too seeks to develop a way out of the constitutive split within our linguistically established identities. Articulating this resolution through recourse to the inexpressible expression that is God's voice beyond all attempts by language (or scripture) to say it would seem to overlap in this sense with Deleuze's reading of Spinoza. That this understanding should lead Deleuze, for his part, to conclude his interpretation and exposition of Spinoza's thought with an immanent notion of "beatitude" that sees no distinction between the body and the soul, would be of equal interest to Agamben.[11] As much as Agamben has of late been interested in erasing all boundaries between the glorious body and the earthly one, there remains in this investigation of immanence an expression of our being beyond all linguistic forms and representations.[12] In this same sense, if our exposure to another in our precarious nakedness is the central ethical experience of Agamben's thought, as we have seen, such a disclosure is also found in Deleuze's Spinoza, for whom "[t]he path of salvation is the path of expression itself: to become expressive—that is, to become active; to express God's essence, to be oneself an idea through which the essence of God explicates itself, to have affections that are explained by our own essence and express God's essence."[13] Bearing this in mind, the relation to Deleuze's Spinoza has certainly become more prominent over time along with Agamben's increased engagement with the theological.

In an essay titled "Absolute Immanence," Agamben takes up the manner in which life and its "errancies" (Deleuze) could be said to produce a knowledge over and above the manner in which we had previously relied upon truth. Here there is an "opening to a world" that allows us to construct an alternative structure of "knowing" (*P* 221). Taking up Deleuze's interest in Spinoza directly, Agamben conceives how the "principle of immanence . . . is nothing other than generalization of the ontology of univocity, which excludes any transcendence of Being" (*P* 226).[14] This understanding, for its part, is built upon Spinoza's elaboration of the "univocity of Being"—its openness as it were over and against the medieval scholastics and their presentation of an *analogia entis* ("analogy of being") which would confine the relation between God and beings to a strict analogical relation. This is, then, an immanence that is immanent with respect to nothing, as being "immanent to" something would necessarily involve a transcendent counterpart. It is a pure immanence which is present within every thought, as the "not external outside" and as the "non-internal inside" (*P* 228).

This is a form of "bare life" which Agamben detects in Deleuze's work on immanence and one that likewise has been prominent in Agamben's work from its inception. Hence, the return to concepts such as infancy and potentiality within the contours of an immanent bare life, even if (or especially if) these are Deleuze's own words quoted by Agamben, brings us full circle to a profaning of transcendence. As Agamben quotes him: "The smallest infants all resemble each other and have no individuality; but they have singularities, a smile, a gesture, a grimace, events that are not subjective characters. The smallest infants are traversed by an immanent life that is pure potentiality, even beatitude through suffering and weakness" (*P* 230).[15] Read closely, this passage would indeed seem to summarize a great deal of Agamben's most poignant theological reflections as have already been noted.

The attempt to posit a transcendental subject, for Agamben, cannot be achieved by the anthropological machinery otherwise constantly at work in our world. As Agamben sees it, it is this figure of absolute immanence which eludes any given subjectivity. Rather, it is the very condition of an "infinite desubjectification" (*P* 232–233). As with the force of the messianic which renders the boundary between the transcendent and the immanent completely obscured, a philosophical movement toward a plane of immanence likewise undoes the representations of thought founded upon a dichotomous logic of transcendence/immanence (cf. *RG* 129ff.). Agamben's entire philosophical and political project is condensed, then, within this context: "The plane of immanence thus functions as a principle of virtual indetermination, in which the vegetative and the animal, the inside and the outside and even the organic and the inorganic, in passing through one another, cannot be told apart" (*P* 233).

For Deleuze, this was a form of "contemplation without knowledge," sensation and habit without act or decision as politics most fundamental gesture. It is rather the preservation of desire, or the "immanence of desire to itself" (*P* 235) that Deleuze seemingly borrowed from Spinoza, where the term *conatus* attempted to define how desire and Being "coincide without residue" (*P* 236). It is a "contemplation without knowledge" then in the sense that it is a presentation without representation, an exposure of the particularities that we ourselves own and which are not grafted onto us as reductionistic generalizations.

If the highest value of nutritive life is to preserve itself, this shift in Spinoza's thought immediately opens us up to an immanent plane of existence that reduces the transcendent to the biological. Therefore, it can be said that "Deleuze (like Spinoza) brings the paradigm of the soul back to the lower scheme of nutritive life" (P 236). And thus the historical project of theology, as Spinoza had already discovered centuries earlier, is called into question, from its most basic propositions on the transcendent, to its ties with the political sphere. From this point on, theological terms are to be consistently reworked upon an immanent plane, redictating what they could mean once they are seen within this immanent light.

Hence, beatitude is no longer something reserved for the saints in heaven, but rather "[i]n Spinoza, the idea of beatitude coincides with the experience of the self as an immanent cause, which he calls *acquiescentia in se ipso*, 'being at rest in oneself,' and defines precisely as *laetitia, concomitante idea sui tamquam causa*, 'rejoicing accompanied by the idea of the self as cause'" (P 237). No longer is God the cause that we seek after, but rather our goal becomes being the creaturely beings that we already are prior to the establishment of the human beings which we have wrongly sought to be—this is the originary figure that Agamben has consistently pursued throughout his work. Accordingly, biological life merges with contemplative life, bare life with the "life of the mind," and a univocity beyond representation occurs as a result of this immanent disclosure of our being (P 239). As a result of this merging of categories that have long been kept separate, the typical associations of contemplation with the divine are torn asunder: "*Theōria* and the contemplative life, which the philosophical tradition has identified as its highest goal for centuries, will have to be dislocated onto a new plane of immanence" (P 239). This is a statement that is then immediately qualified with the words that will effectively define his later work: "It is not certain that, in the process, political philosophy and epistemology will be able to maintain their present physiognomy and difference with respect to ontology" (P 239). And perhaps nothing is more clear at this point than the fact that Agamben has sought to make the revaluation of these most basic philosophical categories almost solely his undertaking.

Alongside this task, of course, lies the central thread that guides each revaluation, the deconstruction of the transcendent and its accompanying theological justifications, bringing that which was once thought to be concerned solely with what was "on high" to its earthly feet. This project is central to his latest writings, such as *Profanations, The Reign and the Glory, The Sacrament of Language* and the essays gathered under the title *Nudities*. And this undertaking is what will enable him to conclude that "[t]oday, blessed life lies on the same terrain as the biological body of the West" (*P* 239). The same basic insight that allows him elsewhere to locate the "glorious body," supposedly appearing after the resurrection of the dead, as within the earthly bodies that we already inhabit (cf. *N* 166; *RG* 371ff.).

Despite the criticism that Agamben's use of Spinoza seems to neglect the latter's preference for "a finite participation" in an "infinite, i.e., nontotalizable, nature," whereas the former opts instead for "an oceanic joining with the whole of nature or life," as Julie Klein has pointed out, there seems yet to be a coincidence of thought between the two thinkers that has yet to be more fully developed.[16] Perhaps, then, what we have before us, in the end, is aptly characterized by Antonio Negri as a "renewal of the theological-political in the Spinozian way"—a theology of immanence.[17] In this, it would seem to share in the Deleuzian project of formulating a completely materialist version of metaphysics.[18] Or, perhaps put another way, it would be a potential "re-enchantment" of our postreligious world, if it were not one that appears paradoxically as an absolute profanation of our world, a complete jettisoning of our transcendent principles (of divinity, of subjectivity) in favor of an immanence that resonates within and returns to us.[19] In this sense, it is difficult to simply and unequivocally define Agamben as a pantheist or pan*en*theist for that matter.[20]

What Agamben sets forth, in the end, is an immanent movement of creaturely life that resists becoming sovereign or perpetuating the violence of representations toward the other.

Rather it is a movement that tries to embody the weakness, precariousness, and delicacy found only in life's very existence. And perhaps the greatest irony lies here as well—not in that Agamben maintains something of the religious in his work and despite his efforts to profane our existence—but in that religion (though Christianity especially for him) seems genuinely to point toward this act of profanation as its own *telos* or end goal. It is as if Agamben intends to demonstrate (once again) the core message of the Christian narrative which has been suppressed almost since the moment Christ died on the cross.

When he suggests near the end of *The Reign and the Glory* that perhaps we are in a situation similar to one wherein God leaves the world as without God (*RG* 422), we are perhaps also left with an impression of Christianity's first moments after their God has truly left them, an emphasis witnessed at the beginning of the book of Acts, for example, that seems to go even a step beyond the demise of their God upon a cross. The messiah had died, been raised from the dead, and then, even after all of this, left the world behind him and departed it seemingly for good. The religious existence of the messiah's followers is now most uncertain, any attachment to belief seems perhaps somewhat muted or at least extremely difficult to express and a sense of abandonment could be said to permeate the air. A threshold has been breached and the religious impulse in its near entirety lies in question. And, then, as if it were Agamben himself whispering to us, we can perhaps hear a small voice provoking us, *People of Galilee, why do you stand looking toward heaven? There is work to be done here on earth, with the things of this earth now seen beyond the veils that had once concealed them. There is life beyond the sacred as you have known it yet to be lived in the time that remains.*[21]

Coda

Agamben begins his loose collection of aphorisms, fables, short stories, and philosophical remarks, titled *The Idea of Prose*, with a historical tale, one concerning the fifth-century Neoplatonist Damascius. As it happened, Damascius devoted the last years of his life to a work to be titled *Aporias and Solutions Concerning First Principles*. He intended for this work to uncover the source or origin of the Whole, the One. Yet, it was also this work that alternately perplexed and engrossed him completely, as he was unable to articulate anything seemingly intelligible on the subject of the beginning of thought. Every attempt seemed to break apart on the rock of a singular question, which was, as Agamben expresses it: "How can one comprehend the incomprehensible?" (*IP* 32).

It should by now be obvious that the question of how we are to comprehend the incomprehensible, or think the unthinkable, is the essential question linking the entirety of Agamben's work. As such, comprehending the incomprehensible is inseparable from the initial questions with which these reflections began: how can one live the "unlivable" in the present moment? How could one express the inexpressible in language? Or the question of our evolution: how can one think outside of our genetic coding, and hence grasp the "unwritten" codes of our biological existence? Historically, as Agamben will deftly illustrate over and again, these are theological questions as well, at least insofar as they all seek in some sense to pronounce the unpronounceable name of God.

As Agamben concludes his tale of a seemingly insoluble problem, Damascius reaches an epiphany of sorts when he in fact finds a kind of solution, one initiated simply by reframing the question entirely:

> The uttermost limit thought can reach is not a being,
> not a place or thing, no matter how free of any quality,
> but rather, its own absolute potentiality, the pure poten-
> tiality of representation itself: the writing tablet! What he
> had until then been taking as the One, as the absolutely
> Other of thought, was instead only the material, only
> the potentiality of thought. (*IP* 34)

Agamben continues, as if to address the question of how we might pronounce with words that which has remained unpronounceable and yet which constitutes our human subjectivity: "what could not cease from writing itself was the image of what never ceased from not writing itself" (*IP* 34). That is, what continues to remain unwritten (the unpronounceable) is what gives us our identity, is what grounds our every reflection. It is the animality "underneath" our humanity, or the divinity "above" it, which perplexes and defies our every attempt to move beyond them, and yet which cannot in any sense really ever be denied because they are both seemingly forever part of us as well. The excluded and abject figures of the world need not be created external to us in order to solidify our sense of political solidarity; rather, there is a "bare life" that thrives in us as well, as an internal limit which we would do well not to ignore any longer. Inside of us, there is a blank slate beyond all representations, a chance to encounter the presence of the other through the (infantile) face before us, looking at us, asking us to love it or at least let its love take place in us.

As for Damascius, though the same could perhaps someday be said of each of us, "now he could break the tablet, stop writing. Or rather, now he could truly begin. He now believed that he understood the sense of the maxim stating that by knowing the unknowable it is not something about it we know, but something about ourselves" (*IP* 34).

Notes

Introduction

1. Alice Lagaay and Juliane Schiffers, "Passivity at Work. A Conversation on an Element in the Philosophy of Giorgio Agamben," *Law Critique* 20 (2009), 325–337.
2. Lagaay and Schiffers, "Passivity at Work," 326.
3. Lagaay and Schiffers, "Passivity at Work," 326.
4. On the phrase "radical passivity" in relation to Agamben's work, see Thomas Carl Wall, *Radical Passivity: Levinas, Blanchot and Agamben* (Albany, NY: State University of New York, 1999).
5. Lagaay and Schiffers, "Passivity at Work," 327.
6. For example, secondary literature on his work is continuing to surface at a great rate, including the present book. Cf. Andrew Norris, ed., *Politics, Metaphysics, and Death: Essays on Giorgio Agamben's* Homo Sacer (Durham, NC: Duke University Press, 2005); Matthew Calarco and Steven DeCaroli, eds., *Giorgio Agamben: Sovereignty & Life* (Stanford: Stanford University Press, 2007); Catherine Mills, *The Philosophy of Agamben* (Stocksfield: Acumen, 2008); Justin Clemens, Nicholas Heron, and Alex Murry, eds., *The Work of Giorgio Agamben: Law, Literature, Life* (Edinburgh: Edinburgh University Press, 2008); Leland de la Durantaye, *Giorgio Agamben: A Critical Introduction* (Stanford: Stanford University Press, 2009); Alex Murray, *Giorgio Agamben* (London: Routledge, 2010); Thanos Zartaloudis, *Giorgio Agamben: Power, Law and the Uses of Criticism* (London: Routledge, 2010); and, William Watkin, *The Literary Agamben: Adventures in Logopoiesis* (London: Continuum, 2010).

Chapter 1

1. Cf. Genesis 10.8–12 for the original biblical portrayal of Nemrod.

2. One thinks here especially of those authors in the Italian context with which Agamben is familiar, such as Italo Calvino, whose novel *If on a Winter's Night a Traveler* (trans. William Weaver, New York: Harvest, 1981) seems to epitomize such an effort. See the depiction of such fictional attempts in relation to Agamben's work in the highly commendable writings of Paolo Bartoloni, such as his *Interstitial Writing: Calvino, Caproni, Sereni and Svevo* (Market Harborough: Troubador, 2003); "The Stanza of the Self: On Agamben's Potentiality," *Contretemps* 5 (2004), 8–15; and, *On the Cultures of Exile, Translation, and Writing* (West Lafayette, IN: Purdue University Press, 2008).

3. The work of Paul Celan, for example, and its affinity with philosophical discourses on the limits of language and intelligibility. Cf. Paul Celan, *Selected Poems and Prose of Paul Celan* (trans. John Felstiner, New York: W. W. Norton, 2001), as well as Jacques Derrida's study of Celan's work in relation to language and its limits in Thomas Dutoit and Outi Pasanen, eds., *Sovereignties in Question: The Poetics of Paul Celan* (New York: Fordham University Press, 2005). Agamben's relation to Celan is briefly explored in Isabel A. Moore, "'Speak, You Also': Encircling Trauma," *Journal for Cultural Research* 9: 1 (2005), 87–99.

4. Currently, the only English translations available of Giorgio Caproni's work are *The Wall of the Earth* (trans. Pasquale Verdicchio, Montreal: Guernica, 1992) and *The Earth's Wall: Selected Poems 1932–1986* (trans. Ned Condini, New York: Chelsea, 2004).

5. On Agamben's understanding of Caproni's poetry, see Paul Colilli, "The Theological Materials of Modernity (On Giorgio Agamben)," *Italica* 85: 4 (2008), 465–479.

6. Cf. Ferdinand de Saussure, *Writings in General Linguistics* (ed. Simon Bouquet and Rudolf Engler, New York: Oxford University Press, 2006); Roland Barthes, *Elements of Semiology* (trans. Annette Lavers and Colin Smith, New York: Hill and Wang, 1967); Umberto Eco, *Semiotics and the Philosophy of Language* (Bloomington, IN: Indiana University Press, 1986); as well as Terence Hawkes, *Structuralism and Semiotics* (London: Routledge, 2003).

7. Cf. Homi K. Bhabha, *The Location of Culture* (London: Routledge, 1994).

8. The influence of Walter Benjamin on Agamben's theory of language should not, of course, be overlooked. Cf. Walter Benjamin, "On Language as Such and on the Language of Man" in Marcus Bullock and Michael W. Jennings, eds., *Selected Writings*, vol. 1 (trans. Edmund Jephcott, Cambridge, MA: Harvard University Press, 1996), 62–74.

9. The study of Agamben's criticisms of Derrida constitute a study in and of themselves, and can only be referred to. See, for example, Adam Thurschwell, "Cutting the Branches for Akiba: Agamben's Critique of Derrida" in Norris, ed., *Politics, Metaphysics, and Death*, 173–197; David E. Johnson, "*As If* the Time Were Now: Deconstructing Agamben," *South Atlantic Quarterly* 106: 2 (2007), 265–290; Simon Morgan Wortham, "Law of Friendship: Agamben and Derrida" *New Formations* 62 (2007), 89–105; Jeffrey S. Librett, "From the Sacrifice of the Letter to the Voice of Testimony: Giorgio Agamben's Fulfillment of Metaphysics," *Diacritics* 37: 2–3 (2007), 11–33; Vernon Cisney, "Categories of Life: The Status of the Camp in Derrida and Agamben," *The Southern Journal of Philosophy* 46 (2008), 161–179; Catherine Mills, "Playing with Law: Agamben and Derrida on Postjuridical Justice," *South Atlantic Quarterly* 107: 1 (2008), 17–35; and Kevin Attell, "An Esoteric Dossier: Agamben and Derrida Read Saussure," *ELH* 76: 4 (2009), 821–846. A substantial review of the tensions between Derrida and Agamben can also be found in Durantaye, *Giorgio Agamben*, 184–191.

10. His use of the phrase "state (or society) of the spectacle" is, of course, greatly indebted to the work of Guy Debord, as Agamben himself acknowledges. See Guy Debord, *The Society of the Spectacle* (trans. Donald Nicholson-Smith, New York: Zone, 1995). Cf. Alex Murray, "Beyond Spectacle and the Image: The Poetics of Guy Debord and Agamben" in Clemens, Heron, and Murray, eds., *The Work of Giorgio Agamben*, 164–180.

11. Cf. Louis Althusser, "Ideology and Ideological State Apparatuses (Notes towards an Investigation)" in Slavoj Žižek, ed., *Mapping Ideology* (London: Verso, 1995), 100–140.

12. According to Agamben, this is what once led Linnaeus to attempt a categorization of humans as the animal which has the capacity to recognize itself (cf. *O* 26).

13. Michel Foucault, *The Order of Things: An Archaeology of the Human Sciences* (New York: Vintage, 1970), 386–387.

14. Cf. Carl Schmitt, *Political Theology: Four Chapters on the Concept of Sovereignty* (trans. George Schwab, Chicago: University of Chicago Press, 2005), 5.

15. Deuteronomy 11.26.

16. Cf. John Llewelyn, "Approaches to (Quasi)Theology via Appresentation," *Research in Phenomenology* 39 (2009), 224–247.

17. Cf. how the concept of the "names-of-the-father" has been developed by Jacques Lacan, *The Seminar of Jacques Lacan: The Psychoses 1955–1956* (vol. 3, trans. Jacques-Alain Miller and Russell Grigg, New York: W. W. Norton, 1997). For his part, however, Agamben does not provide any sustained engagement with Lacan's work, thus demonstrating only a missed opportunity.

18. Essentially, the strength of his critique of signification will ultimately push his views beyond trying to salvage any "antitragic" comic elements within certain Christian literary traditions in favor of a return to the originary "Christ event" found in the writings of Saint Paul, for

example. Hence, in other contexts, he will be able to take up Saint Paul's writings as introducing a (messianic) zone between the public and the private as the grounds for *the* Christian proclamation beyond the forms of both comedy and tragedy because beyond the realm of language itself (cf. *RG* 269; *TR*). If anything, this space could thus be said to be parodic, a parody of language and of the human being established through it, and thus in line with Agamben's reflections on parody in general.

19. In many respects, these comments appear similar to those critical responses to Roberto Benigni's 1997 film *La vita è bella* (*Life is Beautiful*) which read his comic attempts to circulate around, but never attempt to disclose, the horrors of the holocaust as much more "faithful" in its depiction of the *horror mysteriosus* that lurked behind its reality than other films which sought to "accurately" portray the German death camps. Cf. Slavoj Žižek, *Did Somebody Say Totalitarianism? Five Interventions in the (Mis)use of a Notion* (London: Verso, 2001), 70. What I am here terming the "horror mysteriosus" bears a structural affinity with the more traditionally used "horror religiosus." See the introduction to Hent de Vries, *Religion and Violence: Philosophical Perspectives from Kant to Derrida* (Baltimore, MD: Johns Hopkins University Press, 2002).

20. This immediately prompts his discussion of parody to examine the exemplary case of "limbo" from a theological perspective, offering a suggestive reading of limbo as a realm containing a "natural joy" in ignorance of God and thereby demonstrating itself as a "special form of parody" of hell (*PR* 44).

21. Cf. this same theme as it appears throughout Simon Critchley, *Things Merely Are: Philosophy in the Poetry of Wallace Stevens* (London: Routledge, 2005).

22. On the conjunction of "the thing itself" and Agamben's postmetaphysical project, see Fabio Presutti, "Manlio

Sgalambro, Giorgio Agamben: On Metaphysical Suspension of Language and the Destiny of Its Inorganic Re-Absorption," *Italica* 85: 2–3 (2008), 243–272.

23. The literary (poetic) celebration of the split in our modern subjectivities is something he reflects upon elsewhere as the activity which takes place in the writing and keeping of a diary where the self who reads the diary is not the same self (or selves) who had written it. See Giorgio Agamben and Valeria Piazza, [untitled article], trans. Luciana Bellini, *parallax* 9: 3 (2003), 2–4.

Chapter 2

1. The preference for the term "creaturely" which is given to Agamben's use of the phrase "bare life" is something which I will occasionally refer to throughout this chapter, and is adapted from Eric L. Santner's reading of Agamben's notion of "bare life" in his *On Creaturely Life: Rilke, Benjamin, Sebald* (Chicago: University of Chicago Press, 2006).

2. Durantaye, *Giorgio Agamben*, 22ff. Agamben also uses the term "decreation" in his essay on contingency and Bartleby (cf. *P* 270).

3. One thinks here, for example, of the late Jacques Derrida's ample coverage of "différance" within an ethical paradigm. Cf. Jacques Derrida, *Writing and Difference* (trans. Alan Bass, London: Routledge, 1978). See also, Emmanuel Levinas, *Totality and Infinity: An Essay on Exteriority* (trans. Alphonso Lingis, Pittsburgh, PA: Duquesne University Press, 1969).

4. The standard conception of God as an "Actus Purus" is worked out in the first part of Thomas Aquinas' *Summa Theologica*.

5. Cf. the commentary on Agamben's conceptualization of potentiality in relation to the possibility of theology vis-à-vis politics in Alberto Bertozzi, "Thoughts in Potentiality: Provisional Reflections on Agamben's Understanding of

Potentiality and Its Relevance for Theology and Politics," *Philosophy Today* 51: 3 (2007), 290–302, as well as in relation to the work of Jacques Derrida in Sean Gaston, *Derrida, Literature and War: Absence and the Chance of Meeting* (London: Continuum, 2009), 41–53.

6. For a more nuanced and critical interpretation of Agamben's reading of Melville, see Alexander Cooke, "Resistance, Potentiality and the Law," *Angelaki* 10: 3 (2005), 79–89. See also Armin Beverungen and Stephen Dunne, " 'I'd Prefer Not To': Bartleby and the Excesses of Interpretation," *Culture and Organization* 13: 2 (2007), 171–183.

7. Cf. the article of Rad Borislavov on the linkage of ontology and political power titled "Agamben, Ontology, and Constituent Power," *Debatte* 13: 2 (2005), 173–184.

8. Yet, as Andrew Norris has noted, the distinctions being drawn by Agamben between the political and the philosophical vis-à-vis the metaphysical are not always as clear as Agamben might like them to be. Cf. Andrew Norris, "The Exemplary Exception: Philosophical and Political Decisions in Giorgio Agamben's *Homo Sacer*" in Norris, ed., *Politics, Metaphysics, and Death*, 262–283.

9. Walter Benjamin, "Critique of Violence," in Bullock and Jennings, eds., *Selected Writings*, vol. 1.

10. This would perhaps serve to explain, in no small measure, why someone of Jewish descent such as Benjamin would take the time to write to someone with such anti-Semitic tendencies as Schmitt in order to affirm the connection between sovereignty and the state of exception, something which was deeply influential upon Benjamin's work as a whole. See the "Editor's Introduction" in Carl Schmitt, *Political Theology II: The Myth of the Closure of Any Political Theology* (trans. Michael Hoelzl and Graham Ward, Cambridge: Polity, 2008). It would also serve to explain why Schmitt's theories, despite their affiliation with National Socialism and anti-Semitism, have

remained central to articulating "political theology" today (cf. *SE* 1ff.). Despite this affinity between Benjamin and Schmitt, however, it would also seem that their theories of sovereignty diverge in some respect, contra Agamben's attempts to unite them in *Homo Sacer*, precisely on the issue of violence and state sovereignty. See Adam Kotsko, "On Agamben's Use of Benjamin's 'Critique of Violence,'" *Telos* 145 (2008), 119–129.

11. Cf. Schmitt, *Political Theology* and *Political Theology II*.
12. Cf. 2 Corinthians 12.9–10.
13. Cf. Martin Heidegger, *Being and Time* (trans. Joan Stambaugh, Albany, NY: State University of New York, 1996) and Antonio Negri, *Insurgencies: Constituent Power and the Modern State* (trans. Maurizia Boscagli, Minneapolis, MN: University of Minnesota Press, 1999).
14. Cf. Ulrich Raulff, "An Interview with Giorgio Agamben," *German Law Journal* 5: 5 (2004), 609–613. See also Bruno Gullì, "The Ontology and Politics of Exception: Reflections on the Work of Giorgio Agamben" in Calarco and DeCaroli, eds., *Giorgio Agamben*, 219–242.
15. Cf. Derek Gregory's analysis of Agamben's contentions with Guantánamo Bay, for example, in his "The Black Flag: Guantánamo Bay and the Space of Exception," *Geogr. Ann.* 88B: 4 (2006), 405–427.
16. Cf. Kirk Wetters, "The Rule of the Norm and the Political Theology of 'Real Life' in Carl Schmitt and Giorgio Agamben," *Diacritics* 36: 1 (2006), 31–46. On Schmitt's attempts to form a "political theology," see his *Political Theology* and *Political Theology II*.
17. Cf. the transcendental "origins" of Agamben's "state of exception" as explored in Wendell Kisner, "Agamben, Hegel, and the State of Exception," *Cosmos and History* 3: 2–3 (2007), 222–253.
18. Schmitt, *Political Theology*, 5.
19. One of the earliest proponents of the phrase "political theology" was in fact Carl Schmitt, as we have already

seen. It has subsequently acquired a life of its own, how-
ever, and evolved into a veritable field of study in its own
right. Cf. Slavoj Žižek, Eric Santner, and Kenneth
Reinhard, *The Neighbor: Three Inquiries in Political Theology*
(Chicago: University of Chicago Press, 2005); Creston
Davis, John Milbank, and Slavoj Žižek, eds., *Theology and
the Political: The New Debate* (Durham, NC: Duke
University Press, 2005); Peter Scott and William T.
Cavanaugh, eds., *The Blackwell Companion to Political
Theology* (Oxford: Wiley-Blackwell, 2006); Hent de Vries,
ed., *Political Theologies: Public Religions in a Post-Secular
World* (New York: Fordham University Press, 2006); and
Michael Kirwin, *Political Theology: An Introduction*
(Minneapolis, MN: Fortress, 2009).

20. "Biopolitics," as a term drawn directly by Agamben from
the work of Michel Foucault, can be seen in its essence as
the classical force of sovereignty gone "underground" as
it were, directly governing the bodies of subjects in more
veiled, but also more insidious forms. Hence, for Foucault,
as for Agamben, those places in society where bodies are
made to submit to certain inscriptions, disciplined accordingly and marked forever after by this biopolitical power,
are the "hotspots" of biopolitical activity in the modern
era. See, for example, Michel Foucault, *Discipline and
Punish: The Birth of the Prison* (trans. Alan Sheridan, New
York: Vintage, 1977) as well as *The Birth of Biopolitics:
Lectures at the College De France, 1978–1979* (trans. Graham
Burchell, New York: Palgrave Macmillan, 2010). On the
development of the term in relation to Agamben, see
especially Paul Patton, "Agamben and Foucault on
Biopower and Biopolitics" in Calarco and DeCaroli, eds.,
Giorgio Agamben, 203–218; Mitchell Dean, "Four Theses
on the Powers of Life and Death," *Contretemps* 5 (2004),
16–29; as well as Mark Mazower, "Foucault, Agamben:
Theory and the Nazis," *Boundary 2* 35: 1 (2008), 23–34.
For an interesting contrast on their accounts of the

biopolitical, see the recent work of Roberto Esposito, *Bíos: Biopolitics and Philosophy* (trans. Timothy Campbell, Minneapolis, MN: University of Minnesota Press, 2008).

21. These distinctions, of course, recall Schmitt's initial definition of politics as being based on a foundational friend/enemy distinction. Cf. Carl Schmitt, *The Concept of the Political* (trans. George Schwab, Chicago: University of Chicago Press, 1996), 27. As some have contended, however, they are often not as simple to make as we might hope. See, for example, Gil Anidjar, *The Jew, the Arab: A History of the Enemy* (Stanford: Stanford University Press, 2003). Even Agamben's reliance upon the division between *zoē* (our "creaturely" life) and *bios* (our political life) has been critiqued for maintaining a too-strict boundary which perhaps is more permeable than he would like to admit, thus perhaps aligning his division with the sovereign act of signification, a heavy-charge indeed to someone committed to critiquing sovereignty itself. Cf. Jacques Derrida, *The Beast and the Sovereign, vol. 1* (ed. Michel Lisse, Marie-Louise Mallet, and Ginette Michaud, trans. Geoffrey Bennington, Chicago: University of Chicago Press, 2009), 92ff.

22. On the conjunction of the biopolitical and the formation of any "species" in general, see Michael Dillon and Luis Lobo-Guerrero, "The Biopolitical Imaginary of Species-Being," *Theory, Culture and Society* 26: 1 (2009), 1–23.

23. Cf. an article that attempts to deal with refugees in relation to Agamben's notion of "bare life" from an ethical-theological point of view, Luke Bretherton, "The Duty of Care to Refugees, Christian Cosmopolitanism, and the Hallowing of Bare Life," *Studies in Christian Ethics* 19: 1 (2006), 39–61. See also, however, a critique of Agamben's position on refugees in Patricia Owens, "Reclaiming 'Bare Life'?: Against Agamben on Refugees," *International Relations* 23: 4 (2009), 567–582. Related to this redefining of genuine political subjects in

light of contemporary biopolitical norms, see also Mark Rifkin's study of Native Peoples' identities, titled "Indigenizing Agamben: Rethinking Sovereignty in Light of the 'Peculiar' Status of Native Peoples," *Cultural Critique* 73 (2009), 88–124.

24. Cf. how Trevor Parfitt co-opts this notion in relation to concrete political situations today in his "Are the Third World Poor *Homines Sacri*? Biopolitics, Sovereignty, and Development," *Alternatives* 34 (2009), 41–58.

25. The division of our world into sacred and profane, however, does have a long history in and of itself. See, for example, the seminal work of Mircea Eliade, *The Sacred and the Profane: The Nature of Religion* (trans. Willard R. Trask, New York: Harcourt-Brace Jovanovich, 1987).

Chapter 3

1. Judith Butler and Gayatri Chakravorty Spivak, *Who Sings the Nation-State?* (Oxford: Seagull, 2007), 36 and 102.

2. His use of the term "governmentality" stems from the work of Michel Foucault who first developed the concept in his lectures. Cf. Michel Foucault, *Security, Territory, Population: Lectures at the College de France 1977–1978* (ed. Michel Senellart, trans. Graham Burchell, New York: Palgrave Macmillan, 2007). This term has seen numerous subsequent developments since its inception. See also Graham Burchell, Colin Gordon, and Peter Miller, eds., *The Foucault Effect: Studies in Governmentality* (Chicago: University of Chicago Press, 1991).

3. Cf. on Heidegger's use of the term "ontotheology," see Martin Heidegger, *Nietzsche: Vol. IV: Nihilism* (ed. David Farell Krell, trans. Frank A. Capuzzi, 4 vols., San Francisco: HarperSanFrancisco, 1982), 209ff., as well as Iain Thomson, *Heidegger on Ontotheology: Technology and the Politics of Education* (Cambridge: Cambridge University Press, 2005). See also Joeri Schijvers, "On Doing Theology

'After' Ontotheology: Notes on a French Debate," *New Blackfriars* 87 (2006), 302–314.

It should also be noted, however, that Agamben has consistently, though opaquely, insisted that the work of Benjamin played the role of "remedy" to the "poison" in Heidegger's writings, and thus, that the two must be read in conjunction throughout his own work. See the discussion in Durantaye, *Giorgio Agamben*, 310ff.

4. This thesis, of course, shares a remarkable similarity with the work of René Girard on the relationship between violence, religion, and sacrifice, a similarity which Agamben has not yet taken up directly as such. Cf. René Girard, *Things Hidden Since the Foundation of the World* (trans. Stephen Bann and Michael Metteer, Stanford: Stanford University Press, 1987), as well as *The Scapegoat* (trans. Yvonne Freccero, Baltimore, MD: Johns Hopkins University Press, 1989). On the affinities and differences between Girard's position and that of Agamben, see also Christopher A. Fox, "Sacrificial Pasts and Messianic Futures: Religion as a Political Prospect in René Girard and Giorgio Agamben," *Philosophy and Social Criticism* 33: 5 (2007), 563–595, as well as Rey Chow, "Sacrifice, Mimesis, and the Theorizing of Victimhood," *Representations* 94 (2006), 131–149. Moreover, if Girard's thesis can likewise be read as an attempt to conceive of the Christian message as one ultimately doing away with the "false sacred" within our world, a sort of "secularization" thesis as found in the work of Gianni Vattimo, for example, then perhaps Agamben's attempt to "profane" our world can be understood as a similarly minded gesture. Cf. Gianni Vattimo, *After Christianity* (trans. Luca D'Isanto, New York: Columbia University Press, 2002). See also the discussion in Frederiek Depoortere, *Christ and Postmodern Philosophy: Gianni Vattimo, René Girard, and Slavoj Žižek* (London: T&T Clark, 2008).

5. On his distancing of his position from Schmitt, see also *HS* 110.

6. Cf. John 1.1ff.

7. Agamben's use of the figure of the *Muselmann*, as well as his general account of testimony, in *Remnants of Auschwitz* has been the subject of much criticism, including Philippe Mesnard and Claudine Kahan, *Giorgio Agamben: à l'épreuve d'Auschwitz: témoignages/interprétations* (Paris: Kimé, 2001); Alexander García Düttmann, "Never Before, Always Already: Notes on Agamben and the Category of Relation," *Angelaki* 6: 3 (2001), 3–6; Robert Eaglestone, "On Giorgio Agamben's Holocaust," *Paragraph* 25 (2002), 52–67; Philippe Mesnard, "The Political Philosophy of Giorgio Agamben: A Critical Evaluation," trans. Cyrille Guiat, *Totalitarian Movements and Political Religions* 5: 1 (2004), 139–157; J. M. Bernstein, "Intact and Fragmented Bodies: Versions of Ethics 'after Auschwitz,'" *New German Critique* 33: 1 (2006), 31–52; Nicholas Chare, "The Gap in Context: Giorgio Agamben's *Remnants of Auschwitz*," *Cultural Critique* 64 (2006), 40–68; and Ruth Leys, *From Guilt to Shame: Auschwitz and After* (Princeton: Princeton University Press, 2007), 157–179. Substantial engagements concerning these matters can also be found in Catherine Mills, "Linguistic Survival and Ethicality: Biopolitics, Subjectification, and Testimony in *Remnants of Auschwitz*" in Norris, ed., *Politics, Metaphysics, and Death*, 198–221, as well as in Durantaye, *Giorgio Agamben*, 261ff.

8. Cf. also the analysis of the camps within a (bio)political context in Claudio Minca, "Giorgio Agamben and the New Biopolitical *Nomos*," *Geogr. Ann.* 88B: 4 (2006), 387–403.

9. Though a difference between the Muselmann and the *homo sacer*, however, is mentioned in the last remaining analysis of *Homo Sacer* (cf. *HS* 181–188), subsequent elaboration upon the figure of the *homo sacer* seems to align them somewhat more closely, especially as the *homo sacer*

figure approaches to becoming a messianic "vocation" (cf. *PR* 78–79).

10. One is reminded here of Hannah Arendt's discussion of the "banality of evil" in her *Eichmann in Jerusalem: A Report on the Banality of Evil* (New York: Penguin, 2006).

Chapter 4

1. Cf. the charge of "political nihilism" in Agamben's work has been levied by Ernesto Laclau, "Bare Life or Social Indeterminacy?" and William Rasch, "From Sovereign Ban to Banning Sovereignty" both found in Calarco and DeCaroli, eds., *Giorgio Agamben*, 22 and 107 respectively. Catherine Mills also draws attention to the viability of his end to politics in the conclusion to her *The Philosophy of Agamben*. See also her "Agamben's Messianic Politics: Biopolitics, Abandonment and Happy Life," *Contretemps* 5 (2004), 42–62. Paul Passavant, for one, has likewise argued that Agamben presents conflicting visions of the state in his work, and that, in the end, the state should be defended against those, such as Agamben, who would seem to be pointing toward an "ideal" state beyond the political which cannot be actualized as such. See Paul A. Passavant, "The Contradictory State of Giorgio Agamben," *Political Theory* 35: 2 (2007), 147–174. The conflict which Passavant stages in his article is one between politics as a dealing with the actuality before us and religious belief as a potentiality for another world beyond this one, an idealistic vision that others, immersed in the political, may refuse to share. As he puts it,

> [a]s good as love sounds, what if some do not want to be so loved? What of those who do not want to be part of this Judeo-Christian tradition? What of those who might resist the missionary's appeal, fearing that "love" is a cover for colonialism? What of those who

either do not want to be part of this messianic situation or might resist its faithful who live by its law? (Passavant, "Contradictory State," 167)

2. Cf. the close reading of Agamben's use of Benjamin precisely on this point in Anselm Haverkamp, "Anagrammatics of Violence: The Benjaminian Ground of *Homo Sacer*," trans. Kirk Wetters, in Norris, ed., *Politics, Metaphysics, and Death*, 135–144, as well as in Arne De Boever, "Politics and Poetics of Divine Violence: On a Figure in Giorgio Agamben and Walter Benjamin" in Clemens, Heron, and Murray, eds., *The Work of Giorgio Agamben*, 82–96.

3. Cf. Walter Benjamin, "On the Concept of History" in Howard Eiland and Michael W. Jennings, eds., *Selected Writings* (vol. 4, trans. Edmund Jephcott et al., Cambridge, MA: Belknap, 2003); John D. Caputo, *The Weakness of God: A Theology of the Event* (Bloomington, IN: Indiana University Press, 2006); Slavoj Žižek, *In Defense of Lost Causes* (London: Verso, 2009); Jacques Derrida, *Specters of Marx: The State of the Debt, the Work of Mourning and the New International* (trans. Peggy Kamuf, London: Routledge, 1994); and Judith Butler, "Afterward" in Ellen T. Armour and Susan M. St. Ville (eds.), *Bodily Citations: Religion and Judith Butler* (New York: Columbia University Press, 2006).

4. Cf. Jacob Taubes, *The Political Theology of Paul* (trans. Dana Hollander, Stanford: Stanford University Press, 2003); Alain Badiou, *Saint Paul: The Foundation of Universalism* (trans. Ray Brassier, Stanford: Stanford University Press, 2003); Slavoj Žižek, *The Puppet and the Dwarf: The Perverse Core of Christianity* (Cambridge, MA: MIT Press, 2003); and, John D. Caputo and Linda Martín Alcoff, eds., *St. Paul among the Philosophers* (Bloomington, IN: Indiana University Press, 2009). See also, the many articles to appear recently on Agamben's use of the term itself, including Ward Blanton, "Disturbing Politics: Neo-Paulinism and the Scrambling of Religious and

Secular Identities," *Dialog: A Journal of Theology* 46: 1 (2007), 3–13; Eleanor Kaufman, "The Saturday of Messianic Time (Agamben and Badiou on the Apostle Paul)," *South Atlantic Quarterly* 107: 1 (2008), 37–54; John Roberts, "The 'Returns to Religion': Messianism, Christianity and the Revolutionary Tradition. Part II: The Pauline Tradition," *Historical Materialism* 16 (2008), 77–103; Patrick O'Connor, "Redemptive Remnants: Agamben's Human Messianism," *Journal for Cultural Research* 13: 3–4 (2009), 335–352; Job de Meyere, "The Care for the Present: Giorgio Agamben's Actualization of the Pauline Messianic Experience," *Bijdragen: International Journal in Philosophy and Theology* 70 (2009), 168–184; Mike Grimshaw, "Ruptured Romans: A Theological Meditation on Paul, Cultural Theory, and the Cosmopolitan Rupture of Grace," *Stimulus* 17: 2 (2009), 32–40; Paolo Palladino, "Picturing the Messianic: Agamben and Titian's *The Nymph and the Shepherd*," *Theory, Culture and Society* 27 (2010), 94–109; and, Colby Dickinson, "Canon as an Act of Creation: Giorgio Agamben and the Extended Logic of the Messianic," *Bijdragen: International Journal in Philosophy and Theology* 71: 2 (2010), 132–158.

5. Cf. the similarity between this approach and that found in Badiou's *Saint Paul*.

6. 1 Corinthians 7.19.

7. Cf. 1 Corinthians 7.29–32.

8. Cf. Romans 13. See also the ample introduction to this quite problematic relationship between Christianity and law in John Witte, Jr., and Frank S. Alexander, *Christianity and Law: An Introduction* (Cambridge: Cambridge University Press, 2008).

9. On Agamben's relationship to Benjamin with regard to the messianic and history, see Miguel Vatter, "In Odradek's World: Bare Life and Historical Materialism in Agamben and Benjamin," *Diacritics* 38: 3 (2008), 45–70.

10. Cf. Adrian Johnston, *Badiou, Žižek, and Political Transformations: The Cadence of Change* (Evanston, IL: Northwestern University Press, 2009).
11. Cf. Benjamin, "On the Concept of History," as well as Žižek, *The Puppet and the Dwarf*, 92–121. See also, the insightful article by Jayne Svenungsson, "Wrestling with Angels: Or How to Avoid Decisionist Messianic Romances," *International Journal of Žižek Studies* 4: 4 (2010).
12. Benjamin even goes so far as to state that his work is "saturated" with the theological throughout, though he does not always address its thematic directly as such. Walter Benjamin, *The Arcades Project* (trans. Howard Eiland and Kevin McLaughlin, Cambridge, MA: Belknap, 1999), 471. The relationship between Benjamin and Agamben, though undoubtedly clearly defined in many ways, is not without its problematics, however. See, for example, the recent collection of articles by Vittoria Borsò, Claas Morgenroth, Karl Solibakke, and Bernd Witte, eds., *Benjamin–Agamben: Politics, Messianism, Kabbalah* (Würzburg: Königshausen and Neumann, 2010).
13. Walter Benjamin, "On the Program of the Coming Philosophy," *Selected Writings*, vol. 1, 104.
14. Cf. the role of the metaphysical in Benjamin's work in both Susan A. Handelmann, *Fragments of Redemption: Jewish Thought and Literary Theory in Benjamin, Scholem, and Levinas* (Bloomington, IN: Indiana University Press, 1991); and, Eric Jacobson, *Metaphysics of the Profane: The Political Theology of Walter Benjamin and Gershom Scholem* (New York: Columbia University Press, 2003).
15. Thomas Carl Wall, "Au Hasard" in Norris, ed., *Politics, Metaphysics, and Death*, 45.
16. Cf. Raulff, "An Interview with Giorgio Agamben," 613.
17. Or, as he will elsewhere state, each example is treated as a "real particular case" despite the fact that it cannot "serve in its particularity" (*CC* 10). He will also state that Foucault's study of paradigms was "the most characteristic

gesture of [his] method" and in this effort, he "freed historiography from the exclusive domain of meonymic
contexts . . . in order to return metaphorical contexts to
primacy" (*SA* 17). And, likewise, "Paradigms obey not
the logic of the metaphorical transfer of meaning but the
analogical logic of the example" (*SA* 18).

18. There is a significant, though unstated, affinity between
the exposure of our being and Judith Butler's discussion
of "precarious life" in her book *Precarious Life: The Powers
of Mourning and Violence* (London: Verso, 2004).

19. As Lorenzo Chiesa has put it, "the heroic *homo sacer* of
politics is silently turned into the *homo messianicus* of
Christian religion. Furthermore, according to this interpretation, Agamben's notion of 'weak' [*faible*] being, a
being characterized by a 'presentative poverty,' could
qualify his ontology as 'Franciscan.'" Lorenzo Chiesa,
"Giorgio Agamben's Franciscan Ontology" in Lorenzo
Chiesa and Alberto Toscano, eds., *The Italian Difference:
Between Nihilism and Biopolitics* (Melbourne, re.press,
2009), 162. Alain Badiou has also referred to Agamben's
work as being "Franciscan" in its ontology in his *Logiques
des Mondes: L'Être et l'événement, 2* (Paris: Seuil, 2006),
584. Cf. also Justin Clemens, "The Role of the Shifter
and the Problem of Reference in Giorgio Agamben" in
Clemens, Heron, and Murray, eds., *The Work of Giorgio
Agamben*, 57.

20. Cf. Michel Foucault, "Nietzsche, Genealogy, History,"
The Foucault Reader (ed. Paul Rabinow, New York:
Pantheon, 1984), 76–100.

Chapter 5

1. Matthew 18.1–4.
2. Cf. John 3.4.
3. Agamben's interest in Freud has run throughout the course
of his work on several notable levels. See, for instance, his

discussions on Freud and the unconscious (*IH* 55), Freud on both mourning and melancholia (*S* 19ff.) and Freud and the fetish object (*S* 31ff.). On Agamben's relationship to Freud, see Justin Clemens, "The Abandonment of Sex: Giorgio Agamben, Psychoanalysis and Melancholia," *Theory and Event* 13: 1 (2010).

4. Agamben himself notes his indebtedness to the work of Enzo Melandri. Cf. Enzo Melandri, *La linea e il circolo: Studio logico-filosofico sull'analogia* (Macerata: Quodlibet, 2004).

5. Benjamin, "On the Concept of History," 391. For a discussion of this concept within a relevant context to what Agamben is pursuing here, see Matthias Fritsch, *The Promise of Memory: History and Politics in Marx, Benjamin, and Derrida* (Albany, NY: State University of New York Press, 2005).

6. Cf. Michel Foucault, *The Archaeology of Knowledge* (trans. A. M. Sheridan Smith, London: Routledge, 1972).

7. Deborah Levitt, "Notes on Media and Biopolitics: 'Notes on Gesture,'" in Clemens, Heron, and Murray, eds., *The Work of Giorgio Agamben*, 202. On the place of gesture in Agamben's work on the whole, see also Samuel Weber, "Going Along for the Ride: Violence and Gesture: Agamben Reading Benjamin Reading Kafka Reading Cervantes," *The Germanic Review* 81: 1 (2006), 65–83; Anthony Curtis Adler, "The Intermedial Gesture: Agamben and Kommerell," *Angelaki* 12: 3 (2007), 57–64; as well as Alastair Morgan, "'A Figure of Annihilated Human Existence': Agamben and Adorno on Gesture," *Law Critique* 20 (2009), 299–307.

8. Levitt, "Notes on Media," 203. Cf. *ME* 57.

9. The subject of Agamben and his relationship to poetry merits an in-depth analysis of its own. In brief, and as Agamben has elsewhere commented, it is the caesuras within poetry which make representation itself visible or manifest, and which, in fact, express the inexpressible

through their presentation of the fracture within language (and being) itself (*IP* 44). In this sense, the only responsible way that a representation can be said to "present" truth is by illustrating the gap, or the caesura, that separates representation from truth itself (*IP* 107). If this is taken into consideration with what Agamben develops in another context as a form of "being-contemporary," we are left to witness the reality of how "[t]he poet, insofar as he is contemporary, *is* this fracture, *is* at once that which impedes time from composing itself and the blood that must suture this break or this wound" (*WA* 42). Embodying a radical vocation, then, the poet sits at a juncture in history wherein his/her experience is capable of expressing a profound sense the redemption possible *in* life. Perhaps we are now in a better position to comprehend once again Agamben's fascination with the work of Saint Paul, for whom the fracture within our being, theologically registered for him as "sin," was paramount to discovering our vocation before God. Paradoxical as it might appear, it is by moving closer to Paul's theology that Agamben hopes to illustrate the absolute distance which the poetic experience maintains in relation to what is traditionally considered as the domain of the "mystical-theological." Hence, he can assert with full confidence that, in relation to this poetic sense of "being-contemporary," the ultimate example, if you will, is the notion of a messianic realignment of time, one fully espoused in the Pauline corpus. As he puts it, "[t]here is nothing more exemplary, in this sense, than Paul's gesture at the point in which he experiences and announces to his brothers the contemporariness par excellence that is messianic time, the being-contemporary with the Messiah, which he calls precisely the 'time of the now'" (*WA* 52). And, in this sense, it is the time of the poet as well, the time in which the fracture is exposed and therefore most open to the potential of its healing. This will seemingly cement the profound relationship he strikes elsewhere between Paul and poetry, specifically on the point of "rhythm," which Agamben reads as Paul's legacy to the poetic (cf. *TR* 87ff.). In addition, as he sees it, the poem also functions similar to the *katechon* in Paul's writings, a measure which delays the coming of the Messiah (cf. *EP* 114).

10. Cf. Benjamin, "On the Concept of History."

11. Cf. Benjamin on theology and history in *The Arcades Project*, convolute *N*.

12. "We have seen that Nietzsche was mistaken about the origins of nihilism and we see here that he was equally mistaken about its solution, for his Dionysus is not the great antagonist of the Christian God but only his most recent incarnation." Michael Allen Gillespie, *Nihilism before Nietzsche* (Chicago: Chicago University Press, 1995), 254. See also, the central understanding of nihilism at stake in Nietzsche's work in Bernard Reginster, *The Affirmation of Life: Nietzsche on Overcoming Nihilism* (Cambridge, MA: Harvard University Press, 2009). Theologically, some have suggested that nihilism be addressed in a more nuanced fashion, one which explores its potential clearing of ontotheological guises so that a properly theological account of our existence perhaps might be given. See Conor Cunningham, *Genealogy of Nihilism: Philosophies of Nothing and the Difference of Theology* (London: Routledge, 2002).

13. The allusion to Christian notions of community as a theme in Agamben's work has not, of course, gone without notice. Cf. Jessica Whyte, " 'A New Use of the Self': Giorgio Agamben on the Coming Community," *Theory and Event* 13: 1 (2010).

14. Dominick LaCapra, "Approaching Limit Events: Siting Agamben" in Calarco and DeCaroli, eds., *Giorgio Agamben*, 162.

15. Cf. Claire Colebrook, "Agamben: Aesthetics, Potentiality, and Life," *South Atlantic Quarterly* 107: 1 (2008), 107–120.

16. Cf. the application of Agamben's theory of art and its political implications in those artists who deliberately immerse their art in the "zones of indistinction" present in our world today, in Andrew Downey, "Zones of Indistinction: Giorgio Agamben's 'Bare Life' and the Politics of Aesthetics," *Third Text* 23: 2 (2009), 109–125.

17. Cf. Frederiek Depoortere, *The Death of God: An Investigation into the History of the Western Concept of God* (London: T&T Clark, 2008).

18. Friedrich Nietzsche, *The Gay Science* (ed. Bernard Williams, Cambridge: Cambridge University Press, 2001), 199 and 120.

19. Cf. Sigmund Freud, *The Interpretation of Dreams: The Complete and Definitive Text* (trans. James Strachey, New York: Basic, 1955), 463.

20. Cf. Benjamin's fragment: "Historical materialism must renounce the epic element in history. It blasts the epoch out of the reified 'continuity of history.' But it also explodes the homogeneity of the epoch, interspersing it with ruins—that is, with the present." Benjamin, *The Arcades Project*, 474.

21. Samuel Beckett, "The Capital of the Ruins," *As the Story was Told: Uncollected and Late Prose* (London: John Calder, 1990), 27–28.

22. This is not to suggest, however, that a complete overlap between Agamben and Schmitt exists. Cf. the contrast between Schmitt's political thinking and Agamben's attempts to transcend the political in David Pan, "Against Biopolitics: Walter Benjamin, Carl Schmitt, and Giorgio Agamben on Political Sovereignty and Symbolic Order," *The German Quarterly* 82: 1 (2009), 42–62.

23. Cf. the "Radical Orthodoxy" movement within British theology in recent years, including such notable authors as John Milbank, Catherine Pickstock, and Graham Ward who jointly coedited *Radical Orthodoxy: A New Theology* (London: Routledge, 1998) as well as Philip Blond, ed.,

Post-Secular Philosophy: Between Philosophy and Theology (London: Routledge, 1998).

24. On the idea that the term "profanation" lies at the center of Agamben's thought, see Leland de la Durantaye, "*Homo profanes*: Giorgio Agamben's Profane Philosophy," *Boundary 2* 25: 3 (2008), 27–62.
25. On Agamben's relating of "whatever being" to the forms of the poetic, in fact, see Jonathan Monroe's article "Philosophy, Poetry, Parataxis," *The European Legacy* 14: 5 (2009), 599–611.
26. Luke 13.24ff., for example.
27. Benjamin Morgan, "Undoing Legal Violence: Walter Benjamin's and Giorgio Agamben's Aesthetics of Pure Means," *Journal of Law and Society* 34: 1 (2007), 46–64, 61.

Chapter 6

1. Cf. Foucault, "Nietzsche, Genealogy, History."
2. Cf. the manner in which Diane Enns deals with Agamben's attempts to regress to a state prior to typical identity formations in her essay "Political Life before Identity," *Theory and Event* 10: 1 (2007).
3. John 3.4.
4. Watkin, *The Literary Agamben*, 13.
5. Mills, *The Philosophy of Agamben*, 25.
6. On Agamben's appropriation of Heidegger's category of "letting be," see Krzysztof Ziarek, "After Humanism: Agamben and Heidegger," *South Atlantic Quarterly* 107: 1 (2008), 187–209. Cf. the references to the "open" in Martin Heidegger, "The Origin of the Work of Art," *Poetry, Language, Thought* (trans. Albert Hofstadter, New York: Harper, 1971), 43ff.
7. Cf. Galatians 3.28 and Romans 6.
8. Galatians 3.28.
9. It is noteworthy that Agamben does not, here or elsewhere, engage with the work of Emmanuel Levinas on

this point, for whom the face was the central reference for his ethics. Cf. Levinas, *Totality and Infinity*.

10. Julian Wolfreys, "Face to Face with Agamben; or, the Other *in* Love" in Clemens, Heron, and Murray, eds., *The Work of Giorgio Agamben*, 149–163.

11. Cf. his comments on the poetry of Rainer Maria Rilke as a form of this quasi-mystical state, for example, in *IH* 49ff.

12. The conceptualization of "citationality" has a history of its own, ranging from Benjamin to Derrida and Butler. It is with the latter two figures that this notion of citationality merges with a sense of performativity, especially with regard to how we can be said to "cite" and "perform" aspects of our identity, such as gender. Cf. Jacques Derrida, "Signature Event Context" in *Margins of Philosophy* (trans. Alan Bass, Chicago: University of Chicago Press, 1982) and Judith Butler, *Bodies That Matter: On the Discursive Limits of "Sex"* (London: Routledge, 1993).

13. Cf. her defense of our precarious (gendered) selves in Judith Butler, *Undoing Gender* (London: Routledge, 2004). An emancipatory politics such as usually found in feminist and race theorists is conspicuously absent from Agamben's work, which would otherwise seem to offer itself as an ideal platform for deconstructing the arbitrary boundaries of race and gender in our world today. Cf. how this issue is dealt with in Ewa Płonowska Ziarek, "Bare Life on Strike: Notes on the Biopolitics of Race and Gender," *South Atlantic Quarterly* 107: 1 (2008), 89–105, and her subsequent "Feminine 'I can': On Possibility and Praxis in Agamben's Work," *Theory and Event* 13: 1 (2010), as well as in Emma R. Jones, "In the Presence of the Living Cockroach: The Moment of Aliveness and the Gendered Body in Agamben and Lispector," *PhaenEx* 2: 2 (2007), 24–41.

14. Cf. a wide variety of literature, including Mary Daly's early challenges in *Beyond God the Father: Toward a*

Philosophy of Women's Liberation (Boston: Beacon, 1973); and, Grace Jantzen, *Becoming Divine: Towards a Feminist Philosophy of Religion* (Bloomington, IN: Indiana University Press, 1998). See also the stress on immanence in Sharon D. Welch, *A Feminist Ethic of Risk* (Minneapolis, MN: Fortress, 2000). From an interreligious perspective, see also John J. Thatamanil, *The Immanent Divine: God, Creation and the Human Predicament* (Minneapolis, MN: Fortress Press, 2006).

15. Cf. Caputo, *The Weakness of God*.

Conclusion

1. Agamben's project would seem to many to run in contrast to phenomenological accounts of life that would, for their part, posit an "ontology of immanence," thus making his distance from phenomenology seem all that more relevant and prompting at least one person to quip "Agamben *or* Merleau-Ponty," though presumably not both. Cf. Jean-Philippe Deranty, "Witnessing the Inhuman: Agamben or Merleau-Ponty," *South Atlantic Quarterly* 107: 1 (2008), 165–186 (emphasis in the quotation is mine). As is here indicated, Agamben's focus appears to be on the negative, or the nihilistic, the dissolution of boundaries and subjects, rather than on a positive "building up" of concepts from what appears in the phenomena themselves. Yet his relation to the phenomenological remains somewhat unclear. For an alternative stress, one placed upon the "positive" aspects within Agamben's oeuvre, mainly in relation to his earlier work, see Stefano Franchi, "Of the Synthetic and the Analytic," *Contretemps* 5 (2004), 30–41.

2. Thomas Aquinas, *Summa Theologica*, Supplement P. 3, Q. 79, A. 1.

3. "*State of Exception* provides us with a second, more original and powerful perspective—a Spinozist and Deleuzian

one. Here, the analysis does not survey an inert biopolitical plane but traverses it with a feverish utopian anxiety,
grasping its internal antagonism." Antonio Negri,
"Giorgio Agamben: The Discreet Taste of the Dialectic,"
trans. Matteo Mandarini, in Calarco and DeCaroli, eds.,
Giorgio Agamben, 118–119. Negri's attentiveness to the
Spinozistic refrains in Agamben's work is no doubt due to
his own interest in Spinoza's unity of metaphysics and
politics. Cf. Antonio Negri, *The Savage Anomaly: The
Power of Spinoza's Metaphysics and Politics* (trans. Michael
Hardt, Minneapolis, MN: University of Minnesota Press,
1991). On Agamben's relation to Negri's work in general,
see Cesare Casarino, "Time Matters: Marx, Negri,
Agamben, and the Corporeal," *Strategies* 16: 2 (2003),
185–206.

4. Negri, "Giorgio Agamben," 119.

5. Negri, "Giorgio Agamben," 119. Negri's emphasis upon
Agamben's attempt to complete an "immanent theology"
would seem in many ways to give answer to those Marxist
positions which have already noted the affinity between
the Marxist subject and the Christian one without, however, being able to yet ascertain whether or not a genuinely Christian ontological position can provide a
socio-political model of liberation. Cf. Kenneth Surin,
Freedom Not Yet: Liberation and the Next World Order
(Durham, NC: Duke University Press, 2009).

6. Peter Hallward, for one, discerns a distinction between
Agamben and Deleuze in terms of their regard for the
creaturely aspects of being, with Agamben striving to
preserve its core and with Deleuze opting instead to
"evacuate the creatural so as to renew the creating that
sustains it." Peter Hallward, *Out of This World: Deleuze
and the Philosophy of Creation* (London: Verso, 2006), 160.
It remains to be seen, however, whether or not Agamben's
notion of potentiality, which Hallward does cite in this
regard, would not be capable of presenting a notion

similar to Deleuze's of a creative desire at the heart of our creaturely being. For another sustained critique of Agamben's appropriation of Deleuze's form of immanence, see Erinn Cunniff Gilson, "Zones of Indiscernability: The Life of a Concept from Deleuze to Agamben," *Philosophy Today* 51 (2007), 98–106.

7. Gilles Deleuze, *Expressionism in Philosophy: Spinoza* (trans. Martin Joughin, New York: Zone, 1990), 57. The lasting impact of Spinoza's thought in Deleuze's formulation of a "univocity of being" can be seen in the last pages of his *Difference and Repetition* (trans. Paul Patton, New York: Columbia University Press, 1994) where he once again presents a Spinozistic affirmation of life in univocal being. See *Difference and Repetition*, 303–304.

8. Cf. Baruch Spinoza, *Ethics, Treatise on the Emendation of the Intellect, Selected Letters* (trans. Samuel Shirley, Cambridge: Hackett, 1992). On the philosophical legacy of the contrast between representation and presentation, see Alison Ross's astute observations in her *The Aesthetic Paths of Philosophy: Presentation in Kant, Heidegger, Lacoue-Labarthe, and Nancy* (Stanford: Stanford University Press, 2007).

9. The difficulty of affixing to Agamben's thought the understanding of God's relationship to nature is as complex as it was for Spinoza to whom many of Agamben's formulations on this count are indeed indebted. Attempts to label Spinoza's immanent philosophy either as pantheistic, that is, espousing a belief that God and nature are equivalent, or as pan*en*theistic, that is, the belief that God is *in* everything yet distinct from it, have been made throughout history, though both are not entirely adequate in their ability to comprehend his metaphysical system. Such caution, then, in labeling Agamben's thought likewise would no doubt be appropriate here, though an affinity with both positions can certainly be detected in his writing. See Sherry Deveaux, *The Role of God in Spinoza's Metaphysics* (London: Continuum, 2007), as well

as Richard Mason, *The God of Spinoza: A Philosophical Study* (Cambridge: Cambridge University Press, 1997).

10. Deleuze, *Expressionism in Philosophy*, 60ff. Gilles Deleuze, "Immanence: A Life" in David Lapoujade, ed., *Two Regimes of Madness: Texts and Interviews 1975–1995* (trans. Ames Hodges and Mike Taormina, New York: Semiotext(e), 2006). See also, in this regard, Alain Badiou, *Deleuze: The Clamor of Being* (trans. Louise Burchill, Minneapolis, MN: University of Minnesota Press, 1999).

11. Deleuze, *Expressionism in Philosophy*, 314–315.

12. On Deleuze's contestations with the realm of representation, see, among others, Dorothea Olkowski, *Gilles Deleuze and the Ruin of Representation* (Berkeley, CA: University of California Press, 1999).

13. Deleuze, *Expressionism in Philosophy*, 320.

14. Cf. Deleuze, *Expressionism in Philosophy*.

15. Cf. Deleuze, "Immanence: A Life," 387.

16. Julie R. Klein, "Nature's Metabolism: On Eating in Derrida, Agamben, and Spinoza," *Research in Phenomenology* 33 (2003), 186–217, 213. It is noteworthy that Klein's reading of Agamben on Spinoza does not take into account his comments on Spinoza precisely in relation to the materiality (and, ultimately, divinity) of the world in *The Coming Community*, which I attempt to highlight in what follows. In regard to Agamben's reading of Spinoza, see also Dimitris Vardoulakis, "The Ends of Stasis: Spinoza as a Reader of Agamben," *Culture, Theory and Critique* 51: 2 (2010), 145–156.

17. Antonio Negri, "Sovereignty: That Divine Ministry of the Affairs of Earthly Life," *Journal for Cultural and Religious Theory* 9: 1 (Winter 2008), 96–100.

18. Cf. the reading of Deleuze offered, for example, by Éric Alliez, *The Signature of the World: What is Deleuze and Guattari's Philosophy?* (trans. Eliot Ross Albert and Alberto Toscano, London: Continuum, 2004).

19. The label of "re-enchantment" is given to Agamben's work by Dominick LaCapra, for example, who, for his part, appears to misperceive Agamben's explicit intention of "going beyond" the political, which would otherwise seem to counter any forays into dangerous, utopian political movements. Yet, exactly how this form of living without politics is achievable, practically speaking, however, remains to be seen. In this sense, his calls for a "coming community" do seem to mirror those Christian calls to bring the "Kingdom of God" to our world, and perhaps then illuminate the very problematic borders of what (de/re)enchantment would entail in the first place. Cf. Dominick LaCapra, *History and Its Limits: Human, Animal, Violence* (Ithaca, NY: Cornell University Press, 2009), 162ff. See, as well, LaCapra's critical article on Agamben's work titled "Approaching Limit Events: Siting Agamben" in Calarco and DeCaroli, eds., *Giorgio Agamben*, 126–162. On Agamben's possible "utopian" ideals, see Durantaye, *Giorgio Agamben*, 351.

20. Cf. the manner in which a Platonic philosophy can be read as a panentheistic "process" philosophy in Daniel A. Dombrowski, *A Platonic Philosophy of Religion: A Process Perspective* (Albany, NY: State University of New York, 2005). Not only would such a perspective on Plato, as Dombrowski presents him, be applicable to Agamben's work through its presentation of "the thing itself," but also as a general process philosophical outlook could mutually inform Agamben's conceptualization of "potentiality." For other contemporary explorations of panentheism, see especially Catherine Keller, *On the Mystery: Discerning Divinity in Process* (Minneapolis, MN: Fortress, 2008).

21. Cf. Acts 1.10ff.

Bibliography

Works by Giorgio Agamben

Nudités, trans. Martin Rueff, Paris: Rivages, 2009. Originally published as *Nudità*, Roma: Nottetempo, 2009.

Le sacrement du langage. Archéologie du serment. Homo sacer II, 3, trans. Joël Gayraud, Paris: Vrin, 2009. Originally published as *Il sacramento del linguaggio. Archeologia del giuramento, Homo sacer II, 3*, Roma: Laterza, 2008.

The Signature of All Things: On Method, trans. Luca D'Isanto with Kevin Attell, New York: Zone, 2009. Originally published as *Signatura rerum. Sul metodo*, Torino: Bollati Boringhieri, 2008.

What is an Apparatus? and Other Essays, trans. David Kishik and Stefan Pedatella, Stanford: Stanford University Press, 2009. Originally published as *Che cos'è un dispositivo?*, Roma: Nottetempo, 2006; *L'amico*, Roma: Nottetempo, 2007; *Che cos'è il contemporaneo?*, Roma: Nottetempo, 2008.

Le Règne et la gloire. Pour une généalogie théologique de l'économie et du gouvernement. Homo Sacer II, 2, trans. Joël Gayraud and Martin Rueff, Paris: Seuil, 2008. Originally published as *Il regno e la gloria. Per una genealogia teologica dell'economia e del governo. Homo sacer II, 2*, Milano: Neri Pozza, 2007.

Ninfe, Torino: Bollati Boringhieri, 2007.

Profanations, trans. Jeff Fort, New York: Zone, 2007. Originally published as *Profanazioni*, Roma: Nottetempo, 2005.

State of Exception, Homo sacer II, 1, trans. Kevin Attell, Chicago: University of Chicago Press, 2005. Originally published as *Stato di Eccezione. Homo sacer, II, 1*, Torino: Bollati Boringhieri, 2003.

The Time That Remains: A Commentary on the Letter to the Romans, trans. Patricia Dailey, Stanford: Stanford University Press, 2005. Originally published as *Il tempo che resta. Un commento alla Lettera ai Romani*, Torino: Bollati Boringhieri, 2000.

The Open: Man and Animal, trans. Kevin Attell, Stanford: Stanford University Press, 2004. Originally published as *L'aperto. L'uomo e l'animale*, Torino: Bollati Boringhieri, 2002.

Remnants of Auschwitz: The Witness and the Archive, Homo sacer III, trans. Daniel Heller-Roazen, New York: Zone, 2002. Originally published as *Quel che resta di Auschwitz. L'archivio e il testimone. Homo sacer III*, Torino: Bollati Boringhieri, 1998.

Means without Ends: Notes on Politics, trans. Vincenzo Binetti and Cesare Casarino, Minneapolis, MN: University of Minnesota Press, 2000. Originally published as *Mezzi senza fine. Note sulla politica*, Torino: Bollati Boringhieri, 1996.

Potentialities: Collected Essays in Philosophy, trans. Daniel Heller-Roazen, Stanford: Stanford University Press, 2000. Originally published as *La potenza del pensiero: Saggi e conferenza*, Milano: Neri Pozza, 2005.

The End of the Poem: Studies in Poetics, trans. Daniel Heller-Roazen, Stanford: Stanford University Press, 1999. Originally published as *Categorie italiane. Studi di poetica*, Venezia: Marsilio, 1996.

The Man without Content, trans. Georgia Albert, Stanford: Stanford University Press, 1999. Originally published as *L'uomo senza contenuto*, Milano: Rizzoli, 1970.

Homo Sacer: Sovereign Power and Bare Life, trans. Daniel Heller-Roazen, Stanford: Stanford University Press, 1998. Originally published as *Homo Sacer: Il potere soverano e la vita nuda*, Torino: Einaudi, 1995.

The Idea of Prose, trans. Michael Sullivan and Sam Whitsitt, Albany, NY: State University of New York Press, 1995. Originally published as *Idea della prosa*, Milano: Giangiacomo Feltrinelli, 1985.

Bartleby, la formula della creazione (con Gilles Deleuze), Macerata: Quodlibet, 1993.

The Coming Community, trans. Michael Hardt, Minneapolis, MN: University of Minnesota Press, 1993. Originally published as *La comunità che viene*, Torino: Bollati Boringhieri, 1990.

Infancy and History: On the Destruction of Experience, trans. Liz Heron, London: Verso, 1993. Originally published as *Infanzia e storia: Distruzione dell'esperienza e origine della storia*, Torino: Einaudi, 1978.

Stanzas: Word and Phantasm in Western Culture, trans. Ronald L. Martinez, Minneapolis, MN: University of Minnesota Press, 1993. Originally published as *Stanze. La parola e il fantasma nella cultura occidentale*, Torino: Einaudi, 1977.

Language and Death: The Place of Negativity, trans. Karen E. Pinkus and Michael Hardt, Minneapolis, MN: University of Minnesota Press, 1991. Originally published as *Il linguaggio e la morte: Un seminario sul luogo della negatività*, Torino: Einaudi, 1982.

Selected Secondary Literature

Adler, Anthony Curtis, "The Intermedial Gesture: Agamben and Kommerell," *Angelaki* 12: 3 (2007), 57–64.

Agamben, Giorgio and Valeria Piazza, [untitled article], trans. Luciana Bellini, *parallax* 9: 3 (2003), 2–4.

Alliez, Éric, *The Signature of the World: What is Deleuze and Guattari's Philosophy?*, trans. Eliot Ross Albert and Alberto Toscano, London: Continuum, 2004.

Althusser, Louis, "Ideology and Ideological State Apparatuses (Notes towards an Investigation)" in Slavoj Žižek, ed., *Mapping Ideology*, London: Verso, 1995.

Anidjar, Gil, *The Jew, the Arab: A History of the Enemy*, Stanford: Stanford University Press, 2003.

Arendt, Hannah, *Eichmann in Jerusalem: A Report on the Banality of Evil*, New York: Penguin, 2006.

Bibliography

Attell, Kevin, "An Esoteric Dossier: Agamben and Derrida Read Saussure," *ELH* 76: 4 (2009), 821–846.

Badiou, Alain, *Deleuze: The Clamor of Being*, trans. Louise Burchill, Minneapolis, MN: University of Minnesota Press, 1999.

—, *Saint Paul: The Foundation of Universalism*, trans. Ray Brassier, Stanford: Stanford University Press, 2003.

—, *Logiques des Mondes: L'Être et l'événement, 2*, Paris, Seuil, 2006.

Barthes, Roland, *Elements of Semiology*, trans. Annette Lavers and Colin Smith, New York: Hill and Wang, 1967.

Bartoloni, Paolo, *Interstitial Writing: Calvino, Caproni, Sereni and Svevo*, Market Harborough: Troubador, 2003.

—, "The Stanza of the Self: On Agamben's Potentiality," *Contretemps* 5 (2004), 8–15.

—, *On the Cultures of Exile, Translation, and Writing*, West Lafayette, IN: Purdue University Press, 2008.

Beckett, Samuel, "The Capital of the Ruins," *As the Story was Told: Uncollected and Late Prose*, London: John Calder, 1990.

Benjamin, Walter, "On Language as Such and on the Language of Man" in Marcus Bullock and Michael W. Jennings, eds., *Selected Writings*, vol. 1, trans. Edmund Jephcott et al., Cambridge, MA: Harvard University Press, 1996.

—, *The Arcades Project*, trans. Howard Eiland and Kevin McLaughlin, Cambridge, MA: Belknap, 1999.

—, "On the Concept of History" in Howard Eiland and Michael W. Jennings, eds., *Selected Writings*, vol. 4, trans. Edmund Jephcott et al., Cambridge, MA: Belknap, 2003.

Bernstein, J. M., "Intact and Fragmented Bodies: Versions of Ethics 'after Auschwitz,'" *New German Critique* 33: 1 (2006), 31–52.

Bertozzi, Alberto, "Thoughts in Potentiality: Provisional Reflections on Agamben's Understanding of Potentiality and Its Relevance for Theology and Politics," *Philosophy Today* 51: 3 (2007), 290–302.

Bibliography

Beverungen, Armin and Stephen Dunne, "'I'd Prefer Not To': Bartleby and the Excesses of Interpretation," *Culture and Organization* 13: 2 (2007), 171–183.

Bhabha, Homi K., *The Location of Culture*, London: Routledge, 1994.

Blanton, Ward, "Disturbing Politics: Neo-Paulinism and the Scrambling of Religious and Secular Identities," *Dialog: A Journal of Theology* 46: 1 (2007), 3–13.

Blond, Philip, ed., *Post-Secular Philosophy: Between Philosophy and Theology*, London: Routledge, 1998.

Borislavov, Rad, "Agamben, Ontology, and Constituent Power," *Debatte* 13: 2 (2005), 173–184.

Borsò, Vittoria, Claas Morgenroth, Karl Solibakke, and Bernd Witte, eds., *Benjamin–Agamben: Politics, Messianism, Kabbalah*, Würzburg: Königshausen and Neumann, 2010.

Bretherton, Luke, "The Duty of Care to Refugees, Christian Cosmopolitanism, and the Hallowing of Bare Life," *Studies in Christian Ethics* 19: 1 (2006), 39–61.

Burchell, Graham, Colin Gordon, and Peter Miller, eds., *The Foucault Effect: Studies in Governmentality*, Chicago: University of Chicago Press, 1991.

Butler, Judith, *Bodies That Matter: On the Discursive Limits of "Sex,"* London: Routledge, 1993.

—, *Precarious Life: The Powers of Mourning and Violence*, London: Verso, 2004.

—, *Undoing Gender*, London: Routledge, 2004.

—, "Afterward" in Ellen T. Armour and Susan M. St. Ville, eds., *Bodily Citations: Religion and Judith Butler*, New York: Columbia University Press, 2006.

Butler, Judith and Gayatri Chakravorty Spivak, *Who Sings the Nation-State?*, Oxford: Seagull, 2007.

Calarco, Matthew and Steven DeCaroli, eds., *Giorgio Agamben: Sovereignty & Life*, Stanford: Stanford University Press, 2007.

Calvino, Italo, *If on a Winter's Night a Traveler*, trans. William Weaver, New York: Harvest, 1981.

Caproni, Giorgio, *The Wall of the Earth*, trans. Pasquale Verdicchio, Montreal: Guernica, 1992.

—, *The Earth's Wall: Selected Poems 1932–1986*, trans. Ned Condini, New York: Chelsea, 2004.

Caputo, John D., *The Weakness of God: A Theology of the Event*, Bloomington, IN: Indiana University Press, 2006.

Caputo, John D., and Linda Martín Alcoff, eds., *St. Paul among the Philosophers*, Bloomington, IN: Indiana University Press, 2009.

Casarino, Cesare, "Time Matters: Marx, Negri, Agamben, and the Corporeal," *Strategies* 16: 2 (2003), 185–206.

Celan, Paul, *Selected Poems and Prose of Paul Celan*, trans. John Felstiner, New York: W. W. Norton, 2001.

Chare, Nicholas, "The Gap in Context: Giorgio Agamben's *Remnants of Auschwitz*," *Cultural Critique* 64 (2006), 40–68.

Chiesa, Lorenzo, "Giorgio Agamben's Franciscan Ontology" in Lorenzo Chiesa and Alberto Toscano, eds., *The Italian Difference: Between Nihilism and Biopolitics*, Melbourne: re.press, 2009.

Chow, Rey, "Sacrifice, Mimesis, and the Theorizing of Victimhood," *Representations* 94 (2006), 131–149.

Cisney, Vernon, "Categories of Life: The Status of the Camp in Derrida and Agamben," *The Southern Journal of Philosophy* 46 (2008), 161–179.

Clemens, Justin, "The Abandonment of Sex: Giorgio Agamben, Psychoanalysis and Melancholia," *Theory and Event* 13: 1 (2010).

Clemens, Justin, Nicholas Heron, and Alex Murry, eds., *The Work of Giorgio Agamben: Law, Literature, Life*, Edinburgh: Edinburgh University Press, 2008.

Colebrook, Claire, "Agamben: Aesthetics, Potentiality, and Life," *South Atlantic Quarterly* 107: 1 (2008), 107–120.

Colilli, Paul, "The Theological Materials of Modernity (On Giorgio Agamben)," *Italica* 85: 4 (2008), 465–479.

Cooke, Alexander, "Resistance, Potentiality and the Law," *Angelaki* 10: 3 (2005), 79–89.

Critchley, Simon, *Things Merely Are: Philosophy in the Poetry of Wallace Stevens*, London: Routledge, 2005.

Cunningham, Conor, *Genealogy of Nihilism: Philosophies of Nothing and the Difference of Theology*, London: Routledge, 2002.

Daly, Mary, *Beyond God the Father: Toward a Philosophy of Women's Liberation*, Boston: Beacon, 1973.

Davis, Creston, John Milbank, and Slavoj Žižek, eds., *Theology and the Political: The New Debate*, Durham, NC: Duke University Press, 2005.

Dean, Mitchell, "Four Theses on the Powers of Life and Death," *Contretemps* 5 (2004), 16–29.

Debord, Guy, *The Society of the Spectacle*, trans. Donald Nicholson-Smith, New York: Zone, 1995.

Deleuze, Gilles, *Expressionism in Philosophy: Spinoza*, trans. Martin Joughin, New York: Zone, 1990.

—, *Difference and Repetition*, trans. Paul Patton, New York: Columbia University Press, 1994.

—, "Immanence: A Life" in David Lapoujade, ed., *Two Regimes of Madness: Texts and Interviews 1975–1995*, trans. Ames Hodges and Mike Taormina, New York: Semiotext(e), 2006.

Depoortere, Frederiek, *Christ and Postmodern Philosophy: Gianni Vattimo, René Girard, and Slavoj Žižek*, London: T&T Clark, 2008.

—, *The Death of God: An Investigation into the History of the Western Concept of God*, London: T&T Clark, 2008.

Deranty, Jean-Philippe, "Witnessing the Inhuman: Agamben or Merleau-Ponty," *South Atlantic Quarterly* 107: 1 (2008), 165–186.

Derrida, Jacques, *Writing and Difference*, trans. Alan Bass, London: Routledge, 1978.

—, "Signature Event Context" in *Margins of Philosophy*, trans. Alan Bass, Chicago: University of Chicago Press, 1982.

—, *Specters of Marx: The State of the Debt, the Work of Mourning and the New International*, trans. Peggy Kamuf, London: Routledge, 1994.

—, *Sovereignties in Question: The Poetics of Paul Celan*, ed. Thomas Dutoit and Outi Pasanen, New York: Fordham University Press, 2005.

—, *The Beast and the Sovereign, vol. 1*, ed. Michel Lisse, Marie-Louise Mallet, and Ginette Michaud, trans. Geoffrey Bennington, Chicago: University of Chicago Press, 2009.

Deveaux, Sherry, *The Role of God in Spinoza's Metaphysics*, London: Continuum, 2007.

Dickinson, Colby, "Canon as an Act of Creation: Giorgio Agamben and the Extended Logic of the Messianic," *Bijdragen: International Journal in Philosophy and Theology* 71: 2 (2010), 132–158.

Dillon, Michael and Luis Lobo-Guerrero, "The Biopolitical Imaginary of Species-Being," *Theory, Culture and Society* 26: 1 (2009), 1–23.

Dombrowski, Daniel A., *A Platonic Philosophy of Religion: A Process Perspective*, Albany, NY: State University of New York, 2005.

Downey, Andrew, "Zones of Indistinction: Giorgio Agamben's 'Bare Life' and the Politics of Aesthetics," *Third Text* 23: 2 (2009), 109–125.

Durantaye, Leland de la, "*Homo profanes*: Giorgio Agamben's Profane Philosophy," *Boundary 2* 25: 3 (2008), 27–62.

—, *Giorgio Agamben: A Critical Introduction*, Stanford: Stanford University Press, 2009.

Düttmann, Alexander García, "Never Before, Always Already: Notes on Agamben and the Category of Relation," *Angelaki* 6: 3 (2001), 3–6.

Eaglestone, Robert, "On Giorgio Agamben's Holocaust," *Paragraph* 25 (2002), 52–67.

Eco, Umberto, *Semiotics and the Philosophy of Language*, Bloomington, IN: Indiana University Press, 1986.

Eliade, Mircea, *The Sacred and the Profane: The Nature of Religion*, trans. Willard R. Trask, New York: Harcourt-Brace Jovanovich, 1987.

Bibliography

Enns, Diane, "Political Life before Identity," *Theory and Event* 10: 1 (2007).

Esposito, Roberto, *Bíos: Biopolitics and Philosophy*, trans. Timothy Campbell, Minneapolis, MN: University of Minnesota Press, 2008.

Foucault, Michel, *The Order of Things: An Archaeology of the Human Sciences*, New York: Vintage, 1970.

—, *The Archaeology of Knowledge*, trans. A. M. Sheridan Smith, London: Routledge, 1972.

—, *Discipline and Punish: The Birth of the Prison*, trans. Alan Sheridan, New York: Vintage, 1977.

—, "Nietzsche, Genealogy, History" in Paul Rabinow, ed., *The Foucault Reader*, New York: Pantheon, 1984.

—, *Security, Territory, Population: Lectures at the College de France 1977–1978*, ed. Michel Senellart, trans. Graham Burchell, New York: Palgrave Macmillan, 2007.

—, *The Birth of Biopolitics: Lectures at the College De France, 1978–1979*, trans. Graham Burchell, New York: Palgrave Macmillan, 2010.

Fox, Christopher A., "Sacrificial Pasts and Messianic Futures: Religion as a Political Prospect in René Girard and Giorgio Agamben," *Philosophy and Social Criticism* 33: 5 (2007), 563–595.

Franchi, Stefano, "Of the Synthetic and the Analytic," *Contretemps* 5 (2004), 30–41.

Freud, Sigmund, *The Interpretation of Dreams: The Complete and Definitive Text*, trans. James Strachey, New York: Basic, 1955.

Fritsch, Matthias, *The Promise of Memory: History and Politics in Marx, Benjamin, and Derrida*, Albany, NY: State University of New York Press, 2005.

Gaston, Sean, *Derrida, Literature and War: Absence and the Chance of Meeting*, London: Continuum, 2009.

Gillespie, Michael Allen, *Nihilism before Nietzsche*, Chicago: Chicago University Press, 1995.

Gilson, Erinn Cunniff, "Zones of Indiscernability: The Life of a Concept from Deleuze to Agamben," *Philosophy Today* 51 (2007), 98–106.

Girard, René, *Things Hidden Since the Foundation of the World*, trans. Stephen Bann and Michael Metteer, Stanford: Stanford University Press, 1987.

—, *The Scapegoat*, trans. Yvonne Freccero, Baltimore, MD: Johns Hopkins University Press, 1989.

Gregory, Derek, "The Black Flag: Guantánamo Bay and the Space of Exception," *Geogr. Ann.* 88B: 4 (2006), 405–427.

Grimshaw, Mike, "Ruptured Romans: A Theological Meditation on Paul, Cultural Theory, and the Cosmopolitan Rupture of Grace," *Stimulus* 17: 2 (2009), 32–40.

Hallward, Peter, *Out of This World: Deleuze and the Philosophy of Creation*, London: Verso, 2006.

Handelmann, Susan A., *Fragments of Redemption: Jewish Thought and Literary Theory in Benjamin, Scholem, and Levinas*, Bloomington, IN: Indiana University Press, 1991.

Hawkes, Terence, *Structuralism and Semiotics*, London: Routledge, 2003.

Heidegger, Martin, "The Origin of the Work of Art," *Poetry, Language, Thought*, trans. Albert Hofstadter, New York: Harper, 1971.

—, *Nietzsche: Vol. IV: Nihilism*, ed. David Farell Krell, trans. Frank A. Capuzzi, 4 vols., San Francisco: HarperSanFrancisco, 1982.

—, *Being and Time*, trans. Joan Stambaugh, Albany, NY: State University of New York, 1996.

Jacobson, Eric, *Metaphysics of the Profane: The Political Theology of Walter Benjamin and Gershom Scholem*, New York: Columbia University Press, 2003.

Jantzen, Grace, *Becoming Divine: Towards a Feminist Philosophy of Religion*, Bloomington, IN: Indiana University Press, 1998.

Johnson, David E., "*As If* the Time Were Now: Deconstructing Agamben," *South Atlantic Quarterly* 106: 2 (2007), 265–290.

Johnston, Adrian, *Badiou, Žižek, and Political Transformations: The Cadence of Change*, Evanston, IL: Northwestern University Press, 2009.

Jones, Emma R., "In the Presence of the Living Cockroach: The Moment of Aliveness and the Gendered Body in Agamben and Lispector," *PhaenEx* 2: 2 (2007), 24–41.

Kaufman, Eleanor, "The Saturday of Messianic Time (Agamben and Badiou on the Apostle Paul)," *South Atlantic Quarterly* 107: 1 (2008), 37–54.

Keller, Catherine, *On the Mystery: Discerning Divinity in Process*, Minneapolis, MN: Fortress, 2008.

Kirwin, Michael, *Political Theology: An Introduction*, Minneapolis, MN: Fortress, 2009.

Kisner, Wendell, "Agamben, Hegel, and the State of Exception," *Cosmos and History* 3: 2–3 (2007), 222–253.

Klein, Julie R., "Nature's Metabolism: On Eating in Derrida, Agamben, and Spinoza," *Research in Phenomenology* 33 (2003), 186–217.

Kotsko, Adam, "On Agamben's Use of Benjamin's 'Critique of Violence,'" *Telos* 145 (2008), 119–129.

Lacan, Jacques, *The Seminar of Jacques Lacan: The Psychoses 1955–1956*, vol. 3, trans. Jacques-Alain Miller and Russell Grigg, New York: W. W. Norton, 1997.

LaCapra, Dominick, *History and Its Limits: Human, Animal, Violence*, Ithaca, NY: Cornell University Press, 2009.

Lagaay, Alice and Juliane Schiffers, "Passivity at Work. A Conversation on an Element in the Philosophy of Giorgio Agamben," *Law Critique* 20 (2009), 325–337.

Levinas, Emmanuel, *Totality and Infinity: An Essay on Exteriority*, trans. Alphonso Lingis, Pittsburgh, PA: Duquesne University Press, 1969.

Leys, Ruth, *From Guilt to Shame: Auschwitz and After*, Princeton: Princeton University Press, 2007.

Librett, Jeffrey S., "From the Sacrifice of the Letter to the Voice of Testimony: Giorgio Agamben's Fulfillment of Metaphysics," *Diacritics* 37: 2–3 (2007), 11–33.

Llewelyn, John, "Approaches to (Quasi)Theology via Appresentation," *Research in Phenomenology* 39 (2009), 224–247.

Mason, Richard, *The God of Spinoza: A Philosophical Study*, Cambridge: Cambridge University Press, 1997.

Mazower, Mark, "Foucault, Agamben: Theory and the Nazis," *Boundary 2* 35: 1 (2008), 23–34.

Melandri, Enzo, *La linea e il circolo: Studio logico-filosofico sull'analogia*, Macerata: Quodlibet, 2004.

Mesnard, Philippe, "The Political Philosophy of Giorgio Agamben: A Critical Evaluation," trans. Cyrille Guiat, *Totalitarian Movements and Political Religions* 5: 1 (2004), 139–157.

Mesnard, Philippe and Claudine Kahan, *Giorgio Agamben: à l'épreuve d'Auschwitz: témoignages/interpretations*, Paris: Kimé, 2001.

Meyere, Job de, "The Care for the Present: Giorgio Agamben's Actualization of the Pauline Messianic Experience," *Bijdragen: International Journal in Philosophy and Theology* 70 (2009), 168–184.

Milbank, John, Catherine Pickstock, and Graham Ward, eds., *Radical Orthodoxy: A New Theology*, London: Routledge, 1998.

Mills, Catherine, "Agamben's Messianic Politics: Biopolitics, Abandonment and Happy Life," *Contretemps* 5 (2004), 42–62.

—, *The Philosophy of Agamben*, Stocksfield: Acumen, 2008.

—, "Playing with Law: Agamben and Derrida on Postjuridical Justice," *South Atlantic Quarterly* 107: 1 (2008), 17–35.

Minca, Claudio, "Giorgio Agamben and the New Biopolitical Nomos," *Geogr. Ann.* 88B: 4 (2006), 387–403.

Monroe, Jonathan, "Philosophy, Poetry, Parataxis," *The European Legacy* 14: 5 (2009), 599–611.

Moore, Isabel A., "'Speak, You Also': Encircling Trauma," *Journal for Cultural Research* 9: 1 (2005), 87–99.

Morgan, Alastair, "'A Figure of Annihilated Human Existence': Agamben and Adorno on Gesture," *Law Critique* 20 (2009), 299–307.

Morgan, Benjamin, "Undoing Legal Violence: Walter Benjamin's and Giorgio Agamben's Aesthetics of Pure Means," *Journal of Law and Society* 34: 1 (2007), 46–64.

Murray, Alex, *Giorgio Agamben*, London: Routledge, 2010.

Negri, Antonio, *The Savage Anomaly: The Power of Spinoza's Metaphysics and Politics*, trans. Michael Hardt, Minneapolis, MN: University of Minnesota Press, 1991.

—, *Insurgencies: Constituent Power and the Modern State*, trans. Maurizia Boscagli, Minneapolis, MN: University of Minnesota Press, 1999.

—, "Sovereignty: That Divine Ministry of the Affairs of Earthly Life," *Journal for Cultural and Religious Theory* 9: 1 (Winter 2008), 96–100.

Nietzsche, Friedrich, *The Gay Science*, ed. Bernard Williams, Cambridge: Cambridge University Press, 2001.

Norris, Andrew, ed., *Politics, Metaphysics, and Death: Essays on Giorgio Agamben's* Homo Sacer, Durham, NC: Duke University Press, 2005.

O'Connor, Patrick, "Redemptive Remnants: Agamben's Human Messianism," *Journal for Cultural Research* 13: 3–4 (2009), 335–352.

Olkowski, Dorothea, *Gilles Deleuze and the Ruin of Representation*, Berkeley, CA: University of California Press, 1999.

Owens, Patricia, "Reclaiming 'Bare Life'?: Against Agamben on Refugees," *International Relations* 23: 4 (2009), 567–582.

Palladino, Paolo, "Picturing the Messianic: Agamben and Titian's *The Nymph and the Shepherd*," *Theory, Culture and Society* 27 (2010), 94–109.

Pan, David, "Against Biopolitics: Walter Benjamin, Carl Schmitt, and Giorgio Agamben on Political Sovereignty and Symbolic Order," *The German Quarterly* 82: 1 (2009), 42–62.

Parfitt, Trevor, "Are the Third World Poor *Homines Sacri?* Biopolitics, Sovereignty, and Development," *Alternatives* 34 (2009), 41–58.

Passavant, Paul A., "The Contradictory State of Giorgio Agamben," *Political Theory* 35: 2 (2007), 147–174.

Presutti, Fabio, "Manlio Sgalambro, Giorgio Agamben: On Metaphysical Suspension of Language and the Destiny of Its Inorganic Re-Absorption," *Italica* 85: 2–3 (2008), 243–272.

Raulff, Ulrich, "An Interview with Giorgio Agamben," *German Law Journal* 5: 5 (2004), 609–613.

Reginster, Bernard, *The Affirmation of Life: Nietzsche on Overcoming Nihilism*, Cambridge, MA: Harvard University Press, 2009.

Rifkin, Mark, "Indigenizing Agamben: Rethinking Sovereignty in Light of the 'Peculiar' Status of Native Peoples," *Cultural Critique* 73 (2009), 88–124.

Roberts, John, "The 'Returns to Religion': Messianism, Christianity and the Revolutionary Tradition. Part II: The Pauline Tradition," *Historical Materialism* 16 (2008), 77–103.

Ross, Alison, *The Aesthetic Paths of Philosophy: Presentation in Kant, Heidegger, Lacoue-Labarthe, and Nancy*, Stanford: Stanford University Press, 2007.

Santner, Eric L., *On Creaturely Life: Rilke, Benjamin, Sebald*, Chicago: University of Chicago Press, 2006.

Saussure, Ferdinand de, *Writings in General Linguistics*, ed. Simon Bouquet and Rudolf Engler, New York: Oxford University Press, 2006.

Schijvers, Joeri, "On Doing Theology 'After' Ontotheology: Notes on a French Debate," *New Blackfriars* 87 (2006), 302–314.

Schmitt, Carl, *The Concept of the Political*, trans. George Schwab, Chicago: University of Chicago Press, 1996.

—, *Political Theology: Four Chapters on the Concept of Sovereignty*, trans. George Schwab, Chicago: University of Chicago Press, 2005.

—, *Political Theology II: The Myth of the Closure of Any Political Theology*, trans. Michael Hoelzl and Graham Ward, Cambridge: Polity, 2008.

Scott, Peter and William T. Cavanaugh, eds., *The Blackwell Companion to Political Theology*, Oxford: Wiley-Blackwell, 2006.

Spinoza, Baruch, *Ethics, Treatise on the Emendation of the Intellect, Selected Letters*, trans. Samuel Shirley, Cambridge: Hackett, 1992.

Surin, Kenneth, *Freedom Not Yet: Liberation and the Next World Order*, Durham, NC: Duke University Press, 2009.

Svenungsson, Jayne, "Wrestling with Angels: Or How to Avoid Decisionist Messianic Romances," *International Journal of Žižek Studies* 4: 4 (2010).

Taubes, Jacob, *The Political Theology of Paul*, trans. Dana Hollander, Stanford: Stanford University Press, 2003.

Thatamanil, John J., *The Immanent Divine: God, Creation and the Human Predicament*, Minneapolis, MN: Fortress Press, 2006.

Thomson, Iain, *Heidegger on Ontotheology: Technology and the Politics of Education*, Cambridge: Cambridge University Press, 2005.

Vardoulakis, Dimitris, "The Ends of Stasis: Spinoza as a Reader of Agamben," *Culture, Theory and Critique* 51: 2 (2010), 145–156.

Vatter, Miguel, "In Odradek's World: Bare Life and Historical Materialism in Agamben and Benjamin," *Diacritics* 38: 3 (2008), 45–70.

Vattimo, Gianni, *After Christianity*, trans. Luca D'Isanto, New York: Columbia University Press, 2002.

Vries, Hent de, *Religion and Violence: Philosophical Perspectives from Kant to Derrida*, Baltimore, MD: Johns Hopkins University Press, 2002.

—, ed., *Political Theologies: Public Religions in a Post-Secular World*, New York: Fordham University Press, 2006.

Wall, Thomas Carl, *Radical Passivity: Levinas, Blanchot and Agamben*, Albany, NY: State University of New York, 1999.

Watkin, William, *The Literary Agamben: Adventures in Logopoiesis*, London: Continuum, 2010.

Weber, Samuel, "Going Along for the Ride: Violence and Gesture: Agamben Reading Benjamin Reading Kafka Reading Cervantes," *The Germanic Review* 81: 1 (2006), 65–83.

Welch, Sharon D., *A Feminist Ethic of Risk*, Minneapolis, MN: Fortress, 2000.

Wetters, Kirk, "The Rule of the Norm and the Political Theology of 'Real Life' in Carl Schmitt and Giorgio Agamben," *Diacritics* 36: 1 (2006), 31–46.

Whyte, Jessica, "'A New Use of the Self': Giorgio Agamben on the Coming Community," *Theory and Event* 13: 1 (2010).

Witte, John, Jr., and Frank S. Alexander, *Christianity and Law: An Introduction*, Cambridge: Cambridge University Press, 2008.

Wortham, Simon Morgan, "Law of Friendship: Agamben and Derrida," *New Formations* 62 (2007), 89–105.

Zartaloudis, Thanos, *Giorgio Agamben: Power, Law and the Uses of Criticism*, London: Routledge, 2010.

Ziarek, Ewa Płonowska, "Bare Life on Strike: Notes on the Biopolitics of Race and Gender," *South Atlantic Quarterly* 107: 1 (2008), 89–105.

—, "Feminine 'I can': On Possibility and Praxis in Agamben's Work," *Theory and Event* 13: 1 (2010).

Ziarek, Krzysztof, "After Humanism: Agamben and Heidegger," *South Atlantic Quarterly* 107: 1 (2008), 187–209.

Žižek, Slavoj, *Did Somebody Say Totalitarianism? Five Interventions in the (Mis)use of a Notion*, London: Verso, 2001.

—, *The Puppet and the Dwarf: The Perverse Core of Christianity*, Cambridge, MA: MIT Press, 2003.

—, *In Defense of Lost Causes*, London: Verso, 2009.

Žižek, Slavoj, Eric Santner, and Kenneth Reinhard, *The Neighbor: Three Inquiries in Political Theology*, Chicago: University of Chicago Press, 2005.

Index

absolute 18, 23, 39, 43, 51, 63, 70,
  77, 81, 96, 104, 113, 115,
  124, 127, 133, 134, 155, 158,
  168, 171, 172, 174, 177
actuality 18–19, 40–57, 80, 84,
  92, 97, 104, 157, 191n. 1
Actus Purus 40, 43, 46, 183n. 4
Adler, Anthony Curtis 196n. 7
aesthetics 117, 126, 129, 166
Alcoff, Linda Martín 192n. 4
Alexander, Frank S. 193n. 8
Alliez, Éric 205n. 18
Althusser, Louis 181n. 11
Anidjar, Gil 187n. 21
animality 14, 63–4, 67–8, 72, 74,
  89, 103, 105, 118–21, 141,
  145–6, 148, 150, 177
Anselm, Saint 23
anthropological machinery 14–16,
  33, 38, 62, 65, 69, 77–80, 83,
  89, 114, 118–20, 138, 140,
  151, 154, 172
aporia 7–8, 10, 14–15, 31, 47,
  53–4, 58, 92, 102, 109,
  165, 176
apparatus 14, 18, 62–5, 69, 83,
  105, 136
Aquinas, Thomas 25, 43, 52, 152,
  183n. 4, 202n. 2
Arendt, Hannah 3, 58, 61, 168,
  191n. 10
Aristotle 18, 27, 41–50, 97
art 80, 121–9, 133–4, 162, 199n. 16
atheology 11, 62, 163
Attell, Kevin 180n. 9

axolotl 142–3

Badiou, Alain 192n. 4, 193n. 5,
  195n. 19, 205n. 10
bare life 18, 58–9, 62, 66–76, 80,
  103, 114, 120, 134, 140, 171,
  173, 177, 183n. 1, 187n. 23
Barthes, Roland 180n. 6
Bartleby 3, 43–4, 47, 68, 84,
  183n. 2, 184n. 6
Bartoloni, Paolo 179n. 2
Bataille, Georges 3, 168
Beckett, Samuel 128–9, 199n. 21
Benjamin, Walter 3, 47–8, 84–5,
  86, 89, 92, 95–6, 98–9, 111,
  115–17, 128, 137–8, 140,
  160, 163–4, 168, 180n. 8,
  183n. 1, 184n. 9, 185n. 10,
  189n. 3, 192n. 2–3, 193n. 9,
  194n. 11–14, 196n. 5, 196n.
  7, 198n. 10–11, 199n. 20,
  199n. 22, 200n. 27, 201n. 12
Bernstein, J. M. 190n. 7
Bertozzi, Alberto 183n. 5
Beverungen, Armin 184n. 6
Bhabha, Homi K. 180n. 7
biopolitics 57–8, 104, 131,
  186n. 20, 187n. 22, 188n. 23,
  203n. 3
Blanchot, Maurice 3
Blanton, Ward 192n. 4
Blond, Philip 199n. 23
body, the 58, 72, 79, 80, 82,
  115–16, 132–8, 147, 163,
  167, 170, 174

Index

Index

Index

metaphysics 15–16, 30–2, 37–8,
    43, 47–8, 50, 56, 62, 69, 72,
    76, 79, 96–9, 111, 118, 124,
    133–5, 169, 174, 182n. 22,
    184n. 8, 194n. 14, 203n. 3,
    204n. 9
Meyere, Job de 193n. 4
Milbank, John 186n. 19, 199n. 23
Miller, Peter 188n. 2
Mills, Catherine 178n. 6, 180n. 9,
    190n. 7, 191n. 1, 200n. 5
Minca, Claudio 190n. 8
monotheism 21, 33, 36, 61–2, 92,
    95, 112
Monroe, Jonathan 200n. 25
Moore, Isabel A. 179n. 3
Morante, Elsa 3
Morgan, Alastair 196n. 7
Morgan, Benjamin 137,
    200n. 27
Morgenroth, Claas 194n. 12
Moses 19
Murray, Alex 178n. 6, 181n. 10
Muselmann 70, 73, 190n. 7
mystery 1, 21–2, 29–32, 68, 100,
    102, 114, 118, 140
mystical 41, 44, 48, 120, 150,
    159–60, 197n. 9, 201n. 11

name of God 10, 22, 24, 31,
    37, 176
Nancy, Jean-Luc 3, 168
natural law 50–1, 54
Nazism 51–2, 70, 73, 77
necessity 44, 51, 53–6, 60, 97, 171
Negri, Antonio 185n. 13, 203n.
    3–5, 205n. 17
Nemrod 5–11, 179n. 1
Nicodemus 108, 148
Nietzsche, Friedrich 119, 121,
    125, 146, 198n. 12,
    199n. 18

nihilism 20, 39, 84, 108, 119,
    121–9, 134, 154, 165–6,
    191n. 1, 198n. 12, 202n. 1
Norris, Andrew 178n. 6, 184n. 8
nudity 25, 38, 58, 104, 134, 147,
    154, 160, 170

oath 36–7, 147
O'Connor, Patrick 193n. 4
Olkowski, Dorothea 205n. 12
ontology 15, 23, 31, 46, 48, 59,
    79, 90, 98, 104–5, 121, 128,
    148, 173, 195n. 19, 202n. 1,
    203n. 5
ontotheology 32, 37, 56, 61–3,
    79, 83, 89, 96, 98, 101,
    104–5, 116, 133, 154, 169,
    188n. 3, 198n. 12
Origen 115, 166
original sin 5, 11–21, 25–7, 41,
    145, 148
Owens, Patricia 187n. 23

Palladino, Paolo 193n. 4
Pan, David 199n. 22
pantheism/panentheism 157,
    162–3, 168, 170, 174, 204n. 9
parabasis 32–4
paradigm 52, 58, 99–105, 131,
    151, 158, 173
Parfitt, Trevor 188n. 24
parody 28–34, 182n. 18, 182n. 20
particular 18, 53, 86–8, 95,
    97–104, 109, 147, 154,
    156–8, 172, 194n. 17
Pascolini, Giovanni 3
Passavant, Paul 191n. 1
Patton, Paul 186n. 20
Paul, Saint 21, 24, 40, 44, 48, 84,
    86–97, 127, 136–8,
    154, 156–7, 164, 181n. 18,
    197n. 9

Index

philosophy 8, 37, 39, 41, 66, 115
photography 113–15, 132–3
Piazza, Valeria 183n. 23
Pickstock, Catherine 199n. 23
poetry 6–11, 26–31, 44, 115, 117, 148, 166, 183n. 23, 196n. 9, 200n. 25, 201n. 11
political theology 52, 56, 72, 185n. 16, 185n. 19
politics 15, 17–18, 20, 34, 40, 42, 46–62, 66–80, 84–5, 93–7, 101–5, 107–8, 114–15, 117, 130–2, 145, 147–8, 183n. 5, 184n. 7, 187n. 21, 191n. 1, 199n. 22, 201n. 13, 206n. 19
Pollock, Jackson 122
potentiality 15, 18, 34, 38–59, 68, 71, 80–1, 83–4, 92, 96–7, 103–6, 112, 120–1, 125, 127, 150, 157, 166, 171–2, 177, 183n. 5, 191n. 1, 203n. 6, 206n. 20
power 5, 8, 10, 12, 14, 16–19, 40, 43, 45–56, 61–2, 68, 72, 74, 76, 83, 85, 89, 91, 96, 103–5, 127, 130–1, 136, 158, 161, 163, 169, 186n. 20
presentation 30, 33, 105, 151, 159, 161–2, 170–2, 197n. 9, 204n. 8, 206n. 20
Presutti, Fabio 182n. 22
profanation 8, 17, 21–2, 30, 33–4, 38, 45, 60, 63, 71, 74, 76, 79, 81, 96, 114, 129–41, 149, 152–3, 163, 165, 168–9, 171, 174–5, 188n. 25, 189n. 4, 200n. 24

Radical Orthodoxy 149, 199n. 23
Rasch, William 191n. 1
Raulff, Ulrich 185n. 14, 194n. 16
redemption 112, 115–17, 137–40, 145–6, 150, 153, 168, 197n. 9
Reginster, Bernard 198n. 12
regression 24, 60, 92–3, 105, 107–13, 128, 142–3, 148, 151, 165, 168
Reinhard, Kenneth 186n. 19
remnant 76, 90–1, 95–7, 150
representation 2, 11, 13, 19, 32–3, 40, 42, 55, 57, 61–6, 72, 80–1, 85–6, 89–106, 107, 109–10, 112, 116, 119–23, 127, 132–5, 138–40, 146, 149, 154–68, 170, 172–4, 177, 196n. 9, 204n. 8, 205n. 12
revelation 8, 21–3, 27, 30, 44–5, 110, 118–19, 165, 168, 169
Rifkin, Mark 188n. 23
Rilke, Rainer Maria 201n. 11
ritual 30, 60, 63–4, 69, 72, 131
Roberts, John 193n. 4
Ross, Alison 204n. 8
Rousseau, Jean-Jacques 72–3

Sabbati Zevi 92
sacrament 36–7
sacred 17, 22, 30, 36–40, 45, 49, 60, 61–6, 67, 71–9, 114, 130–1, 134–9, 149, 160, 175, 188n. 25, 189n. 4
sacrifice 49, 60–80, 91, 93, 99, 136, 189n. 4

228

Index